WHY DO WOMEN LOVE MEN AND NOT THEIR MOTHERS?

WHY DO WOMEN LOVE MEN AND NOT THEIR MOTHERS?

Marie-Christine Hamon

Translated by Susan Fairfield

OTHER
Other Press
New York

Library of Congress Cataloging-in-Publication Data

Hamon, Marie-Christine.
   [Pourquoi les femmes aiment-elles les hommes? English]
   Why do women love men and not their mothers/Marie-Christine Hamon ; translated by Susan Fairfield.
      p. cm.
   Includes bibliographical references and index.
   ISBN 1-892746-46-8 (pbk.)
   1. Femininity—History—20th century. 2. Freud, Sigmund, 1856–1939—Contributions in psychology of femininity. 3. Mothers and daughters—History—20th century. 4. Women—Psychology—History—20th century. 5. Women and psychoanalysis—History. I. Title.
BF175.5.F45 H3513 2000
155.3'33—dc21

                                                     00-055069

Contents

Introduction   1

1. Freud on Women   7
    Ignorance from 1923 to 1931. The homology be-
    tween boy and girl postulated up to 1920. Reti-
    cence and caution after 1923. Cause of the uncer-
    tainty. Difference between castration anxiety and
    castration complex. Asymmetry of the Oedipus ac-
    cording to sex in 1925. In the girl, it is a second-
    ary formation with a prehistory. Not all is said; the
    summations of 1931 and 1932.

2. Female Cases before 1920   13
    The parameters: the Oedipus (dreams and wish for
    parents' death, wish for a child from the father);
    sexuality in the broad sense; masturbation (Dora
    and the girl with the pillow). No lack of material
    or knowledge, but thinking the unconscious im-
    plies letting part of the meaning escape.

3. Retroaction (*Nachträglichkeit*)   21
    Misrecognition. Taking time into account. A work
    in stages. 1923: primacy of the phallus and castra-

tion of the mother; 1924: castration threats, the "feminine" position presupposing castration, the problem of the girl's superego; 1925: the Oedipus in girls—they enter it, but do they leave? Penis envy is the manifestation of their castration complex and governs their development. If they do not leave the Oedipus, what of the superego?

4. Everything Has to Be Reexamined 29
The theoretical revision of 1931. Certainties reconquered: everything has already been revised. Composition of the 1931 paper on feminine sexuality: four stages. The contribution of disciples in the fourth stage: indebtedness and dodging. The 1932 lecture on femininity: correction prevails over debt. Freud's appeal, his pupils' response.

5. The Girl's Oedipus 35
The initial attachment to the mother in the different phases (oral, anal, and phallic). No difference between girls and boys in the phallic phase. Devaluation of the castrated mother. Abandonment of phallic *jouissance* and love for the mother: the connection between the two. Primacy of the phallus for the girl. Delayed effects: the case of homosexuality in a young woman (1920); some characteristics of women's nature explained (modesty, narcissism, object choice, masculinity complex, dependency, and superego).

6. The Girl as Little Man 49
Girls ask their mother for what they know she cannot give them. How Freud was anticipated by H. W. van Ophuijsen in 1917 and Jeanne Lampl-de Groot in 1927. Scarcity of clinical reference to femininity in Freud. Others provide casuistry. Two analysts, one case. Masculinity complex and expressions of the demand for the male organ. H. W. van

Ophuijsen is the first to note these. Matrix of this complex. The clinical case and the symptoms. Identification with the father's organ. Jeanne Lampl-de Groot oversees the second stage of the treatment. Identity of the girl and the boy in the phallic phase, where the girl, like the boy, wants to seduce the mother.

7. Castration and the Loss of the Breast   57
Why is the phallic signifier the signifier of lack? What is really lacking is the breast. Three dreams to illustrate the "mother complex." Signified and signifier of castration. The first difference is that of the genital organs. Clinical practice wins out. Redefinition of castration. Hiatus between signification and primacy of the phallus. The inferences drawn by Freud.

8. Helene Deutsch and the Mater Dolorosa   63
Deutsch's starting point: the difficulties of motherhood. How activity is opposed to femininity. The phallic mother is a nursing mother. Ferenczi's model and the reference to Abraham. Deutsch's question about passivity. Freud's reservations. Phallic activity.

9. Motherhood, Frigidity, Masochism   73
Feminine masochism in women. Where Deutsch takes Freud literally. Her reconstruction of female development and her invention of a postphallic phase. A masochistic oedipal fantasy. Sexual inhibition in women is the result of avoidance of masochistic dangers. The refusal of masochism is a refusal of castration. The sublimation of maternity. Why women tolerate frigidity. Emphasis on fantasy, elision of desire. The unconscious phase of fantasy is a reconstruction. Division of the girl between masculinity and femininity, activity and passivity.

10. Deutsch on Female Homosexuality   83

Eleven female cases. The aftermath of the first case
(1920). Preoedipal hate and desire for the mother.
Emergence of oedipal material; the patient is directed to an analyst of the other sex. In the second
case (1928–1931), the model of the homosexual
relation is the mother–child relation. Dreams and
history of the patient overlap. A stage of identification with the father. What blocks the passage to the
father is guilt connected with the mother. The maternal prohibition of *jouissance*. The girl's oedipal
position is passive and masochistic. Deutsch's priority in the matter of hatred for the mother. Freud's
acknowledgment.

11. Regressions and Fixations   93

Two cases of women attached to their fathers.
First case: the mother is a witch who seduced her.
The pleasure was fatal. Fantasy of revenge: a partial
incorporation of the father. Guilt and the fulfillment of desire. A vengeful and rescuing father
unites desire and the law. Second case: the dead
father is idealized. Oral symptoms, mystical communication. Castration ascribed to the mother.
The prevalence of orality comes from the reference to Abraham. Castrating mother, not castrated
mother. The question of the mother's desire: "What
does she want of me?"

12. Castration and Love for the Father   103

A brief remark of 1923. The detour through Karen
Horney (1922). The 1919 paper, "A child is being
beaten."

13. The Origin of Hatred for the Mother   107

Change of opinion. Hate is always retroactive. Castrated mother, not castrating mother: difference

from Fenichel and Melanie Klein. For both sexes
the mother's lack determines the exit from the
Oedipus. The phallus as cause of love through its
presence, of hate through its absence. The preoedipal is the stage before the recognition of the
sexes; it does not announce the Oedipus. It is hate
that enables Freud to affirm the primacy of the phallus for the girl in 1932. His debt to Helene Deutsch.

14. The Disagreement with Abraham   113

Abraham's clinical vignette of 1924. Everyone
refers to it, but Freud is silent. Displacement of
the debate on femininity. Progress on love. From
narcissism to object love. The case and its use by
Abraham and his followers. Cannibalistic identification with the father. Disgust for the mother. Oral
penis envy and oral symptoms in women. Complexity of identifications. Freud's distinctions between
primary identification and secondary (oedipal)
identification. Abraham's advantages. Hypotheses
and reconstruction, not synthesis. The stage theory.
Development or retroaction. The temporal order
is merely an artifact. How to approach Abraham's
clinical account. The aftermath of castration.
Freud's warnings. His censure of Abraham.

15. Melanie Klein and the Early Oedipus   127

Freud's rejection of the 1928 paper. Its aim is polemical. Klein is serving not two but three masters,
and hence none. The early Oedipus complex. Oral
sadism. No Oedipus that is not conflictual. Introjection. The loss of the breast. The castrating mother.
The mother's *jouissance* and the enigma of her
desire. The mother as described by Klein is a
mother before the recognition of castration. The
fierce mother of *jouissance* and the father of the
primal horde.

16. The Theoretical Shift   139

What guided Melanie Klein up to 1926. The later
modification. The example of sadism. Oedipus
and weaning. Anna Freud's opposition. The reference to Abraham is overdetermined.

17. The Phase of Femininity   145

A contestation of the phallic phase. Oral frustration,
cause of identification, and feminine receptivity.
The boy's femininity complex. Is the identification
with the mother feminizing or masculinizing? Klein
notes the weak point of Freud's pronouncements
on femininity up to 1925.

18. Between Klein and Freud   153

Freud's corrections of 1931 and 1932 have no effect on Klein. His remarks on the mother's castration are too elliptical: the function of the father is
not situated there. One text returns to the other.
Two explicit formulations of castration by Freud.
The father as bearer of the phallus and as castrator. Freud's paper on Leonardo da Vinci via Ruth
Mack Brunswick. Nostalgia for the mother: two aspects. The mother's desire. Fantasy of the phallic
mother as a refusal of castration. The purpose of
the father's presence.

19. Objections, Fidelity, Disagreements   165

Klein's opposition to Freud is a request for explanation. Vicissitudes of the drive: aims and pregenital source, oedipal object. Absorption and expulsion of the parental objects. Splitting of the object.
Mirror and fragmentation effects. The extension of
the concept of identification. Limited acceptation
of the Oedipus in Freud. Three indissociable terms:
Oedipus, phallic phase, and castration. Convergence of the primacy of the phallus and the cas-

tration of the mother. Freud's indirect responses to Melanie Klein.

20. Freud and Ruth Mack Brunswick 175

Freud speaks of Ruth Mack Brunswick in 1931 and 1932–1933, and forgets her in 1937. Two texts that do not have the same status. One, from 1928, is a detailed case description; the other, from 1940, a reflection on the preoedipal period.

21. A Case without an Oedipus 179

Delusional jealousy in a woman. Composition of the paper and presentation of the treatment. A female "Wolf Man." The analyst's construction and its effects. Transference dreams and interpretation. The fantasy of the phallic mother allows repression of both castration threat and abandonment. A transference psychosis through forcing of transference effects. Repetition. Recognition and denial of castration. Reality of early seduction. How the primitive homosexual nucleus remains untouched. Threats to the transference. Three dreams. A specific penis envy. The repression of hate. What the patient does not want to see but wants to continue to believe. Hallucination and resolution of the delusion. A successful treatment of a psychotic. We grasp the meaning of the Oedipus and castration in a case where the Oedipus is lacking. What Freud has to say about this. Brunswick's demonstration and the further step regarding Freud. Round trips between the texts. Need for retroactivity.

22. Primitive Identification and Castration 217

Brunswick's 1940 paper is the theoretical result of a clinical problem arising in her 1928 case. Conjoint work with Freud and its echo in the 1931 and 1932–1933 papers on femininity. But she is the one who enables us to understand and situate Klein's conceptualization. The concept of castration gains intensity. Brunswick's failure. Fertility of the error and difficulties of fidelity.

Afterword: How the Meaning of the Oedipus Changed   227

References   231

Index   239

Introduction

When it came to women, Freud was quite sure of himself for a long time. He knew what they wanted. At the risk of giving offense to some, he named it: *Penisneid* (penis envy). Women, he said, envy what they do not have—the male organ. Suddenly (Freud 1923b), he is no longer sure. And he even pleads the lack of clinical material available to him.

1931. Now Freud is as confident as he was formerly confused: it is their mother whom they loved at first, not their father. Everything has to be revised. The Oedipus as it had been conceived up until then—the boy's preference for the mother, the girl's for the father—is disproved by clinical experience. In becoming women, girls change both sex and object. In order to love men, girls must renounce a virility that from the outset belongs to them as much as it does to boys, and, like boys, girls must drop their first love object. And so it is urgently necessary for them to undo the tie to the mother, the core of neurosis for girls, who are partly out of danger if they have managed to transfer their love to their father. They seek refuge there and cling to it: "[W]e cannot understand women unless we appreciate this phase of their pre-Oedipus attachment to their mother" (Freud 1932–1933, p. 119). Freud has finally understood and confirmed what the girl's castration complex is like. Everything he had formulated up to now about the girl's

phallic activity and her penis envy is reaffirmed, but reordered as
a function of the mother: it is to her that all the girl's demands
are addressed, and this includes the wish to have a child. As with
boys, the shift toward the father occurs only with the recognition
of the mother's castration. Freud also understood the meaning
of the hate that arises in girls at the moment of detachment from
the mother. From now on he will see it as a sign of their entry
into the feminine form of the Oedipus complex.

Freud was hardly convincing. The idea that he misunderstood
femininity persisted: nothing he said about the mother was valid.
This resistance had to be taken seriously—and the texts had to be
taken up once again. Two hypotheses were advanced.

One proposes that what he says can be used against him. That
he gives insufficient weight to the tie to the mother. That he has
not yet fully penetrated into a clinical case. That he is a man, when
all is said and done, and is aware of his disadvantage with regard
to women analysts: they have a greater opportunity to occupy the
place of the mother in a treatment and to evoke the return of this
archaic repressed material that he, as father, found it difficult to
reach. And is it implied that he has conceded defeat, leaving to
others—women—opportunities for clinical experience that would
confirm the thesis.

The second hypothesis claims that his exposition of the theory
is not quite convincing. On the one hand, he shows a kind of reserve towards his contribution: everything had already been said
in the analytic literature on this subject, and all he is doing is to
put it into order. On the other hand, he summarily measures the
contributions or inadequacies of everyone else against his own
conclusions, and we cannot tell whether these are purely logical
deductions or whether he is basing his statements on particularly
revealing clinical material. On several occasions he lays claim to
personal experience, yet without giving the details of any specific
case. Where does he get the proof for his statements? What happened between the earlier years, when he suddenly suspended his
opinion, and the present time, when he speaks so definitively?

The theorem was there; the demonstration had to be revised.
In other words, the clinical experience that could have led Freud
to this change of doctrine had to be discovered. And to that end I

had to reread the texts—Freud's own earlier papers, above all—those that had referred to women patients but no longer seemed to be adequate to what he was trying to establish after 1920. I then noticed, and with surprise, that from the beginning Freud had been constantly concerned with women: it was not that he lacked clinical material, but that he did not see what it implied.

As for other papers, those by his pupils, cited at the end of the 1931 paper on female sexuality, I found that several of them reported cases, but I observed that Freud's summation omits certain contributions and is in error in certain respects. Thus Freud is careless about the actual content of one of Helene Deutsch's papers, attributing to the second paper he cites what in fact belongs to a third. Likewise, although he praises a paper by Jeanne Lampl-de Groot based on a case report, he forgets to mention that it concerns the second phase of the treatment, and that the first had been reported ten years earlier by another analyst, H. W. van Ophuijsen, to whom he himself owes certain concepts. Explicitly manifesting his disagreement with some (Ernest Jones, Karen Horney, and Melanie Klein), when it comes to others (such as Otto Fenichel) he holds back from criticism that would be equally justified. Finally, though he pays homage to an old text by Karl Abraham, he says nothing about a more recent paper referred to in nearly all the ones he cites.

If Freud had not insisted on decoding the meaning of such lapses of memory, voluntary or not, we would be able to ignore them. As it is, since we have spotted them, we have to find why they occurred.

Freud's two papers on femininity (1931, 1932–1933) can no longer be regarded in the way he presents them, or as they seem on a first reading: the state or the endpoint of solitary reflection, in which he remarks in passing that other analysts have also ventured forth on this terrain and that he is using this opportunity to note matters of similarity or disagreement with one or the other of them. These papers must be read as a palimpsest, beneath which the erased text has to be restored.

The reference to other texts, those he mentions and those he forgets, shows that his conclusions—his "personal conceptions," "new ideas," or "observations"—sometimes bear a strange resemblance, nearly word for word, to the arguments put forth by one or the other of his pupils for whose discoveries, and even their formulation, he takes credit. To a great extent they brought him the clinical material he himself lacked, material he drew on extensively without attribution. He made incisive claims but sorted out no confusions, and it remains unclear why he argued against one and not the other, or on what issue.

Everything had to be looked at again, in a back-and-forth movement among texts. In rereading, we find something else: the constant borrowings of one paper from another, a circulation of concepts and a community of work that has been forgotten. It becomes apparent that the contributions mentioned by Freud in 1931, as well as those relegated to silence, are those that enabled him to develop his own thought in new ways. It is to those papers that he is responding, and it is with regard to them that he clarifies a point here and there when he notices, given the way his words have been understood, that he had not placed the emphases where they belonged. His two texts on female sexuality are in fact responses and statements of position in a debate that he had been the first to engage on this subject.

Such an approach reveals a figure unknown up to now: no longer a master who is the possessor of knowledge, but a researcher set to work by his pupils. Although Freud invites them to break through what he claims to be his ignorance, he most of all needs the sounding board that they represent for him. Others send him questions that challenge him to explain himself, and to assess what is missing in his exposition.

To understand the Oedipus of girls, how girls come to love men, we have to take Freud at his word: not to rest content with the final statements, but, as in an analysis, to use the results to reconstruct the concatenation of facts, the gradual formation and modification of concepts, their passage from de facto claims to de jure assertions. Ignorance is a method. And it is with ignorance, with Freud when he makes a point of it in regard to the girl, that I began. This was the first stage of my study.

The rest, the second stage, followed when I read what I had not known how to read: that, in 1931, he had gotten responses and was drawing up a balance sheet. I realized how much of what was decisive for him he took from the observations of H. W. van Ophuijsen, Jeanne Lampl-de Groot, August Stärcke, Otto Fenichel, and Helene Deutsch.

It was fitting that at the end of the 1932–1933 paper his account of femininity, "certainly incomplete and fragmentary," would also "not always sound friendly" (p. 135). It seems to me that the very similar terms he used in a 1935 letter to Carl Müller Braunschweig (Freud 1960) are more revealing: he notes that the abundance of writings on this topic suggests that something is missing, unknown, or unexpressed. If something is lacking, or is not expressed, this is sometimes because he did not wish to say it or could not. I analyze this in connection with Karl Abraham and Melanie Klein. What is unknown is what is unrecognized when there is not enough time to stand back and assume a necessary distance. We see this in Ruth Mack Brunswick, who, in my opinion, provides the demonstration missing in Freud. This third stage of my argument is intentionally longer, because this is where I point out the remaining obscurities and at the same time the elements, in the work of another analyst, that were already available to resolve them. If what is crucial for psychic structure (the choice of neurosis or psychosis) has to do with the desire of/for the mother and her castration, it is extremely hard, at the outset, to discern in Freud a register of castration that is not solely imaginary or anatomical. What Melanie Klein has been reproached for not seeing is thereby explained: it was not spelled out in Freud. It was a major task to find this out and formulate it.

1   Freud on Women

The ignorance that Freud professes with regard to the sexual development of girls, and professes with a special insistence from 1923 to 1930, has to be seen as suspect, not only in order to invalidate some hasty judgments on phallicism or misogyny but to rediscover a process that, I hypothesize, is his own and that is none other than working through. This is a theorization based on experience, to be sure, but experience closely linked to interpretation, to the expectations we have for it even if (as Freud constantly emphasizes) analytic listening calls for the forgetting of prior "knowledge" that can function as a prejudice.

The hesitations and reworkings of the theory are thus allied with resistance, the struggle that has to be mounted against the theory for the sake of awareness of unconscious phenomena and for the reinterpretation of these phenomena in a sense that upsets the initial convictions, threatens the initial discoveries, and, what is more, opposes any harmony of the sexes.

In the first edition of the *Three Essays* (Freud 1905a), in connection with the man's sexual overvaluation of the object, Freud notes that the erotic life of women is still "veiled in an impenetrable obscurity" (p. 151) that does not allow him to ascertain whether such a phenomenon exists for them. At this time, he attributes the obscurity to the atrophy imposed by civilization and to women's conventional modesty in matters of sex.

This reserve on the part of the woman concerning her sex life: is it because Freud avoids it by approaching it through dreams whose shocking sexual nature is not apparent to the woman dreamer[1] that, as late as 1920 (cf. 1920a) we are free to postulate oedipal wishes and orientations on the part of the girl that are entirely homologous with those of the boy, every bit as intense and decipherable as his, as far as the change of object is concerned? ("[Men] dream mostly of their father's death and women of their mother's. . . . It is as though . . . a sexual preference were making itself felt at an early age: as though boys regarded their fathers and girls their mothers as their rivals in love, whose elimination could not fail to be to their advantage" [1900, p. 256]).

Before 1920 there are numerous declarations of the spontaneous nature of the Oedipus complex in the child. We note them in the *Introductory Lectures*: "Things happen in just the same way with little girls [as with boys], with the necessary changes: an affectionate attachment to her father, a need to get rid of her mother" (1916–1917, p. 333) and in the paper on beating fantasies: "Something like a premonition of what are later to be the final and normal sexual aims governs the child's libidinal trends. . . . With boys the wish to beget a child from their mother is never absent; with girls the wish to have a child by their father is equally constant" (1919a, pp. 187–188).

Why, then, the reticence after 1923, Freud's repeated claims that all this holds true only for the boy? He says that all he had at his disposal were the masculine parameters, established and verified in only the one sex; as for the girl, everything becomes much more obscure, difficult to grasp, complicated: he knows nothing about women and lacks clinical material (cf. 1923b, 1924a, 1925a). In a note to his autobiography (1924b), he once again observes that his studies of infantile sexuality were developed only with regard to the male child. Is this a well-founded caution? The claim is nevertheless paradoxical once we consider Freud's career, in which he began with a question about women (hysterics, first of all), then immediately went on to reveal what was sexual about this question and then, in short order, what was infantile about this sexuality.

In all the cases of women that Freud presents without interruption, from before *Studies on Hysteria* (1893–1895) and continuing into the 1920s, what was it that blinded him to the point where he denied them all heuristic merit and all truthfulness?

If the only reliable material comes from the analysis of men, isn't this primarily due to the persuasiveness of Freud's self-analysis, in which he discovered, and confided to Fliess, his *libido ad matrem*, a shattering revelation of his own incest fantasy and thus of the Oedipus complex in himself, a revelation that caused him to risk the entire psychoanalytic edifice by renouncing the theory of traumatic seduction to which the hysterics had led him? This conviction was supported by his observation of Little Hans (1909a), which came just in time as a stunning confirmation of the hypotheses about infantile sexuality derived from the analysis of adult neurotics. Furthermore, doesn't Freud's (1923b) uncertainty regarding the girl reflect his theoretical concern at this period? What is in question for him is no longer simply the reconstruction of supposed stages of development, pregenital stages inferred from the libidinal fixations evident in the various neuroses, but the exact delineation of what distinguished adult genital organization from that of the child. He is no longer looking for the Oedipus but is concerned to link this kernel of the neuroses with the castration anxiety that he would soon (1926a) make the force behind repression in the three neuroses (phobia, hysteria, obsessional neurosis), since, even if this anxiety is evident only in phobias, all three types result in the destruction of the Oedipus complex. This key role assigned to castration anxiety entails a number of qualifications. First of all, the term "castration anxiety" is surely inapplicable to the girl, Freud says; she cannot fear a castration that has already taken place. She can have a "castration complex" but not the related anxiety. What she fears is of another order, namely the loss of the love object.

These are not at all the same thing for Freud, whose uncertainty (*non liquet*) can be seen in "The infantile genital organization" (1923b), where the primacy of the phallus—the only representation of sexual difference for the child being the all-or-nothing male genital organ, present or castrated—is explicitly described only for the boy. Yet, in a footnote, the belief in the maternal penis is said to be shared by the girl: "I learned from the analysis of a young married woman who had no father but several aunts that she clung, until quite far into the latency period, to the belief that her mother and her aunts had a penis. One of her aunts, however, was feeble-minded, and she regarded this aunt as castrated, as she felt herself to be" (p. 143). Why, then, not ascribe to the girl, just as to the boy, the generalization of the primacy of the phallus?

We find the same argument (to the effect that, for girls, matters are different) in a paper of the following year, "The dissolution of the Oedipus complex" (1924a). Here Freud says that, for the boy, castration anxiety leads not so much to the repression as to the suppression of the complex. It clears the way for the super-ego once the child's disbelief in the fulfillment of the castration threat has been overcome by the sight of the female genital. But for the girl, although there is likewise an Oedipus complex, a latency period, and a type of superego, matters are different: the girl accepts castration as a *fait accompli*, while the boy fears that it may come to pass.

A third paper, "Some psychical consequences of the anatomical distinction between the sexes" (1925a), provides the key to this qualification: there is a difference, and, Freud says, it is not easy to ascertain where it appears in the course of development. What is this discovery? It is the asymmetry of the Oedipus complex:

> *Whereas in boys the Oedipus complex is destroyed by the castration complex, in girls it is made possible and led up to by the castration complex.* . . . The difference between the sexual development of males and females at the stage we have been considering is an intelligible consequence of the anatomical distinction between their genitals and of the psychical situation involved in it; it corresponds to the difference between a castration that has been carried out and one that has merely been threatened. [pp. 256–257, emphasis in original]

And in fact, in a letter from May 10 of the same year (1972), Freud confides to Lou Andreas-Salomé his shame at not having discovered this difference earlier on. Nevertheless, "Some psychical consequences" was given to Ferenczi to read in the course of the summer, and Freud had his daughter Anna deliver it orally before the Hamburg Congress that autumn.

The first observation of 1925 was that, beyond the child's oedipal desire for the father, which in certain women appears as a basic reality that cannot be further analyzed, a detailed analysis of this same material also shows that this oedipal attachment has a long prehistory and is a secondary formation. We can thus understand Freud's insistence on his ignorance of how the girl's developmental processes correspond to those of the boy. If, as seems to be the case, we assume he had an inkling of this discovery that should have been made earlier, we can better assess the implications for any analogy that might seem too contrived as well as the threat that such a discovery might pose to a conception of the Oedipus as the core of neurosis. The second observation, which follows from the first, is that, if there is indeed a prehistory of the Oedipus complex in the girl, a relation to the mother that precedes the orientation to the opposite sex, then we must also posit an oedipal prehistory for the boy (though its nature, Freud tells us, is unclear), and we must view this prehistory as the origin of certain forms of passive attachment or even simply of tender identification with the father. Nevertheless, several years after the analysis of the Wolf Man (1914a), his initial assumption that the Oedipus is the first recognizable stage in the boy appears unchanged. In contrast, the girl's clearly oedipal desire (to have a child by her father) is established and remains so firm, with all the force of a demand, only because it was so hard won, having been preceded by an entire "male" phase in which she was prey to penis envy and resentment.

Yet between this paper and the 1931–1933 studies on femininity, Freud neglects this fundamental discovery in which he had established an oedipal process proper to each sex, to the point where, in his autobiography (1924b), he speaks of the concentration of sexual desire in infancy as being that of the boy toward his mother, the girl toward her father. We find the same formulation and a similar forgetfulness in the paper on lay analysis (1926b), whereas, in the *Three Essays* (1905a) he had said that the first sexual object for both boy and girl is the mother. We can read these wavering statements as ellipses or as denial: "I know well, . . . but nevertheless" (cf. Mannoni 1969). Things were said, but that does not matter; they do not take on the force of truth right away. There has to be a time for understanding and for new material to confirm the interpretation.

Before 1925 and the thesis of the asymmetry of the Oedipus, every-thing was already there in a certain sense: the manifestations of the castration complex in the form of penis envy, the difference between castration accomplished and castration threatened, the initial mas-culinity of the little girl, and the symbolic equivalence penis = child. Everything was there, except the connection, for the girl, between the Oedipus and the castration complex.

What is still missing, between 1925 and 1933, to give demon-strative power to the theorization of the girl's development? Every-thing, or at least a large part of what will be taken up again in the 1930s, has already been set forth: the mother as first object; the grievances addressed to her insofar as she is held responsible for the loss of the desired object; the repression, owing to shame, of masturbation; and the turn to the father because of penis envy. Yet all has not been said, since the paper "Female sexuality" (1931) and the lecture "Femininity" (1932–1933) return to the question raised in 1925: what leads women to desire men and thus to aban-don their first love object? No longer does Freud invoke the lack of material, or ignorance, or even the risk of challenging his pre-vious theories; instead he refers to the difficulty of the work of uncovering, and to the very archaic, repressed, and thus distorted nature of the material, and, finally, to the obstacle posed by the paternal transference that, like the hard-won oedipal refuge, masks the force of the first aspirations.

From the alleged lack of clinical material to its reinterpretation in terms of the role of the mother: this is where we are, with Freud, in the understanding of his approach. Let us look at his early cases of women to see how he was confirmed in his initial positions, sometimes immovably so, or what modifications he would go on to make.

Note

1. Compare Dora (1905b) and the dreams of the disgusting piano, the market where nothing is to be found, and the candle in the candle-stick (Freud 1900, pp. 183–187).

2   Female Cases before 1920

As we know from his correspondence with Fliess and his early, "pre-analytic" papers, even before the *Studies on Hysteria* (1893–1895) where he reports on five women patients, Freud had dealt with both female and male cases. And, if he had formed any hypotheses about the sexual etiology of the neuroses, both sexes were involved.

Freud gives three examples of obsessions, all women, in "The neuro-psychoses of defence" (1894). "Further remarks on the neuro-psychoses of defence" (1896a) presents eleven cases of female hysteria (compared to two male cases) and more than one observation of paranoia in a woman, while "The aetiology of hysteria" (1896b) mentions twelve cases of women to six of men.

The Dora case (1905b) appears four years after it was written. But in that interval there was *The Interpretation of Dreams* (1900), where many dreams of women are described—apparently innocent dreams, like those of the market, the piano to be tuned, and the candle in "an intelligent and cultivated young woman, reserved and undemonstrative in her behaviour" (p. 183). They are enigmatic with regard to wish fulfillment, like the dream of the butcher's wife and the dinner of smoked salmon (pp. 147–151), and definitely oedipal when they have to do with the disappearance or death of the mother (pp. 259–260).

Between Dora and the case of female paranoia (1915a), if we are to believe Strachey (1925a, p. 245), Freud is no longer interested in the psychology of women. To be sure, the larger studies published during this period deal with males: Little Hans and the Rat Man (1909a, b), Leonardo da Vinci (1910), and Schreber (1911). But are we to disregard the 1907 paper "Obsessive actions and religious practices," which reports a series of obsessions and their mechanism in the woman patient who will reappear in the *Introductory Lectures* of 1916–1917 (pp. 257–272) as the woman with the tablecloth? Are we supposed to believe that the renewed consideration of hysterical attacks (1908a; cf. 1892) and hysterical fantasies (1908b) has no bearing on cases of women?

And how can we ignore the three papers of 1913 (1913 a, b, c) that contain portions of the analyses of women? The first analysis, to which Freud refers in the paper on transformation of instinct (1916a) and in *Inhibitions, Symptoms, and Anxiety* (1926), provides the clinical material that leads him to postulate the existence of an anal-sadistic stage between the autoerotic and narcissistic stages and that of genitality. This is a case of anxiety hysteria—the name Freud gives at the time to phobia accompanied by anxiety—that, after a second trauma, " a second experience, which had completely wiped out the first" (1913a, p. 319), is transformed into a major obsessional neurosis: "a compulsion for scrupulous washing and cleanliness and extremely energetic preventive measures against severe injuries which she thought other people had reason to fear from her. . . . Her sexual need was obliged to find expression in these shapes after her genital life had lost all its value" (p. 320). A more detailed analysis of the oedipal elements in this same case (or another one very similar with regard to the initial phase of anxiety hysteria) is presented twice, in "Psycho-analysis and telepathy" (1921a) and, eleven years later, in the thirtieth of the *New Introductory Lectures* (1932).

In addition to the case of the woman with the tablecloth, whose wedding-night trauma is related to the trauma that sparked the change of neurosis in the earlier (1913a) case, a further example in the same part of the *Introductory Lectures* (1916–1917), the case of the girl with the pillow, is noteworthy for the meaning of the ritual that Freud highlights and also for its points of contact with the interpretation he offers in the study of paranoia in a woman (1915a). Moreover, Freud is careful to explain that the detailed study of six cases, four of them woman patients, is the basis of his paper on childhood beating fantasies (1919a). I would add that, although "The psychogenesis of a case of homosexuality in a woman" (1920a) is, after Dora, his second extensive account of an analysis of a woman, two earlier papers, "On transformation of instinct" (1916a) and "The taboo of virginity" (1918), offer precise, though brief, insights into the issue of the masculinity complex.

What are the presuppositions, the clinical findings, and the endeavors on Freud's part that color his perception of the cases of women he analyzed? The Oedipus (after 1896), sexuality in the broad sense (that is, not confined to genitality), and childhood masturbation seem to provide the conceptual framework for his research. These are, at any rate, the points of departure, the constants, that I propose to follow.

The first parameter, and a common denominator for both sexes, is the Oedipus. It is fully set forth in *The Interpretation of Dreams* (1900) in the form of dreams of the death of parents. If they are evidence of a wish, it is one whose origins go back to early childhood:

> We learn from [such dreams] that a child's sexual wishes—if in their embryonic stage they deserve to be so described—awaken very early, and that a girl's first affection is for her father and a boy's first childish desires are for his mother. Accordingly, the father becomes a disturbing rival to the boy and the mother to the girl; and I have already shown . . . how easily such feelings can lead to a death-wish. [p. 257]

The analysis of adult neurotics, Freud says here, provides "certainty beyond all doubt" of the mutual attraction of the sexes and the wish to get rid of the rival. The most flagrant manifestation, one that need not shock us as it does the dreamer, is thus, in the case of the girl, the death wish toward her mother. In the section on typical dreams, even before his discussion of Sophocles' *Oedipus*, Freud mentions two women's dreams of their mother's death. There can be no doubt, he says, of their meaning: they represent a childhood wish. Hence, in each patient, we find an extreme reaction formation, in one case the woman's feeling that "her rela-

tions must think her horrible" (p. 259), while the other, a girl with
an excessive worry about her mother, leads Freud to conclude that
"it is no longer hard to understand why hysterical girls are so often
attached to their mothers with such exaggerated affection" (p. 260).

The death wish also goes in the opposite direction, from father
to son or mother to daughter. Thus, when a woman dreams of her
15-year-old daughter lying dead in a box or case, Freud notes that
the child in the box represents the embryo in the womb, English
"box," like the German "*Büchse*," being "a vulgar term for the female genitals" (p. 154). *Noli tangere matrem* in connection with the
same case, fifteen years later, in the thirteenth of the *Introductory
Lectures*:

> How many mothers, who love their children tenderly, perhaps over-
> tenderly, today, conceived them unwillingly and wished at that time
> that the living thing within them might not develop further! They
> may even have expressed that wish in various, fortunately harmless,
> actions. Thus their death-wish against someone they love, which is
> later so mysterious, originates from the earliest days of their rela-
> tionship to that person. [1916–1917, p. 202]

Such a mother has to overcompensate for her hatred toward her
children (cf. 1926a). Another, like the mother of the young lesbian
(1920a), shows a special tolerance for her daughter's deviant sexuality only because she cannot accept the latter's femininity; still young
herself, she wants to attract male attentions and welcomes the girl's
withdrawal from competition. A dream of Freud's, added to *The
Interpretation of Dreams* in 1919 and revisited in "Dreams and telepathy" (1922a), provides confirmation of the ambivalence of unconscious desire when he himself dreams of the death of one of his sons:
envy, he concludes, of the younger generation.

Besides the death dream, the animosity, inconsiderateness, or
overt hostility of the girl toward her mother are posited as natural
and not put in question, since the Oedipus—the wish to sleep with
one parent and kill the other in order to replace him or her—is
sufficient explanation. So it is with Dora's (1905b) scorn and disregard for her mother and with the woman, mentioned in "Dreams
and telepathy," who associates her mother's giving birth with her
own anxiety when pigs were being slaughtered.

Another sign of the Oedipus is the infantile wish to have a child by the father. The frustration of this wish leads to neurosis (1913a, the case taken up again in "Dreams and telepathy"). It triggers regression to the female object in the young lesbian (1920a), although she had negotiated the Oedipus, and it is unmistakable in beating fantasies. This wish is concurrent with that other "basic reality," penis envy (cf. 1916–1917 and 1918), to the point where, for Freud, although one part of the defiance involves the mother complex, the symbolism of birth and the defiance itself are primarily based on the wish for a child from the father.

The second parameter is sexuality in the broad sense: the partial drives, the erogenous zones, and the extension of the sexual function beyond the genital function. Early on Freud emphasizes the perverse knowledge of sex among the most innocent. The imaginary sexual geography (1905b) is evident in Katharina's throat constrictions (1893–1895) and the woman who dreamed of the market (1900). Freud is likewise quick to note the sexual nature of infantile investigations (1905a, 1908c). And he enumerates the more or less censored forms of sexual intercourse as imagined by children: being naked together, urinating in front of the other, exchanging blood or money, or having a child (1913b, c). The stages preceding the focus of interest on the genital organs have an explicitly sexual character, incontrovertible proof of which are the regressions that occur during an impasse—for example, to the anal-sadistic stage, a degraded but secure form of sexual life after devaluation of genitality. This mechanism leads to the conclusion that all of the child's aggressive impulses, like his easily observable interest in excretion, are a stage of his sexuality. We also see this in the nursery, where the child's pleasure in nursing and later in sucking, independent of hunger, is clearly sexual in nature and leaves traces in later life (cf. 1905b and Lecture 20 in 1916–1917).

The third and last parameter is the certainty of "masculine" masturbation in the little girl, a certainty that Freud similarly acquires very early on from the analysis of hysterics: hysterical neurosis in a woman represents the excessive repression of male sexuality. During the developmentally prescribed discharge of "genital" sexuality, which, for the little girl, is first associated with the clitoris, the repression of masturbation is excessive if it is partially annihilated through the formation of hysterical substitutes. This confirms the infantile sexual theory that the woman, like the man, possesses a penis, since phenomena of excitation and erection can be displaced from the genital organs to other parts of the body, such as the head and the face. Hysterical symptoms, like those of obsessional neurosis, are substitutes for masturbatory gratification (cf. 1912).

Thus it is no longer the trauma of more or less premature seduction experienced actively or passively (cf. 1896c), but repressed masturbation and the associated fantasy that must be seen as the origin of the defense against an irreconcilable representation. Freud is certain of this as early as 1905, even though he sees some risk of a false construction in proposing his theory of infantile masturbation to Dora (1905b; cf. Cottet 1982, p. 36). In this analysis, originally entitled "Dream and hysteria," the interpretation of the dream is intertwined with the account of the treatment— thereby, Freud explains, allowing him to elucidate symptoms, fill in amnestic gaps, and especially to supply what he calls the missing piece of the puzzle. He sets out from one observation, namely that, when hysterics are asked for memories, they reply with dreams. A fragmentary history, disconnected accounts, unclear chronology: all this parataxis that betokens hysteria justifies "reconstruction."

In the case of masturbation, Freud bases his conclusions on Dora's first dream, that of the jewel box. He interprets an equivocal expression (one might have to leave the room at night) and appeals to typical symbolism (playing with fire, not getting the box wet) to conclude that infantile enuresis is an admission of masturbation, for which he finds supporting evidence in the identification with the mother's catarrh, Dora's allusion to her white discharge, and her symptomatic playing with her reticule during the analytic sessions. Another symptomatic act of Dora's during the treatment, her hiding a letter so as to appear to have a secret, is assigned the same meaning: Dora's unconfessed secret, repeated in the transference, is masturbation. If further proof were needed, there are her cousin's stomach pains and the substitution of psychogenic asthma for urinary incontinence as a symptom providing masturbatory gratification.

After the abandoning of the seduction theory, Freud came to believe that masturbation was the primary need underlying addictions and a need that played an important role in hysteria; this is the hypothesis already mentioned in "The aetiology of hysteria" (1896b). Behind the most recent trauma, even beyond the memory that explains the form of the trauma and the reaction that represents a reactivation, a piece of the puzzle is missing. In the case of Dora, the scene at the lake prompts the search for the initial trauma, namely the scene on the staircase, and, still further beyond that, the reconstruction of masturbation.

This "construction" to which his hysterical patients led Freud also serves him in making sense of an obsessional girl's ritual and of a delusional formation. In the first instance, the case of the girl with the pillow, the protection against noise and the removal of all clocks are grounded in her fear of sexual arousal:

> Our patient's anxiety . . . was directed in particular against being disturbed in her sleep by the ticking of a clock. The ticking of a clock may be compared with the knocking or throbbing in the clitoris during sexual excitement. She had in fact been repeatedly woken from her sleep by this sensation, which had now become distressing to her, and she gave expression to this fear of an erection in the rule that all clocks and watches that were going should be removed from her neighbourhood at night. [1916–1917, pp. 266–267]

Other elements of the bedtime ritual—one in flagrant contradiction of the need to remove any source of noise, since it consisted in keeping the door of the parents' bedroom open by means of various objects that could make some noise, the other involving the careful placement of the pillow so that it would not touch the wood of the bed—were explained, Freud tells us, when the patient realized that, for her, the pillow was feminine and the vertical bedstead masculine. (As Freud noted in *The Interpretation of Dreams* [1900], anything can serve as a sexual symbol.) This was the patient's unconscious and figurative way of preventing the sexual intercourse of her father with a mother whose place she hoped to take. Her ritual enabled her to spy on her parents, to which end she also developed insomnia lasting several months.

Is this an actual account of childhood? A screen memory? What is juxtaposed in this example—infantile masturbation, the Oedipus complex—is closely linked in the case of paranoia in a woman

(1915a). The sexual arousal that makes her fear noise (a chiming or beating [cf. 1919a]), Freud explains, goes back to the primal scene, the observation of parental intercourse. A chance noise, the click of a camera, forms the basis of this young woman's delusion that, at her lover's behest, she was spied on and photographed during their intimate encounter; this, Freud says, merely serves to activate the typical aural fantasy of the parent complex, to the point where it is not at all clear that the noise was accidental. Referring to Rank, he notes that the noise represents either the sounds made during parental intercourse or those that the child fears will betray him.

Thus we see that, before 1920, Freud has no lack of clinical material. Nor of discoveries, since it is hysterical symptoms that enable him to infer a phallic or masculine phase of infantile masturbation, and it is the double neurosis of a woman, more than the analysis of the Rat Man, that leads to the hypothesis of an anal-sadistic phase. Freud accepts Abraham's proposal of an even earlier libidinal period, the oral stage, once he sees it validated in the strong need for sucking in hysteria (cf. 1905a, b). Nor does he lack knowledge, being assured of his accurate decoding of girls' oedipal dreams and of the validity of his reconstruction of infantile masturbation.

The suspension of judgment that appears in 1923 is undoubtedly based on the new questions that arise at the time of the structural theory (cf. 1920b, 1921b, 1923a), but it is also the result of the very way in which psychoanalysis was conceptualized. If the unconscious arises where "it" does not think (*Wo Es war, soll Ich werden*), thinking of the unconscious always entails the risk of losing part of its meaning: where "it" was, there was no thinking about it. This is Freud's discovery, one that he makes a methodological principle consistent with the logic of its object, the unconscious, in which all knowledge is always just a drawing back from repression. He learned to yield to it, to take time into account. What might have been seen in the material from the preceding years never appeared, because it could not have been seen unless the emphasis had been placed where it belonged. Truth arose as if by chance— but often, in fact, from the perspective of a question that had not been asked.

3　　Retroaction　(*Nachträglichkeit*)

As examples of ideas arising from the perspective of truth and the time it takes for facts to become obvious, I want to look again at the papers Freud published in 1923, 1924, and 1925 that bear explicitly on the issue of castration. They are exemplary because of the displacement of emphasis from one to the next, along with the correlative "forgettings." I shall also look at the papers of 1931 and 1932–1933 on femininity. A single year separates these, yet the difference in formulation, slight though it may be, is decisive.

It was in the first of these papers, "The infantile genital organization"(1923b), which concludes with the primacy of the phallus, that I discovered what, up to that time, I had managed not to see: not only the admission but the affirmation that what impedes the advancement of knowledge in psychoanalysis has less to do with ignorance than with misrecognition. "The difficulty of the work of research in psychoanalysis," Freud says at the beginning of the paper, "is clearly shown by the fact of its being possible, in spite of whole decades of unremitting observation, to overlook features that are of general occurrence and situations that are characteristic, until at last they confront one in an unmistakable form" (p. 141). Everything was almost there, he says, except what the neglect of one point prevented him from seeing. He reviews the findings from the original 1905 publication of the *Three Essays* to the additions made in 1915 and 1920, since the new element noted in the meantime must be integrated into the general theory of sexuality. Each time, he says, there is a different emphasis, and he recalls the steps in this increase of knowledge. First there was the recognition of a difference between adult sexual life and that of children, then the pregenital organizations and the diphasic establishment of sexuality (the latency period). Finally, in the note of 1922, there was the closeness of definitive sexual life to that of childhood, as evidenced in the outcome of infantile sexual investigation in which the choice of object is already made, the sole difference being the incompleteness of the synthesis of the partial drives and their subordination to genitality.

This last proposal of 1922 is no longer satisfactory in 1923: the closeness is even greater, Freud declares. In addition to the choice of object, the dominant interest in the genital organs and the associated activity are already there; the difference is that for both sexes a single genital organ, the male one, plays a role: what is primary is not the genital, but, specifically, the phallus. Once this conclusion has been stated, though restricted to the boy, it calls for proof. Freud therefore returns to the account of the development of infantile sexual investigation, highlighting the retroactivity that the child needs in order to achieve the recognition of sexual difference. The sexual nature of the division into men and women, he states, is not immediately perceived. The move from generalizing the possession of the male organ (everyone has it) to marking the exception (not everyone has it, since certain females are deprived of it) is a first step, integrated with difficulty and requiring justification. In the child's view, it is the result of a punishment. This conclusion has great affective resonance, and the idea of the lack of the organ as the consequence of an act of castration calls for a slow maturation; the child at first denies the lack and believes that he sees a penis nonetheless.

A further step, the recognition that the mother herself is castrated, is necessary for the generalization of this fact to all women. One part of the world, the male part, possesses the organ; the other, the female part, does not. The representation of sexual difference, at this culmination of infantile sexuality, is formulated (and this is what distinguishes it from puberty) not in terms of *masculine* or *feminine* but in the contrast between the male genital and the castrated one. Initially denied, attenuated, or rationalized, this "discovery" is accepted and generalized only after a long period of reservation, that is, of retention of the original beliefs.

Whereas "The infantile genital organization" (1923b), beside the attempt to establish the primacy of the phallus, stressed the time needed to arrive at a representation of the difference between the sexes under the elaborated form of castration, the paper of the following year, "The dissolution of the Oedipus complex" (1924a), similarly based on the effects of retroactivity, tries something else in proposing to connect the threat of castration and the exit from the Oedipus.

Here the emphasis is on the parental prohibition of masturbation, contrary to the 1923 paper that took as its point of departure the shock of discovering the lack of a male organ in the female alter ego. The visual experience, central in the earlier text, is here placed in a sequence, since before this the child had formed a concept of loss in the experiences of weaning and defecation. But, Freud emphasizes, there is no reason to suppose that these experiences are still in force on the occasion of the castration threat. It is the observation of the female genital that overrides the child's disbelief, when he has to acknowledge the lack of a penis in a being otherwise so similar to himself. Yet this is determinative only because it retroactively allows the castration threat to take effect. Determinative, but nevertheless not radical: the child still hesitates, reluctant to trust his observation.

At this point in Freud's argument, he makes two comments that do not appear in the 1923 paper. The first concerns the relation between infantile masturbation and the Oedipus complex. The child's sexual life is not reducible to masturbation but consists in the link between it and the oedipal position. And the importance of masturbation has to do with the fact that, as the discharge of oedipal excitation, it forms part of that complex. The second comment indirectly points to the twofold orientation of the Oedipus.[1] Before the castration threat takes effect, the child finds two possibilities for gratification: an active form, in which he takes the place of the father, or a passive form, in which he identifies with the mother, who is still believed to have a penis. The idea that the woman is castrated puts an end to these possibilities, the loss of the penis now affecting both sexes.

This is an important distinction. It is because sexual gratification is also expected from the father, even if one is a boy, that the first encounter with lack in the image of the female other's body—an encounter that, up to now, could be denied—is associated with the threat of castration of one's own body, from the perspective of the mother's castration. Once one has the idea of sexual difference, being loved as a woman by the father means belonging to the class of castrated beings like the mother. Thus the abandonment of the Oedipus is motivated by a conflict between the ego (the narcissistic interest in that part of one's body) and the id (the libidinal investment of the parental objects). Normally, Freud says, the ego prevails; the reference to the structural theory (ego, id, superego) is clear (cf. 1923a). Under the threat of castration, object cathexes are replaced by identification, and paternal, or parental, authority is introjected into the ego, where it forms the basis of the superego. Oedipal wishes are renounced, and incestuous libidinal inclinations are partly desexualized and sublimated, partly inhibited with regard to their aim and transformed into tender impulses. But, according to Freud, this "repression" of the Oedipus that interrupts the child's sexual development and brings on the famous "latency period" is, ideally, much more than a repression. It must be a destruction or a "dissolution" of the complex if it is not to linger in the id and produce pathogenic effects later on.

What he had set out to show, namely that the Oedipus complex collapses as a result of the threat of castration, is, Freud assures us, proved by analytic observation, which enables us to understand how the phallic organization, the Oedipus complex, the castration threat, the formation of the superego, and the latency period are all connected. But the problem remains unsolved. Why? Because, for the girl, things are different. The morphological difference must be reflected in psychic development, and here Freud admits that his clinical material is scanty and obscure.

The girl does not escape castration. Evidence of this can be found in the anatomical homology, in early imagination, of the clitoris and the penis, and then in the feeling of disadvantage that overcomes the child when she discovers her organic inferiority (though she does not see this as decisive; she believes that she will acquire a larger penis as she grows up). It is precisely in the girl's denial, whether this takes the form of awaiting the organ at a later time or believing that she once possessed it, that Freud locates the woman's masculinity complex. Moreover, the girl, like the boy, attributes her castration to an operation—it was taken from her— and, like him, she does not generalize this punishment to all adult women. The difference, stated for the first time in this 1924 paper, depends on her accepting this castration as a *fait accompli*, whereas the boy fears its accomplishment in the future. This difference entails another one: if there is no castration anxiety, there is no strong motivation for superego formation or for the undoing of the infantile genital organization. And in fact, although something like a superego is formed in the girl, Freud sees this as being much more the result of an external intimidation than of an internalized prohibition. Because she does not have castration anxiety, the girl is not easily dislodged from the Oedipus complex (substitution for the mother, feminine position with regard to the father), especially since it is through the oedipal turn that she can compensate for her missing organ. She therefore makes the symbolic equation of penis and child, and her Oedipus complex culminates in the wish to receive the gift of a child from her father, to give him a child. Since this wish is never fulfilled, her Oedipus is never completely abandoned.

"Some psychical consequences of the anatomical distinction between the sexes"(1925a) returns to this difference, stating once again, and in a very assured rhetoric, the difficulty of making progress in psychoanalysis: knowledge was already there, but one did not know that one knew it. Freud thus announces a research finding of great importance, a discovery that cannot wait for further study and that "stands in urgent need of confirmation": "we have been in the habit of taking as the subject of our investigations the male child, the little boy. With little girls, so we have supposed, things must be similar, though in some way or other they must nevertheless be different. The point in development at which this difference lay could not be clearly determined" (p. 249). On the other hand, he ends by stating definitively: "In their essentials . . . our findings are self-evident and it should have been possible to fore-see them" (p. 257), as though the establishment of a somewhat certain fact, the effect of certainty in analytic knowledge, could be attained only on the basis of a prejudice rejected, a misrecognition dispelled: that's how it was, and I never even thought of it.

The shift in emphasis in this third paper makes the comparing term into the compared. What we thought we knew about—the boy—involves matters that are unknown. What we thought we did not know about was merely unrecognized. In the case of the boy, the only one for whom up to now there was some certain knowl-edge, Freud clarifies and even modifies the features of the preced-ing papers. In 1924, as we have seen, Freud announced but did not further specify the twofold gratification (active and passive) of the boy-child in the oedipal position. This doubly oriented Oedipus, which includes a tender identification with the father entailing no sense of rivalry for the mother, will from now on be firmly situated as the "prehistory" of the boy's Oedipus. It will, Freud admits, remain unclear to us for a long time to come.

This poorly understood prehistory will revolutionize the theo-rization of the Oedipus. We must return to a point that Freud had made earlier on (1905a, 1914c, 1916–1917) but that had remained undeveloped until now: the original love object for both sexes is the mother, an object choice made on the basis of the satisfaction of vital needs. The girl's Oedipus, to the extent that she reaches it, thus presupposes a disengagement from the mother that must be explained. We now wonder not only about the end, but also about the entry into the Oedipus, its beginnings and what precedes it. The parallelism between the sexes can no longer be maintained on this point.

In effect, far from being, as with the boy, "the first stage that can be recognized with certainty" (1925a, p. 249), the girl's Oedi-pus complex is a *trompe l'oeil*, a deceptive appearance. The strong bond with the father and the wish for a child by him, which seems to be "an elementary and unanalysable fact," reveals instead that "the Oedipus complex has a long prehistory and is in some respects a secondary formation" (p. 251). The wish for a child from the father, a typical feature of the female Oedipus, is the end of a long trajectory. Between autoerotism (from the oral, sucking stage to masturbatory genital activity) and the new object choice (father instead of mother), penis envy, already recognized in 1924 as a manifestation of the girl's castration complex, now turns out to be of crucial importance: the force of this initial trauma that, for the girl, constitutes the discovery of sexual difference and her own anatomical inferiority, obliges us to take a closer look at her earlier relation to the maternal object and at what she loses in the transition. Penis envy, for Freud, explains not only reaction formations (like the masculinity complex) and certain otherwise inexplicable features of female behavior, but also the disengagement from the mother, who is held responsible. The same is true for jealousy as a character trait and as a motive for the beating fantasies regularly found in the early childhood of women patients. Here we have the explanation for the intensity with which masturbation is repressed, an effect of penis envy that Freud calls "the most important of all" (p. 255), as well as for the change of object from mother to father. The girl agrees to this repression in return for a trade-off, the child she can expect in place of the penis she had been refused.

This is a consequence that has not been emphasized up to now, and its formulation is the discovery that, Freud says, should have been foreseen, namely the radical asymmetry of the sexes with regard to the castration complex and the Oedipus: "*Whereas in boys the Oedipus complex is destroyed by the castration complex, in girls it is made possible and led up to by the castration complex*" (p. 256, emphasis in original). Despite this advance in knowledge, Freud notes that we still do not understand what prompts the destruction of the Oedipus in women. He relies on the theoretical absence of castration anxiety in women to posit a less demanding, or even nonexistent, superego in them: "I cannot evade the notion (though I hesitate to give it expression) that for women the level of what is ethically normal is different from what it is in men. Their superego is never so inexorable, so impersonal, so independent of its emotional origins as we require it to be in men" (p. 257).

In these three papers ("The infantile genital organization," "The dissolution of the Oedipus complex," and "Some psychical consequences of the anatomical distinction between the sexes"), castration is the subject matter. Yet each time the approach to it is different. The first paper describes the process of recognition and symbolization of lack in the boy, ultimately relating it to the mother's castration. The second, attempting to specify how the boy separates from his mother and what enables him to leave the Oedipus, sees castration in terms of a threat, but a threat aimed more at the boy's own body than at that of the maternal Other. (I am using the Lacanian concept here, since it precisely designates the one to whom every demand of the child is addressed.) The mother is mentioned only in the margin, in no way as a starting point or basis of the demonstration. The third paper, finally, which begins with a similar question with regard to the mother—what causes the girl to separate from her?—discusses penis envy and the girl's dissatisfaction without any mention of the mother's castration or lack. The result is that the symbolic equivalence of "penis" and "child from father," which, according to Freud, prompts the turning to the father, could be taken as a rationalization, a presupposition whose motivations are not always clear.

Note

1. This formulation does not appear as such until 1925 ("Some psychical consequences . . ."), though Freud mentions the "complete" form of the Oedipus in *The Ego and the Id* (1923a); compare also 1914b.

4 Everything Has to Be Reexamined

Although they do not provide answers to all the questions raised in Freud's papers of 1923–1925, especially when it comes to the superego and the end of the Oedipus, the two papers on femininity of 1931 and 1932–1933, because they likewise involve a shift in emphasis, reveal connections that had not been noticed before and articulate what had been named but not assigned a specific place in the theoretical structure.

Though they are close in time to one another and identical in their subject matter, these two studies are indispensable for an evaluation of Freud's approach and of the time he takes between a discovery (a reversal of previously held beliefs, a step-by-step progress) and its affirmation. It is as if the discursive artifact, the *New Introductory Lectures* of 1932, supposedly addressed to a less-informed audience, allowed him to omit the retracing of the demonstrative process (as in the 1931 text) and simply to present the results as already acquired knowledge. This change in the mode of utterance from one paper to the next (the one more reflexive, the other more declarative) is, however, not a change of discourse in the direction of mastery—the return, for example, from a hysterical position of ignorance to a position of knowledge (cf. Lacan 1970, Wajeman 1982). The unknown remains, and this can be seen in the fact that the resumption of the same line of questioning highlights the gaps in the sequences (between, say, the mother's castration and the end of the love directed to her). And it enables us to see relationships that had not been conceptualized before, relationships that are elucidated from new perspectives with reference to femininity: narcissism, object choice, feminine shame, or frigidity. The illumination of certain points in 1932–1933, their more assured presentation, is merely an effect of the lecture format. The resulting clarity comes from outside, from the listener, who presumably requires further exposition. But the second paper cannot be read without the first if we are to see how Freud gradually built a more secure theoretical edifice.

The 1931 paper "Female sexuality" can be said to have the form of an investigation: establishing the facts, deducing the causes, seeking proof, and corroborating evidence. The enigma was not where one thought it would be. The structure, in four parts, reflects the movement of thought like a progressive revelation opening out from a small paradox, namely the absence of neurosis in many women who, clearly, have nevertheless not given up their oedipal father fixation.

The first phase is resolution of the paradox. Experience, as well as the necessary postulate formulated in 1925, shows that the girl's Oedipus conceals something else (1925a). It is not a simple matter as with boys, for it has behind it an entire history, the *preoedipal,* which Freud had been unable to see or assess because, he tells us, he is a man and thus naturally evokes a paternal transference in his patients. In contrast, the women analysts he cites (Helene Deutsch and Jeanne Lampl-de Groot), as mother-substitutes, were better able to see where matters stood.

The second phase is displacement of the paradox. If the preoedipal is attested by the details of the woman's Oedipus (the tenacity, or, on the contrary, the fragility of the position when it has been reached), the problem shifts. What is paradoxical is no longer the exit from the Oedipus but the entry into it. How does it happen that some women are able to leave their mother and turn toward their father? The girl's motives in leaving the original object, if we are to believe Freud here, are her discovery of her own castration and the effect of the maternal prohibition of *jouissance.*

The third phase of the enigma is the girl's sexual activity with regard to her mother. Clinical experience has to be reinterpreted in terms of the wishes of each stage (oral, anal, and phallic) in which the mother is involved, even if they appear in a form far from its origin: transference onto the father or anxiety in the wake of repression.

We shall return to these three phases of the paper as corrections of an illusion. They perform the theoretical reversal called for by the awareness of the girl's libidinal attachment to her mother beyond the demand for love addressed to the father, that same demand that had recently led Freud astray. For the moment, let us focus on the fourth phase of this argument, the contributions of other analysts. The fourth phase is the debt owed to these colleagues; all Freud has done, he tells us, is to put them in better order. He mentions seven names, omitting those of Ruth Mack Brunswick, van Ophuijsen, Stärcke, and Joan Rivière. The ones he retains are Karl Abraham, Jeanne Lampl-de Groot, Helene Deutsch, Otto Fenichel, Melanie Klein, Karen Horney, and Ernest Jones; he briefly notes his disagreement with the last three, picking out features in the work of the others that are in accord with his own views and, at the same time, pointing out that each has seen only a part of the whole.

Nor do these contributions by others play a major role in the second paper, "Femininity" (1932–1933). In contrast to the 1931 piece, which was concerned to trace the steps in the evolution of the theory, it recapitulates the "fictive" chronological order of the girl's development, describing first the early stages of libidinal relations with the mother and then the motives behind the girl's hostility and detachment. Freer in style of presentation, it is also more liberal in the acknowledgment of debts. Now it is not so much Freud who is speaking, noting points of agreement and disagreement and making use of the work of others, as it is psychoanalysis itself, the new science, as it is set forth through this intermediary. A collectivity of researchers is to be presupposed, and if only three names are mentioned—Ruth Mack Brunswick, Jeanne Lampl-de Groot, and Helene Deutsch—this is only to be expected in a lecture whose aim, among other things, is to refute allegations of misogyny.

We may also view this paper, with its subordination of indebtedness to others in the interest of rectification, as an attempt to shed light on the 1931 study, in which the reference to the work of others was the object of the conclusion. As we have seen, the entire 1931 text was deductive in approach. It set out from the facts to return to the causes, from pathological formations to the reconstruction of normal development. Only what comes later can illuminate the beginnings. So, then, may we not infer that what comes at the end of this paper, the literature review, could be what stirred Freud to his reflections, or at any rate to his exploring them in greater depth?

Why does Freud place the literature review where it has only marginal relevance? As we see when we read it, the work of his students is what gave him the firm clinical support for his theorizing; he himself, he tells us, had never seen a case all the way through. If this imbalance cannot be justified, it can at least be better understood if we recall the slowdown in the preceding decade, when Freud stated his ignorance and ascribed it to the paucity of material, the bias of researchers, and the assumption of a homology in the development of the girl and the boy on the basis of the analysis and observations of males alone. Freud's texts were taken literally, as an admission of impotence, instead of being seen as an expression of what I would like to call the Freudian *cogito* and an example of theorization of clinical fact, similar to the recognition of repressed material in analytic treatment: *that's what It/ the id was, and I didn't know that I knew it.* This is a Freudian *cogito* in the mode of doubt, of appeal to the knowledge of the Other. Others respond to this request between 1925 and 1932–1933, bringing case material, interpretations, a new configuration of knowledge based on uncertainty: each asks Freud for a guarantee, and he himself (1925a) had asked for his colleagues' help: "An eager crowd of fellow-workers is ready to make use of what is unfinished or doubtful" (p. 249). The fact that he later tends to refer to this help in terms of synthesizing others' contributions or putting them in order did not keep him from acknowledging, in the nascent analytic community, the work that he had made possible and often encouraged, helping along the efforts of his colleagues, as we learn from Ruth Mack Brunswick (1940) and Helene Deutsch (1973). He thus assumed responsibility for the statements of those he had trained, serving as guarantor at the cost of ignoring matters of intellectual property and the narcissism of small differences.

The reconceptualization of femininity in the early 1930s is in part based on that "working through" in theorizing that Freud noted (1923b), a matter of retroactivity, of return to the same issues but with a different emphasis. And it is also a matter of insisting on taking the time to achieve certainty on a given point of doctrine. We can therefore try to define his new positions by seeing how he was led to them in the *Nachträglichkeit* of his own experience. But the experience he had asked for, that of his students, is largely responsible for the rectification of his findings, if only because, in this same effort against repression, Freud must be attentive to what they noticed and he himself had not seen. As I have mentioned, when Freud fears that he will not have time to conduct new experiments he urgently asks for outside confirmation of his discovery (cf. 1925a). I shall be looking separately at the colleagues who replied in their papers and observations, compelling Freud to revise or corroborate his suggestions, whether or not he himself acknowledged these colleagues individually or even recognized their contributions. We shall see that all of them, each in his or her own way, illustrate a constant tension between clinical phenomenology and its conceptualization.

5   The Girl's Oedipus

We shall understand nothing about women, Freud says in the 1932–1933 paper, if we do not consider everything that precedes and threatens to prevent the girl's entry into the Oedipus, namely the quality, intensity, and unsuspected duration of her love for her mother. For the boy, the kernel of neurosis is the Oedipus. But not for the girl; what counts, for her, must be sought elsewhere, in the preoedipal period that, moreover, will determine how she approaches the Oedipus.

This is a major revision. And yet—what is perhaps most surprising of all—such a reexamination of prior conceptions does not affect either the assurance or the firmness of the tone: we find neither reticence nor assertions of mastery. It is as though, at the moment when Freud states that everything must be reexamined, everything, for him had already been revised or designated for reinterpretation. I shall try to show how this assurance is based on observations that, however fragmentary or remote, had already been made. In other words, he claims the authority of clinical experience that, at this time, he does not feel the need to present fully and that acquires its meaning only later.

In "Some psychical consequences . . ." (1925a), Freud had asked how the girl was able to separate from her first object, her mother. The 1931–1933 papers start from the same point: how does she get to the father? But now, instead of spending time on the motives for separation, they retrace the steps of, and exactly specify the reasons for, the attachment to the mother. The positive Oedipus of the boy remains the preoedipal phase—the negative Oedipus, if you will—of the girl.

The mother is the first love object for girl and boy alike because she provided care and food, and it is to her that all desires are addressed at each stage of infantile sexual development: oral, anal-sadistic, even phallic, as we know from their pathological manifestations in fixations and regressions. The girl's anxiety that she will be devoured or killed, the beginnings of a later paranoia, refers to the oral stage; the aggression of the anal-sadistic stage, often converted to anxiety, is at least equal to that of the boy. The analysis of children's play by our women analysts tells us as much, Freud says. The accusation of seduction, like the wish to impregnate the mother or to bear a child for her, are ideas "belonging to the phallic phase and sufficiently surprising, but established beyond doubt by analytic exploration" (1932–1933, p. 120). "With their entry into the phallic phase the differences between the sexes are completely eclipsed by their agreements. We are now obliged to recognize that the little girl is a little man" (p. 118).

The child's desire for the father thus has at least one precedent, since it was originally a demand addressed to the mother. Freud once again sets out from the point he had made in the 1925 paper: because he had encountered in nonneurotic women the intensity of the fixation to the father and the persistence of a demand for a child from him, he was obliged to consider the relation to the mother, the relation to the father being merely its heir. There was also the fact of clinging to the Oedipus—for, once this position had been attained, women were not quick to leave it—that made Freud (1925a) take a new look at femininity.

Then, too, difficulties in women's love lives put the primacy of the Oedipus into question. Thus the hostility of certain women toward a husband they themselves had chosen according to the paternal prototype shows that the repressed, here the bitterness toward the mother, can always return. This is preoedipal hostility, since getting from the father or his substitute what the mother gets, in other words, mitigating the oedipal rivalry, is not sufficient.

Likewise, the birth of a child can unsettle a marriage, Freud says in 1932–1933, because the woman, now a mother herself, identifies with her own mother and repeats the unhappy relationship of her parents. The husband in both cases (preoedipal or oedipal hostility) bears the brunt of his wife's feelings toward her mother. The failure of a first marriage that "The taboo of virginity" (1918) had ascribed to the father, on the grounds that no later love object can equal a woman's father or brother, is now, in 1932–1933, seen in terms of the relation to the mother. The original love experience with the mother poses a risk to the attempt to turn to the father. Everything, therefore, must be reconceptualized. The fantasy of seduction by the father, though it is the typical expression of the woman's Oedipus complex, signals her entry into that complex just as does her hatred toward her mother. But this is not the original state of things. The seducer who appears in the preoedipal history of little girls is not the father but the mother. Similarly, the accusation that the father has castrated her is a transposition of the earlier situation in which, for the girl, the mother is responsible for her castration. Clearly, the Oedipus is only a fallback position.

The Oedipus is precarious when the penis envy that pushes the girl toward her father can just as easily lead to the rejection of all sexuality or to a sexuality that remains, or once again becomes, conflictual. What Freud had observed fifteen years earlier takes on new significance. The regressive desire that some women show toward their husband's organ when they want to keep it for themselves, the hostility that may accompany sexual gratification, the common occurrence of frigidity as the female form of psychic impotence: all these signs of repressed masculinity that Freud had analyzed (1915a, 1918) gave an idea of the crooked path leading to femininity, an essential aspect of which is the passage through a masculine identity. First there is the wish for the organ, then the wish for the man as an appendage of the penis, then the wish for a child, which allows for the passage from self-love to object love.

What Freud establishes in 1931–1933 is the structural role of penis envy, that is, its role in the construction of the girl's "Oedipus," her turning toward her father. Insofar as the wish for a child is an oedipal wish for a child by the father, penis envy must precede it. This is so because what the girl in the phallic phase wants is, as with the boy, to have impregnated the mother. This is the active wish to have a child by the mother that Freud finds in little girls' doll play, but he finds here, in this identification with the phallic-active mother, evidence of their masculinity. The wish for a child by the father is found only after the onset of penis envy. This wish was at first addressed to the mother; when the girl turns to her father, she does so because her attempt with her mother ended in disappointment, in the recognition of the mother's lack. All the reasons given for the girl's hostility toward her mother when she separates from her (premature weaning, preference for siblings, the ambivalence of intense love, the aggressivity triggered by the prohibition of masturbation) are not unique to the girl. The only specific cause is her inferior organ, her "castration," and for these she blames her mother, especially so when she becomes aware of the latter's castration and, generalizing this lack, devalues all women along with her mother.

The 1931 paper, however, does not place the depreciation of women in direct causal relation with the detachment from the mother. The clarifications supplied in 1932–1933 are based on a slight difference in the way the problem is formulated: "No doubt her turning away from her mother does not occur all at once, for to begin with the girl regards her castration as an individual misfortune and only gradually extends it to other females and finally to her mother as well. Her love was directed to her *phallic* mother; with the discovery that her mother is castrated it becomes possible to drop her as an object" (p. 126, italics in original). The connection between hatred for the mother and penis envy finally appears: "the little girl has hitherto lived in a masculine way, has been able to get pleasure by the excitation of her clitoris, and has brought this activity into relation with her sexual wishes directed toward her mother, which are often active ones; now, owing to the influence of her penis envy, she loses her enjoyment in her phallic sexuality" (p. 126).

The change of sex—passing from masculinity to femininity—comes at the cost of abandoning the belief in the maternal phallus and, simultaneously, renouncing the clitoral sexuality that was associated with the mother. If this repression does not achieve its aim, Freud had noted (1925a) and repeats in 1931, the return of the repressed can occur in the form of obsessive masturbation and the struggle against it. Between the recognition of the mother's castration and the turn to the father, then, the girl normally gives up both phallic *jouissance* and the fantasy of possessing the penis. The missing link has now been found. The primacy of the phallus, for the girl as well as for the boy, is what determines the separation from the mother and the turn to the father. This phallic primacy could have been foreseen. It was already there at the level of the symptom and noted in clinical experience as early as the *Three Essays* (1905a), where Freud observes that, when the dominant erotogenic zone changes and masculinity is repressed, a predisposition to neurosis, especially hysteria, can arise.

Does the emphasis on the girl's early masturbation and the assumptions about the equation penis envy = wish for a child find a retroactive explanation that bears them out? As we have seen, Freud was always concerned with the girl's masturbatory pleasure—the "phallic *jouissance*" of the 1932–1933 paper—and assigned it a decisive place, if only because of the damage that may accompany its repression. Yet this repression is inevitable and prescribed, since the girl must eventually pass from this active and "virile" phase, associated with the fantasy of possessing the penis, to the passive "feminine" phase that is properly hers, when, before she expects to get something from her father, she has to acknowledge her own lack. She first encountered this lack in comparing her genitals to those of her male alter ego, to her own disadvantage. This imaginary prejudice, said in 1925 to be traumatic, supposedly led the girl to give up her first zone of "male" *jouissance* in favor of what we later find to be the investment of the specifically "feminine" zone, the vagina, the existence of which, Freud maintains, is suspected neither by the girl nor by the boy in the first phase.

Yet Freud does not immediately understand the traumatic experience that leads to the girl's repression of her love for her mother and puts an end to clitoral masturbation. To be sure, penis envy had been noted early on (cf. 1915a and 1916–1917), but in the form of the conscious demand, made by little girls and later by women, for compensation of a wrong done to them. I have the impression that there was not enough clinical evidence for recognizing this claim as having the instinctual force of unconscious wishes; in the *Introductory Lectures* (1916–1917) the allusions to it come only from direct observation, and, in "Some character types met with in psycho-analytic work" (1916b), Freud appeals to common experience. It was not until 1916a ("On transformation of instinct") and 1918 ("The taboo of virginity") that clinical evidence was offered for the unconscious manifestations of the castration complex in women. In the latter paper, he notes that the dream of a young bride revealed her wish to castrate her husband and keep his penis for herself. Such a dream, says Freud, is a typical reaction to defloration: "Behind this envy for the penis, there comes to light the woman's hostile bitterness against the man" (p. 205). The oddity of a compulsive hostility towards the husband is explained in the same way:

> Light is thrown on the riddle of female frigidity by certain pathological cases in which, after the first and indeed after each repeated instance of sexual intercourse, the woman gives unconcealed expression of her hostility toward the man by abusing him, raising her hand against him, or actually striking him. In one very clear case of this kind, which I was able to submit to a thorough analysis, this happened although the woman loved the man very much, used to demand intercourse herself, and unmistakably found great satisfaction in it. [p. 201]

We need to note the point at which the allegedly damaging equation of the penis and a child from the father is not self-evident. The 1916a paper discusses the linguistic and symbolic overdeterminations that lead from one to the other: little one = penis = child // penis = excrement = gift = child (cf. also 1914a). But getting the organ through the partner who really possesses it does not always lead to the anticipated effects. Far from placating the woman, Freud observes, it can unleash her aggression, even when she has been satisfied on the level of need. In other words, instead of making up for an imaginary lack, the offer of the real organ makes the woman incomplete, dephallicizes her, thereby reactivating her castration: "a woman's *immature sexuality* is discharged onto the man who first makes her acquainted with the sexual act" (1918, p. 206; emphasis in original).

What is it in Freud's clinical experience that, in 1923, was not enough to warrant his drawing conclusions, but that, in 1932–1933, reassures him about the girl's turn to her father as the one who possesses the desirable object and can give what the mother does not have? There can be no doubt that the case of the young homosexual woman (1920a) is retroactively decisive here, even if it seems to involve just the opposite, a failure to receive the phallus. The fact that the father does not give proves that something is expected from him. He does not give it, as we see, because he is exclusively preoccupied with the mother, and so, when he gives, it is to her. What leads Freud to confirm the equivalence of penis and child in this case is the coincidence between the inversion of the girl (aged 16 at the time) and the moment when the mother has gotten a baby boy from the father, a baby that the girl, experiencing in puberty the revival of her childhood Oedipus, believes should have been given to her.

The result, her intense love for mothers—substitutes for a real mother not well suited for the role—tends to prove that the phallus, the power of the gift, has now entirely reverted to the maternal side. The adoration of the Lady can have no other explanation, Freud concludes, than this initial, now manifest, homosexual stream into which the "deeper, heterosexual libido-stream" had been deflected (p. 228). The Lady was not her first love but the last in a series of women with whom the girl had been in love, to her father's great anger. These were "mature" women who represented the "rephallicized" mother by being both mothers and women of easy virtue, "women who were not celebrated for specially strict propriety. . . . Moreover, in all these affairs it had never been a question of women who had any reputation for homosexuality, and who might, therefore, have offered her some prospect of homosexual gratification; on the contrary, she illogically courted women who were coquettes in the ordinary sense of the word" (p. 218). The Lady's bad reputation was a condition for sexual life that is in all ways similar—astonishingly so, as Freud emphasizes— to what he describes in the case of men who have a mother complex.

The father had returned this phallic value to the mother, the real child he gave her indicating that it was she whom he desired. Hence she can no longer be considered lacking or castrated. As the father's exclusive attention shows, she is everything that can be desired. The search for the phallus in the beloved Lady is confirmed, Freud tells us, by another remarkable point, namely that the girl sees in her a resemblance to an older brother whose attributes she had envied as a child. The masculine ego ideal and the revival of childhood love for the phallic mother form an alliance when the father's love fails. He has not dephallicized the mother nor, a fortiori, phallicized the girl by enabling her to symbolize her "castration" through the symbolic gift of an imaginary object (a child she could hope for) in exchange for a real penis.[1] Thus she defies her father in her exhibition of love for the Lady, who, as she knows, is someone he disapproves of. To love, as she loves the Lady, as her father loves her mother, is to offer proof of what one does not have, and this holds just as true for him as for her.

We can see that, though the symbolic equation of the penis with a child from the father is normative and accounts for the destiny of a number of women, it is in itself a complex process of substitutions and transformations, one that is threatened, moreover, by the slightest failing on the part of the father, given that what is at issue is determining what the desirable object is and where it can be found. Thus, in 1920, Freud condemns the demand for the phallus in the girl and the boy alike. There is a great risk that the real organ and the child-as-substitute will both be found inadequate to signify it.

In the same sense, even before the 1925 paper that emphasizes penis envy and the penis/child equation, Freud had noted the hysterical phenomenon of the identification of the girl with her father (cf. Chapter 7 of 1921b). He describes this masculine identification in the 1923–1924 additions to the Dora case (1905b) in terms of homosexuality and gynecophilia, which he had not taken into account in the relationship of Dora and Frau K.: what, beyond Dora herself as the intermediary promoting the affair between her father and Frau K., is her father seeking in this woman he loves? This question keeps Dora in her position, since she herself, loved by Herr K., is beyond the love he has for his wife. If the latter means nothing to him, as he claims, then the belief that there is something desirable about a woman collapses.

There is another way in which, early on, Freud indicates that the phallus is not necessarily a male prerogative. He observes that the real lack of the male organ does not stand in the way of male phenomena, readable as such, in the symptoms of hysteria. And we do not have to force the texts of 1916a and 1918 to see that they allow us to conceptualize castration in terms other than the possession or lack of the real organ. The phallus is not the male organ when the obtaining of this organ in the sex act can revive a feeling of castration in a woman.

The perplexity of the years 1923–1925 was justified not, as Freud claimed, by a paucity of clinical material but by material that was evasive (as when the ground gives way under one's feet) because it had not been fully decoded. Experience preceded its apprehension and theoretical formulation. For in fact it is this same material, partially illuminated, that returns in 1931–1933, this time as the irrefutable weight of experience that, in place of ignorance, yields certainty—even if, here too, all is not said or said again. It is as though theorization, in its separate steps, had temporarily paused on this side of the issues, favoring instead the case material.

Hence we find, at the end of the 1932–1933 paper, some other "psychical peculiarities of mature femininity" (p. 132) associated with penis envy. He lists shame, narcissism, and object choice, without noting the implications for what remains, for him, a presupposition: the absence of castration anxiety and of a superego in women, although he has already given, elsewhere, the wherewithal to rethink them. We can rely on Freud's own comments to confirm that the phallus is not reducible to the organ that signifies it imaginarily. This explains why women and men alike, independently of anatomical sex, can be situated in a problematic of "having" or "being" it.

Let us reread Freud: "Shame, which is considered to be a feminine characteristic *par excellence*, but is far more a matter of convention than might be supposed, has as its purpose, we believe, concealment of genital deficiency" (1932–1933, p. 132). A lack or a secret? What one hides behind the veil can just as well be a secret, something to be kept safe. Shame, given the extreme variability of its historic and somatic manifestations (redness of this or that body part, the *erythema pudicum* of virgins, well known to derma-

tologists, that stops where the gaze ought to stop—at the décolleté),
clearly shows the displacement onto the female body of what is
desirable. The entire body may be invested with phallic value and,
simultaneously, blushing or covered.

The reflux of libido onto the entire body, the falling in love with
her own body when, at puberty, she takes on the shape of the
mother: this, too, is the phallicization of herself that explains the
woman's narcissism, her vanity as well as her fragility on this point,
which is not unrelated to the boy's castration anxiety. All the same,
being the phallus, as is shown by men's attraction to narcissistic
women and their agitation, well attested in literature, at the signs
of feminine shame (cf. Hamon 1986), presupposes the gaze of the
Other and the constant possibility of disgrace.

The narcissistic object choice of some women is, according to
Freud, another consequence of penis envy. One loves a person who
has all the qualities one would like to possess oneself. Such a choice
corresponds to the ego ideal, already analyzed in the paper on
narcissism (1914c), reaffirmed in the study of group psychology
(1921b, Chapter 8), and linked in 1932–1933 to the castration
complex. And such a choice contradicts the assertion of superego
weakness in women, when the ascription of all the qualities of the
self to this ideal figure, at the same time as it leads to falling in love,
also leads to subjection: the one who occupies this ideal place can
ask anything of you. The narcissism of this choice is emphasized
in "The taboo of virginity" (1918), where a certain young woman,
the one whose behavior toward her husband was so hostile, reports
that before she turned to her father, it was her favored younger
brother, possessor of the envied organ, who was the object of her
interest. For the young lesbian as well (1920a), envy of her older
brother, who was endowed with qualities considered preferable,
preceded the inversion and reinforces her unconditional love for
the Lady. The love object, the person one would have loved to be,
is loved as bearer of the phallus.

If it is not possible to give up the fantasy of having a penis, the
masculinity complex is merely another form of narcissistic protest,
a denial, in women, of the lack of the desirable object via identification with the father as bearer of the phallus. Though it occurs at

the same point (after the rejection of the phallic mother), the girl's identification with the father does not have the same implications as for the boy, who, in identifying with the father, drops his demand for love and thereby becomes independent. A modulated, integrated superego protects the boy from parental authority and marks the end of the Oedipus (cf. Freud 1925a, Millot 1984 [reprinted in Millot 1988]). In the case of the girl, however, the paternal identification can lead both to castration anxiety if she imagines that she has the male organ (cf. Braunschweig 1926) and to an increased dependence. Castration anxiety of this kind can be seen in the young lesbian (Freud 1920a), who has to get her father to acknowledge her "masculinity," to demonstrate defiantly before his eyes that she lacks nothing. But her dependence increases because that attempt does not suffice. The gaze of the (oedipal) father is conjoined with that of the Lady, loved in the same way as the (preoedipal) mother.

The dependence on the male Other, in this search for ways to symbolize the desirable object, finds a remarkable illustration in "The disposition to obsessional neurosis" (1913a), as in the *Introductory Lectures* (1916–1917) and in "Dreams and telepathy" (1922a). If these examples allow us to infer the persistence of the Oedipus in girls, an indefinite clinging to the demand made on the father, they also suggest that what is expected from him or his substitute, beyond the wish for a child, is recognition that one is a sexuated being. A woman has no other way of recognizing herself as a woman, of symbolizing her sex, than by trusting the good will of her partner: if he does not desire her, then what is she? The wedding-night trauma of the "woman with the tablecloth" (described in 1916–1917), and the repeated evocation, however fleeting, of her husband's impotence, can be understood by such a woman as a denial of her womanliness and can entail a devaluation of her genitality that can be expressed only in obsessional symptoms. This dependence on the whim of an Other[2] shows the point to which a woman's superego, like that of a man, can be embodied by the partner.

Identification with the phallus constantly threatened with inadequacy, idealization of and subjection to the object, identification with the bearer of the phallus who arouses castration anxiety, dependence on the Other in obsessional neurosis: all these points made by Freud run contrary to what he maintains, even if without special emphasis, in 1931–1933, namely the absence of castration anxiety and the minimal superego demand in women. Yet he does note that women have a superego that, instead of freeing them, alienates them in their relation to the mother. Freud indicates in connection with the case of female paranoia (1915a), as with the young lesbian (1920a), that there is an inevitable encounter with maternal prohibition and that, in the case of girls, this is sanctioned by society. Here the parental authority is external, but what he says in 1932–1933 about the harsh struggle against masturbation, in which the girl takes on the role of the prohibiting mother, leaves no doubt about the existence and the inexorability of the super-ego in women.

Yet Freud explicitly underestimates the female superego, and this surely has to do with the fact that he attaches, or, rather, as-similates it to the girl's irresolution of the castration complex, since it is this irresolution that, for him, necessarily brings her into the Oedipus. It is in this sense that we may understand Freud's remarks on women's identifications as residues of their object cathexes (cf. 1923a): each romance leads to an ideal. In other words, a woman's superego is often just her masculine ego ideal. Let us anticipate: Klein's assertion (1932, Chapter 11) that the paternal superego is always stronger in girls than in boys is not inconsistent with Freud's concept of the identification of certain women with their aban-doned male love objects. As we shall see, this is the stage in which both Freud and Klein will locate the mechanism of introjection (a primitive form of identification), though in a different way: for one, it follows the Oedipus; for the other, it precedes it.

The link between the Oedipus, the phallic phase, and castra-tion, as Freud points out in the case of the girl, does not have the same consequences as with the boy. At any rate, the connection with the superego is lost. But he says this himself. He is concerned, in 1932–1933, only to place certain phenomena into relief. Doesn't his recommendation that the reader refer to the analytic literature on the subject suggest that we are to search out the reasons for his omissions, that we read him in terms of what he distinguishes him-self from and in terms of the perspective he lacks, or in terms of a kind of economy of demonstration in which what he does not say will be found in others?

Notes

1. These Lacanian distinctions among *real, symbolic,* and *imaginary* are to be found, among other texts, in his rereadings of the Dora case and the present case in his seminar on the object relation (1956–1957).

2. I use this expression, which is Lacan's, to indicate the radical heterogeneity of the Other of the demand (the one to whom the demand is addressed), whatever sex he or she may be, identical or not to that of the subject, given that this Other may counter you with a rejection, an absence of response, or a flat refusal.

6   The Girl as Little Man

One of the difficulties presented by the set of texts in which Freud discusses femininity (1923b, 1924a, 1925a, 1931, 1932–1933) is their abstract nature. In reconstructing the stages of feminine sexuality and the vicissitudes of the Oedipus, they offer no case material and rely on none of the observations that, in earlier papers, justified Freud's claims and explicated them in the work of theorization that followed. The scarcity of clinical references is possible, it seems to me, only because those colleagues whom he is addressing when he communicates the results of his thinking are the ones who supplied the casuistry, that is, the cases than enabled him to draw his conclusions.

So it is with van Ophuijsen, whose major paper, "Contributions to the masculinity complex in women" (1924), was known as early as 1917, in which year it was given as a lecture. Freud cites it in "A child is being beaten" (1919a) and even says that it is his source for the expression "masculinity complex," something he would later forget. Yet van Ophuijsen's formulations of the girl's demand for the penis, denial of its absence, and expectation of acquiring it are quite close to those that Freud will take up again from 1923 to 1933, this time without forgetting that the girl's demand is at first addressed to her mother, something that, to my knowledge, van Ophuijsen was the first to state.

This paper is of twofold interest, first of all for the clinical material van Ophuijsen adduces—five cases of obsessional women—in explaining his theoretical starting points and framework, and then because (as I believe has not been noted before) the young woman whose case is reported in greatest detail is also the object of Jeanne Lampl-de Groot's paper, "The evolution of the Oedipus complex in women" (1928), which Freud praises in 1931.

Thus the same case history is discussed by two analysts. Did the first believe that he had come up against the limits of the paternal transference and needed to hand over the case to a woman? We do not know. Still, Lampl-de Groot notes that certain difficulties relating to the transference had not been resolved, and she concludes that the negative Oedipus was so deeply repressed in this patient that it could not be reached except in a lengthy treatment and perhaps could not be revealed with a male analyst. Because a woman could not compete with a father-figure analyst, the treatment could not reach beyond the positive oedipal stage. It was from the nature of the transference in this second analysis (declarations of passionate and jealous love followed by manifestations of hatred) that the analyst became convinced that she was dealing with a repetition of the patient's relationship with her mother. And, on the basis of the analysis of a childhood dream, she emphasizes the extent to which the little girl's phallic activity is addressed to the mother or her substitute. We may note that here she is simply confirming, in different terms, the interpretation van Ophuijsen had already made of this dream; he too spoke of homosexuality and pregenital fixation, but, more than Lampl-de Groot, he was concerned—this was before 1925—to show how the patient's later dreams and neurotic difficulties revealed the identification with the father.

Van Ophuijsen found confirmation of his intuitions and a wish to theorize his observations in Freud's paper "Some character types met with in psycho-analytic work" (1916b), where Freud notes the prejudice that girls feel they have suffered because they were born girls instead of boys, for which they reproach their mothers. His starting point is the *masculinity complex*, a phrase with which he describes a form of the castration complex in women that does not involve guilt. On the contrary, what is most pronounced is the bitter feeling of having been mistreated. Protest and a feeling of injustice are what stand out in those cases of women who behave as though they had male genitals (for example, making room to accommodate them when they sit down). Where does this childhood fantasy come from, and why does it take this form no matter what disconfirmation later experience or information might bring, or whatever repression of these early instinctual drives might have been achieved?

Van Ophuijsen notes that one of his women patients, when she had the feeling of being useless, would often feel like asking her mother for something the mother could not give. Here he finds what is without a doubt the heart of the complex. First, then, there is an unconscious reproach addressed to the mother. To this he adds that three of his five women patients described themselves as exceptional because of an anatomical peculiarity, Hottentot nymphae. The feeling of being an exception (cf. Freud 1916b) is clear. Manifested as a "secret" in some women, it is explicitly related, in the case discussed at greatest length, to an experience of *jouissance* dating from a dream in the patient's fourth year.

When the memory of an observation or an exceptional event forms the point of departure for a fantasy of this kind, we are dealing, van Ophuijsen tells us, with the return of a repressed wish in a recent definition, that is, with a screen memory. According to him, the girl's reactions upon discovering the difference between the sexes reveal just such an unconscious wish, later repressed. Earlier than Freud, he traces its manifestations: bitterness at lacking what the boy has, anxiety and guilt, hope that the organ will grow larger as she herself grows up, or denial—all admissions that the penis is fervently desired, at least when the lack is not felt as a wound and gives rise to anger or dejection.

The reactive fantasy that one does, after all, possess the male organ is thus equivalent to the idea of "being a man." Though other expressions of this same fantasy may be less stark, according to van Ophuijsen they still have to be taken literally: the wish to claim possession of a person instead of being the devotedly attached one, feeling like penetrating someone instead of being penetrated herself, remarking that a tension state would disappear if only she could *let go of* something instead of being burdened by it. This last formulation is that of the woman patient who is van Ophuijsen's primary example and the case he sets forth at greatest length.

He first reports her symptoms. This young woman, a musician from a very early age, suffered from extreme shyness around men and inhibition in her public performances. Attuned to the desire for her father, who encouraged her musical gifts, she identified with his penis, which would calm the tension she felt before an audience or with a composer. Her associations enabled van Ophuijsen to trace the origin of the fantasy. The little girl's toilet training had been intimately connected with the attentive and loving presence of both parents: the mother's words and closeness, the father's sounds stimulating urination. In this sphincter education the child, summoned to give up something of herself, was encouraged by the more or less perverse expectations of the parents, which the analyst thus interprets as a seduction. The erotic charge of such childhood situations determined her vocation, itself erotized to the point of becoming inhibited, via projection of a paternal trait. Often, while seated on the toilet, the patient would emit a thin stream of water so as to make a melody. When giving a concert, she often had the impression that her playing put an end to the tension she felt when before the public.

The analyst deduces a fixation to urethral erotism and tracks it down in the patient's anamnesis: the way in which she practiced masturbation, exhibitionism, and scoptophilia; her ambitiousness; and her infantile sexual theory of intercourse (one "wets the bed" in urinating, as she imagined the father does inside the mother during sexual relations). And he suggests that identification with the father's genital is the key to the childhood dream, the very dream that Jeanne Lampl-de Groot analyzed as proof of phallic desire directed at the preoedipal mother. The patient reported that, when she was not yet 4 years old and was still sleeping in her parents' bedroom, she dreamed, or had an originary fantasy, that she was in bed next to her mother. She felt a very pleasant bodily sensation that surprised her, and her mother told her that this was fine, there was nothing wrong with it. She then experienced a kind or orgasm and awoke. Astonished and dismayed, she discovered that she had soiled her bed. She called her mother, who helped her without scolding.

Van Ophuijsen relates this pregenital (anal and urethral) fixation back to the manner in which her parents toilet trained her: "I'll give you the words (from the mother) or sounds (from the father) of love, so that you'll give me what you owe me, urine or feces." The feeling of injustice—due, he says, to castration—comes from the sudden privation of what had hitherto assured fulfillment. She recalls as the decisive moment a slap from father when, seeking assistance as she did every night in these erotically invested functions, she asked for extra help. Renouncing love, she no longer made any demands; instead she identified with the father, or with his organ, at the cost of maintaining an extreme shyness toward him. The screen memory thus enables us to understand the passage from seduction to prohibition.

The same injustice was experienced, at other times in her childhood, whenever she was surprised by the maternal imperative without any advance preparation. This was the case when she was sent off to school; it was as though something had been taken from her that she could not quite put into words. This was relived in the transference when the analyst set a date for ending the treatment before the patient felt ready, before she had had sufficient time for infantile modes of gratification. It was as though she had been abruptly weaned, without knowing why, from an early *jouissance* that was hers by right.

What strikes us in this case report, even before the discovery by Freud of the primacy of the phallus in the boy—a fortiori in the girl—and his assertion of a phallic phase in girls, is van Ophuijsen's insistence on the mode of pregenital sexuality (and fixation) that is closest to it, for urethral erotism is connected with this same "male" organ. The patient's fixation enabled the analyst to account for both the modes of expression of the felt privation (something the patient could not name had been taken from her) and also her symptoms. Her shyness, van Ophuijsen observes, was overdetermined, due to the renunciation of the demand for love but also to the phenomena of hysterical displacement, the shocking meaning of which did not escape the girl and hence produced her inhibition. She compared her facial congestion (associated in her fantasy with bowel training) to tumescence; outbursts of weeping took on the value of ejaculations; the erogenous displacement from anus to mouth was such that, when someone spoke to her, she could not help noticing whether the person had some sort of mouth odor.

If we follow van Ophuijsen, this same pregenital fixation explains the identification with the father's organ. Why does pregenital phallicism persist in this case as a denial of castration instead of inducing the turn toward the father? The analyst explains that this has to do with a renunciation of the demand for the father's love. When an oedipal attempt (a love affair with a brother of her father's) fails, it triggers a brief homosexual episode that brings the patient to the analyst—to a man. This oscillation from the female object to the male one, and vice versa, is also noted by Jeanne Lampl-de Groot, who mentions the patient's having come to her from a male analyst.

The two other cases reported by van Ophuijsen (a woman whose masculinity complex is manifested in her desire to urinate like a man, another female patient who acts as though she really possesses a male organ) confirm his interpretation, before the fact, along preoedipal lines. Indeed, van Ophuijsen tells us, in the first case the father's death and the mother's debilitating illness that made her totally dependent on the patient led to the reactivation of a major portion of infantile libido, the attachment to the same-sex object no longer being threatened by external prohibitions. The patient's bitterness, in the second case, remained attached to the mother who refused her the male organ that, in the shadow puppetry of childhood, she tried hard to project onto her own genital region.

What do we see here if not the prefiguration of the connection Freud would later try to highlight in order to explain phallicism in the girl, the connection between the investment or disinvestment of the "male" (clitoral) erogenous zone and the attachment to or detachment from the maternal object?

And it is not coincidental that Lampl-de Groot's conclusion, taken up literally by Freud, to the effect that in the phallic stage the girl is really a little man, is based on material from analyses first conducted by van Ophuijsen. The nature of the transference persuades Lampl-de Groot that the romantic conquest she sees in the patient's behavior is above all aimed at the mother. For her, the childhood dream is evidence of the reality of the primal scene, and she interprets it as a clear representation of intercourse with the mother who was so intensely loved at that time, the bedwetting being a substitute for masturbation or the result of it. She uses terms proposed by Freud (1925a): the girl's phallic phase (penis envy) and narcissistic feeling of inferiority lead her to separate from the mother and simultaneously to give up masturbation, without the link between the two being perfectly clear for Freud.

Lampl-de Groot examines this link, emphasizing the wishes of the girl-child in this phallic period. There is not just the narcissistic wish for the coveted organ but also an active wish directed to the mother, the love object, whom she wants to seduce and conquer just as the boy does. And so, reasoning in terms of the "complete Oedipus" in order to compare the boy and the girl (a negative oedipal phase and a positive oedipus phase for each sex), Lampl-de Groot explains the disparity of the risks incurred with the abandonment of the first oedipal position, "positive" for the boy, "negative" for the girl. The renunciation of the negative phase for the boy, when he drops his father as love object, at least preserves his genital, the feminine position vis-à-vis the father having presupposed castration. The renunciation of the positive phase (when he drops his incestuous love for his mother) preserves not only his genital, but also, in a way, his object—though for later on. The abandonment is merely a provisional one.

In contrast, Lampl-de Groot says, when the girl recognizes the fact of her castration, she must definitively abandon both the fantasy of possessing a penis and also the maternal object, drinking the cup of her bitter loss to the dregs. If the girl is really a little man in the early period of development, this is because in her masturbation, as well as in her erotic aim and object choice, she behaves like a boy. The struggle against masturbation, much more intense for the girl than for the boy, is justified by the fact that masturbation reminds her of her first romantic disappointment, the pain of the first loss of a love object. In other words, having a penis serves to conquer and possess the object.

To have or to be the phallus? For it is in these terms of identification with the phallus, *for* the mother, that Lampl-de Groot analyzes a later fantasy dating from the patient's seventh or eighth year.

Van Ophuijsen had noted this "hospital fantasy" but had not spent time on it; according to him it stemmed from the young woman's ambition and her concern to live up to her father's wishes by being a Christ figure flying over the hospital beds and bringing comfort to the sick. Lampl-de Groot sees in the flight image not only a sexual symbol but a fantasy of parthenogenesis: Christ, conceived without a father, was thus the only man to possess the mother. This doubly phallic Christ figure, omnipotence and castration incarnate, is also found in another part of the fantasy. The patient saved the sick people (with whom she identified) after they had undergone extreme torture, including being skinned alive. In any case, the identification with Christ, the man born without a father, implies the neglect of the paternal object in this fantasy (cf. Freud 1931). Does this explain the regret Freud shows in connection with Lampl-de Groot's work? He says that she has not sufficiently considered the hatred accompanying the change of object. But this reproach is to some extent unfounded, insofar as the alternations of the transference, both negative and positive, that Lampl-de Groot conceptualizes in terms of maternal transference point to seduction followed by hostility toward the mother substitute and detachment from her (stopping the treatment). Still, I would say that these remarks suggesting hostility toward the mother fall short of van Ophuijsen's, since in each case he indicates that the request and the reproach are first made to the mother.

And, in my opinion, the shortcoming of Lampl-de Groot's analysis is not the one that Freud observes. What we do not find in her, as opposed to van Ophuijsen, is the mother's lack, the nature of the mother as *phallic* or *castrated*, and this is because Lampl-de Groot does not take up the forms of the demand that the girl addresses to her mother. For Freud in 1931–1933, this lack in the mother is the only way to account for the passage to the father.

7   Castration and the Loss
of the Breast

Another reference integrated by Freud without explicit mention in the 1931–1933 papers on femininity is August Stärcke's 1921 study of the castration complex. Its main point is well known, since Abraham, Freud, Helene Deutsch, and especially Melanie Klein mention it: weaning is the prototype of castration. Freud alludes to this indirectly in a note to "The infantile genital organization" (1923b), though he cites Stärcke in another note added in the same year to the beginning of the account of the analysis of Little Hans (1909a).

This paper is of the greatest interest. It formulates for the first time that the breast belongs to the subject's own body, so that its removal is experienced as a severance between the me and the not-me. But it is especially valuable for its tight argumentation, whose logical rigor, along with the priority granted to clinical fact, ends up demonstrating the opposite of what the author sets out to prove.

Let us say, to schematize, that there are four phases of reply to an initial question of why, for the unconscious, the phallic signifier is the signifier of lack, despite the fact that (1) it is the breast that is really missing; (2) if it is not the breast, this is because the breast is unable to be represented; (3) and yet it comes first and is what determines the fantasy of the phallic mother, so that, if we don't find it, this is because it is archaic, autoerotic, and hence repressed; moreover, it is what enables us to account for sadism. Finally, (4) if the phallus is not the breast, it amounts to the same thing; expressing castration as loss of the breast is just a manner of speaking.

My thesis, then, is that, despite its aim, Stärcke's paper paradoxically and unwittingly acknowledges the primacy of the phallus. All Freud has to do in order to confirm it is take one step beyond this self-refuting effort. This is because of the question posed at the outset: how can we understand, rationalize, this experiential fact that is the castration complex? Like van Ophuijsen, Stärcke explains the unconscious grammar of the complex, the wishes (for the missing organ), fears (of privation), or maintenance of belief (in the woman's penis). The paper is a proposition, weighing all its consequences (especially the logical difficulties it may encounter), noting the elements on which clinical experience will not shed further light, and stating what the proposition amounts to in the end. There is no dogmatism. The reticence internal to the demonstration is an effect of its rigorous reasoning; the tenacity that returns to the same points and delays conclusions is a way of not making concessions on his findings beyond his chief preoccupation, namely the signification of the phallus.

Let us note how the works of this period encounter one another, though they do not agree. The distinction introduced by van Ophuijsen between the masculinity complex, without guilt, on the one hand and the castration complex on the other is one that Stärcke rejects from the outset. For him, there is no distinction but a conflation: "I also consider as effects of the castration complex those cases in which the feeling of guilt is not perceived as such, but is projected onto the surroundings and contributes toward the intensification of the feeling of hate against them, and is expressed by a marked feeling of having been unjustly treated, together with that of embitterment" (1921, p. 179).

Is this the first possible motivation for castration anxiety? Let us admit, Stärcke says, that the point of departure is a castration threat by the parents to deter infantile masturbation. In many cases where this anxiety is plain, however, we discover no trace of such direct threats. If there is a threat, it does not concern the organ or it involves a simple prohibition. There is also the fact that the idea of punishment that we find in girls—that they have been robbed of a penis they previously had—was surely not the effect of this kind of threat. What must be considered above all, therefore, is this representation, absurd to the conscious mind, of the girl's prior castration. For, indeed, how can one feel that one has been deprived of something that one never had in the first place?

The first explanation for the mysterious origin of this complaint is that the originally missing organ is the breast. If a penis is imagined on a body where it does not belong—a woman's body—we must, according to Stärcke, look back to the childhood experience common to both sexes, where a body part similar to a penis is taken from another person and given to the child as its own, its withdrawal causing unpleasure: in other words, the experience of the child at the breast.

Stärcke illustrates this "mother complex" with three dreams. The first of these proves that a castration dream does not always refer to the penis. Behind a woman patient's conscious fantasy of sucking the penis, a fantasy associated with an oral perversion (drinking urine), lay another fantasy, an unconscious one, of drinking blood from a woman's breast. What predominates here, he says, is the maternal fixation, ascertained through a series of symbolic equations (urine = menstruation = blood = blood of the pelican when it feeds its young), a series that may owe more to the analyst's construal than to the patient's anamnesis. Matters of confidentiality, Stärcke tells us, limit what he can report about the dream.

But, I would suggest, isn't this just as much a dream about the castration of the Other? An appropriation of the male organ, which the dreamer lacks, is hidden by more "innocent" material of the kind likely to escape censoring. In drinking from a woman's breast, even if what is drunk is blood, the sadistic tonality of the sucking fantasy is merely dissociated and thus representable.

Likewise, the second dream—a man's—of the mutilation of the breasts of a neglectful mother, understood by Stärcke to refer to vengeful castration of the maternal Other, seems to me to refer to the castration of the subject himself; this interpretation is supported by Stärcke's insistence elsewhere in the text on the lack of a boundary, the undifferentiation of the "me" and the "not-me," of mother and child, in the nursing situation. This is a dream of the subject's own castration, since, if the breast belongs to him as much as to the mother, it is he who lost it. The loss of a part of one's own body is attributed to the body of the Other, as is the responsibility for the loss. For it was the mother who did not sufficiently desire, and hence did not sufficiently "phallicize," the child.

The third dream is Stärcke's own and is much clearer in this regard. He describes the jealousy he felt when he saw a younger rival at his mother's breast, jealousy that, in the dream, evoked older material reconstructed according to the account of a mother who spoke of the mastitis that made it necessary for her to wean her baby. Stärcke turns the fiction of weaning into the original disappointment. Now, what does envy of the usurper signify if not the moment when one is displaced as the desired object, the favorite, the one who was the mother's phallus before being demoted? Moreover, the material that promotes the return of the screen memory (nostalgia for the maternal breast and jealousy) is explicitly phallic: two storks *flying* along the seashore, one of which, more brightly colored than usual, is held under the arm of the dreamer, who feels extremely happy, before it disappoints him by changing into a *walking stick* when he enters a *cheese store* (representing, he tells us, the mother whose milk has curdled).

What is this, if not the gap between the reality of the organ (it is just what it is) and what one imagined as paradise, the magnificent bird, the magic stick, the phallus that opened mother's door? And this goes to show that the analysis of one's own dreams is unreliable, since where we are supposed to see the loss of the breast as symbolic of castration, what we see is that this very loss is represented by the metamorphosis of the phallic organ. Stärcke makes a clear distinction between the signified of castration (which can signify all losses beside that of the penis) and its signifier, which is always the phallus, or the male organ raised to the dignity of the phallus by the alternation of its presence and its absence.

The clinical evidence resists the analyst's construction of the loss of the breast as the first castration. The organ is not simply what is found (the breast) but always the phallus, the male genital organ. Why, Stärcke asks, is there displacement from above to below, from the mouth to the genitals, from the oral to the genital? This is the case, he says, because there is no difference that is perceptible or representable on the level of this initial oral loss that we presuppose: every person has a mouth that is like everyone else's. The first difference is that of the genital organs. Why this privileging of the absence of the male organ and not of female secondary sexual characteristics like the breasts? Because, Stärcke, concludes, that difference does not exist at the early age at which the castration complex arises. The first symbolization of the difference between the sexes occurs only at the moment of comparison of the genitals, possibly with the threat that compels a belief in castration.

But instead of a displacement from above to below, as Stärcke says, what I see here is a displacement, more in accord with censorship, from below to above. If there is representation of the mutilated breast, therefore, this is because there was an earlier representation of a loss at the genital level.

Though the clinical material resists his interpretation, Stärcke brings his own logical resistance. If the first loss was indeed that of the breast, we could explain that odd reality of analytic experience, namely the persisting belief in the woman's penis. For, he says, what we cannot give up, because it involves the first satisfaction really experienced by everyone, is the woman's organ that is similar to the penis. The breast is the first organ allowing for that joining of the sexes that is held in nostalgic memory. Freud sees in the fantasy of the phallic mother first a refusal of castration (since this would be to accept the threat of such a loss for oneself) and, second, a retroactive fantasy that overlaps with this refusal and, later on, is borrowed from material that is much older and much more innocent (nursing as the first sexual relation; cf. Freud 1905a, b), but Stärcke merges the logical phases and privileges chronology. He creates a genesis, to the detriment of the process of symbolization, when he names the loss of the breast as the ultimate reason for the impossible renunciation of the mother's phallus. The same genetic "fiction" can, he says, account for sadism: the situation of the child at the breast is the model for sadism, intense satisfaction based on the pain of the object. His evidence for this connection is the pain of nursing, such as the breast abscesses that mothers complain of.

When clinical material contravenes reasoning, Stärcke admits, it is the clinical material that must prevail. The loss of the breast that—chronologically—inaugurates a series of similar losses (of feces, of the penis) is only one of the meanings of what is represented by castration, the lack of the male organ. This loss of the breast is perhaps a loss only when it is assigned the task of representing a primal castration that is the separation of the primitive ego from the external world, the distinction between the pleasure-ego and the unpleasure-ego, the loss of an initial undifferentiated *jouissance* (in the fusion with the environment or the mother) that is found as a residue only at the cost of the distance allowed by the organs of perception (eyes, nose, ears). Our final pleasure-ego, Stärcke says, "is a remnant—a remnant which owes its origin to the fact that something is removed from us of which the sense organs have taken possession, and which they have stamped with their seal and offer us as external world" (1921, p. 48). In conclusion, he states: "It is this separation in the primitive ego, the formation of the external world, which, properly speaking, is the primitive castration; and when I spoke of the withdrawal of the nipple as castration it is only another way of expressing the same thought" (p. 48).

Thus castration has been redefined. What represents it is of another order. Stärcke's reflections and supporting arguments prove that what we are dealing with is structure.[1] No real event, such as Stärcke and some others are searching for, can alter its figuration as always being a function of the male *or* castrated organ. There is no other representation of loss, for the unconscious, than this. This paper admirably shows the hiatus between signification and the primacy of the phallus on the level of unconscious representation, and does so before Freud saw its implications and formulated them explicitly in 1923.

Note

1. Compare Lacan: "But what is not a myth, and which Freud nevertheless formulated soon after the Oedipus complex, is the castration complex" (1960, p. 318).

8   Helene Deutsch and the Mater Dolorosa

Helene Deutsch is cited by Freud as from 1925 on (1925a, 1931, 1932–1933). Yet in neither of the papers he mentions in 1931— "The psychology of women in relation to the functions of reproduction" (1925) and "The significance of masochism in the mental life of women" (1930a)—do we find the implications he draws from them: in the first, an oedipal schema applied to the preoedipal, which he criticizes, and in the second the emphasis on the girl's hatred as well as on her phallic activity and intensity of attachment directed toward her mother, for which he credits Helene Deutsch in contrast to Jeanne Lampl-de Groot.

Freud is making use of displacement here, since these themes, whose agreement with his views he claims, appear as full-fledged arguments only in a third paper, "On female homosexuality," published in 1932, a year after he referred to them. Moreover, although she pays tribute to Freud in a note on the first page, Deutsch makes it clear in the course of this text that the first female case that oriented her to the girl's hate for and attachment to the mother preceded the attention Freud paid to it in 1931. Because of these issues of interference or priority, but also because of the misunderstandings to which they led, I propose to reexamine these three papers by Helene Deutsch. Readers have found in them a glorification of motherhood; an interpretation of masochism that differs from Freud's view and that posits masochism as inherent in femininity; and the phallicism of Helene Deutsch herself, her denial of castration. And yet the question she asks (the same question in all her diverse undertakings), the way she answers it, and her distinctive clinical ethos deserve attention, even if this means redefining her position and the clinical and theoretical findings ascribed to her.

The first paper, "The psychology of women in relation to the functions of reproduction," is remembered for the extremity of its statements to the effect that childbirth is the height of sexual pleasure or an orgy of masochistic pleasure, that intercourse followed by ejaculation is like childbirth, and that the vagina is a sucking mouth or is to be equated with the anus. At the very least, it has been read as a paean to passivity, with no examination of what it was that Deutsch was attempting to show.

This paper is characterized by declarations of allegiance to Freud at the same time that it takes rather large liberties with his concepts, so that it gradually becomes clear that Deutsch is speaking about herself. The clinical case that is missing in the text is her own, illustrating the difficulties that a woman can encounter in motherhood, though motherhood is considered to be the culmination of femininity. Deutsch sets out to account for sterility and frigidity in women, seeing these as a refusal to accept the female role. The analytic attention brought to bear on the functions of reproduction reveals a series of traumatic psychic events, in other words, a *real*, that is hard to integrate and that, in turn, might explain why it is impossible for some women to consent to their assigned female role. In addition, the awakening of "true femininity," understood as the erogenization of the vagina, is said to presuppose the woman's "being masochistically subjugated by the penis" (1925, p. 406), since "the task of conducting the libido to the vagina . . . devolves upon the activity of the penis" (p. 408). And this awakening involves a restriction of the libido with regard to an originally polymorphous-perverse *jouissance*: "the female, owing to the lesser tyranny of the clitoris, may all her life remain more 'polymorphous-perverse,' more infantile; to her more than to the male 'the whole body is a sexual organ'" (p. 408). And, finally, this transition implies the renunciation of phallic clitoral activity.

The text then goes on to offer questions and answers in alternation. Why, to begin with, do the stages associated with maternity pose an obstacle to the fulfillment of femininity? The reason, says Deutsch, is that they are defined as much by the masculinity associated with them as by their femininity. Paradoxically, phallicism (activity) is found in all of the stages: the phallic activity of the female orgasm, a process of secretion and ejaculation as in men; the oral activity of the vagina, a fantasy of sucking the penis; and the anal-sadistic activity of childbirth, which explains the ambivalence toward the child during pregnancy and, no doubt, in symptoms found at this time. How, then, are we to explain the erogenization of the vagina, the absence of frigidity? Deutsch proposes a series of equivalences. These are not linguistic or symbolic, and hence unconscious, as in Freud, but anatomical, based on the passive or active function of the organ. On the active side is the equation breast = fecal column = penis; on the passive side mouth = anus = vagina.

The activity and passivity of each phase of infantile sexuality are superimposed to account for the feminine, and hence passive, position already to be found at each stage. In the oral phase the active organ is the breast, the passive organ the mouth; the fantasy is of oral impregnation. In the anal phase, the active organ is the fecal column, the passive organ the anus, the fantasy that of the anal child. In the phallic phase the active organ is the penis, the passive organ the vagina if the "masculine" clitoris does not intrude. At the time of puberty a set of detours becomes necessary: the flowing of libido onto the entire body; the transfer, for the residue of clitoral activity, to the partner's organ; and the return, first with coitus and then with motherhood, to the model of the first phase, the oral sucking that reconciles activity and passivity.

The relation of the mouth to the breast, and of the breast to the mouth, thus permits the discovery and the erogenization of the vagina in coitus. Welcoming the penis, the vagina is a sucking mouth, the final term of the infantile fellatio fantasy. Could we not say, if we were to follow Deutsch, that every sexual relation is thus to be thought of as being under the constraint of the original model? This would be a restoration of the mother-child relationship in which activity and passivity are interwoven according to the

pole with which one identifies. The reversibility of roles characteristic of suckling would be found once again in the sex act.

There is no question, for Deutsch, of loss of the organ. Castration is already there, somehow prefigured in the relation to the
breast. For just as the child's interest is focused on and reduced to
the activity of the mouth sucking the breast, the libido, in the case
of women, must be withdrawn from the body as a whole and con-
centrated in the vaginal organ. This does not prevent an image of
the fusion of bodies, in nursing as in coitus, from leading to the
momentary idea of a recreation of the primitive union, banishing
separation and castration. Hence, if coitus takes on the sense of a
return to the maternal breast, suckling, conversely, is "a repetition
of coitus, rendered with photographic faithfulness, the identification being based on the oral incorporation of the object in the act
of sucking. Here again we have the equation: penis = breast. . . . That
which the semen accomplished in the one instance is accomplished
in the other by the jet of milk" (p. 417).

Accordingly, if passivity is imagined in oral terms, it is so only at
the time when there is still a confusion of subject and object, ego
and external world, the incorporation of the penis in intercourse
or of the breast in suckling. The trauma of weaning is, to be sure,
survived, but Deutsch's remarks leave no doubt that the overcoming of this trauma is just a fantasy. The primal situation and passivity
are threatened despite the period of fusion. From the very fact of
the role to which she is summoned, as a mother nursing her child,
a woman once again becomes active—at least in the revival, within
her, of the infantile fantasy. The nursing mother, Deutsch tells us,
is a phallic mother. Difficulties in nursing, too, are likewise conceptualized in terms of masculinity, assimilated to premature ejaculation.

Though it went unnoticed, this male feature of a symptom in
maternity is what guides Deutsch's thinking throughout the paper.
She was influenced by Ferenczi, whose two opening chapters in
Thalassa (1924) were known as early as 1922, having been deliv-
ered at a conference in Berlin in September of that year. Ferenczi
mentions that he himself is drawing on a major paper by Karl
Abraham (1917) on premature ejaculation. Contrasting this male
symptom to female frigidity, Abraham had noted, in both cases,

an investment of the primary erogenous zone of the other sex: in women, there is the predominant infantile excitability of the clitoris, which is homologous to the penis and can interfere with vaginal erogeneity; in men, the surface of the glans is not very excitable, but there is a special sensitivity of the perineum and the posterior wall of the scrotum corresponding to the entry to the vagina and the surrounding area.

Abraham also noted a form of homage to the mother (the son's delicacy as opposed to the father's brutality) as he analyzed the ambivalence of such a "gift": submission to the mother, but simultaneously retention, refusal, and scorn for and fear of women. In any event, this a fixation to urethral erotism in that the sexual function strictly speaking rests on an excretory function. The first loss is thought of as a loss of *jouissance*, since an organ serving a gratifying, erotized function (urination) must also serve the purpose of penetration.

Ferenczi is also interested in another form of psychogenic impotence in men, namely the delay or the impossibility of ejaculation. Abraham had emphasized urethral manifestations, but now the anal aspect of penile functioning, retention, completes the symptom picture. Such neurotic genital problems lead Ferenczi to posit what he calls "amphimixis" of erotic currents in genitality. Deutsch cites this term, which refers to the fusion of two or more partial erotic drives into an overarching unity. The hypothesis is deductive: if, according to Freud, prior stages of organization (anal, urethral) persist as forepleasures in genital organization, we may posit their fusion in genitality. Freud had not yet written on the primacy of the phallus at this time, and Ferenczi's theory of the primacy of the genital organs is based not on their difference but on a teleological line of reasoning inferred from the narcissism attached to the organ. There is a convergence that analysis will resolve once again into its component parts. Not only are all of the libidinal stages represented by the genital organ but all body parts as well, displaced from above to below. Thus, Ferenczi states, the penis is a miniature version of the entire person, the incarnation of the pleasure-ego, and hence the primary condition for the narcissistic investment of the ego. Deutsch echoes this directly:

"The vagina . . . becomes the 'second ego,' the ego in miniature, as does the penis for the man" (1925, p. 410).

Since it is not castration but the identification of the whole with the part that justifies the primacy of the male organ, it follows logically that there is no concept of loss in Ferenczi. What is lost in one way, he says, is found again in another; there is no unpleasure without compensation. The amphimixis of anal and urethral erotic impulses in coitus shows how the child's upbringing leads it to transform early pleasures into unpleasure by combining pleasures into one. The bladder no longer lets urine flow freely, but it has recourse to a different sort of pleasure, namely retention, and the intestines renounces the pleasure of constipation only when they can share in the anal pleasure of evacuation: pleasure is retained in one way or another.

Exchange of a loss of *jouissance* for a gain elsewhere, the repetition of this evolution in each sexual act, the threefold identification in coitus (of the entire organism with the genital organ, of the ego with the partner, of the ego with the genital secretion), parturition as fusion of anality and urethrality, the anality of the vagina in coitus and in childbirth, the "genitality" of the clitoris flowing back to the entire body: all these theses are taken up, for the most part without modification, by Deutsch. On the whole, then, when she investigates what a woman gains by agreeing to passivity, what she is doing is simply responding to Ferenczi's question as to what is gained in return for each renunciation. The enigma of frigidity has become the enigma of femininity-as-passivity. Her reply involves motherhood, itself enigmatic and difficult to conceive except as a castration. But, since women accept it, the pain of childbirth must be associated with another pleasure, which she sets out to define.

The problematic aspect of this 1925 paper of Helene Deutsch's— its overelaborate and apparently unbridled fantasy—vanishes when we understand what she is aiming at. The organization of the text seems confused, reversing its ostensible approach. The clinical data, her point of departure, come only at the end. At the beginning we find the reconstruction based on Ferenczi's model. From this theoretical fiction, Deutsch offers a developmental hypothesis with which she accounts for the Freudian postulates of reversal of activity into passivity and change of genital zone in the transition from the clitoris to the vagina. And yet her own question is a different one. She is preoccupied with female passivity because she presupposes an equation between activity and sadism on the one hand, passivity and masochism in the other, and also because the process of motherhood seems to her to represent pleasure in suffering.

Deutsch's statements about maternity and breastfeeding have been interpreted as a denial of the woman's castration. What I see here, however, is Deutsch's own way of analyzing the fantasy of the phallic mother, this strange formation of the unconscious that, like other analysts, she encounters in clinical experience. Let me explain. In projecting this fantasy of completeness and activity figured by breast-feeding onto the sex act that implies, for the woman, the abandonment of phallic clitoral activity, Deutsch, it seems to me, is simply trying to understand how such a renunciation is possible. What is she describing, after all, if not the woman's phallic incompleteness? A woman must renounce the *jouissance* of the entire body in favor of a localized *jouissance*, leave the concern for this pleasure to her partner, and undergo suffering and the fear of death, or at least of the loss of part of her own body, at the time of labor and the expulsion of the child. And, throughout pregnancy, she is supposed to overcome her ambivalence toward an other, this child who can narcissize her but also vampirize her or persecute her as an ego ideal. A woman's role as an active mother is thus merely a fantasy of recompletion or rephallicization that enables her to accept her castration. This castration is not just an imaginary prejudice but is confirmed by the series of real events that constitute her destiny as woman and mother.

And so it is going too far to conclude that Deutsch is presenting a phallicist fantasy. If she has such a fantasy, it serves merely to validate and illustrate the fantasy of another analyst, for the denial of castration in the form of the relation to the mother comes first from Ferenczi. How, he asks, can we explain the monotony and regularity of oedipal desire, if not by the desire for a return to the maternal womb? Such a return is conceivable if, like Ferenczi, we posit the identification of each person with his or her organ or its secretion. He grants that men are privileged here, since they are able to penetrate into the mother's body; women must content themselves with fantasmatic compensations and welcoming a child. It is to this loss that Deutsch offers a solution. If the man refinds a mother external to himself, the woman, when she is breast-feeding, refinds not only the mother that she herself is but also the male organ.

Freud's reservations with regard to this first paper by Helene Deutsch can be understood, I would suggest, as an indirect criticism of the so-called mother complex as described by Ferenczi. In *Inhibitions, Symptoms, and Anxiety* (1926a) Freud sets himself apart from such notions. For, although he does not reject the idea of nostalgia for the maternal womb or the fantasies of intrauterine return as oedipal manifestations, he states that one must account for the exit from the Oedipus, and hence for the prohibition of incest, something that Ferenczi's "bioanalysis" leaves unexplained. Ferenczi (1924) says that castration is inherent in development: at the oral-sadistic stage, the nursing child who wants to penetrate the mother's body uses his teeth for this purpose. Hence the mother must wean him. Ferenczi concludes from this that the tooth is the first loss; it is not the tooth that is the symbol of the penis, but the penis that later comes to symbolize the tooth as first instrument of penetration. Freud disagrees. For him, castration can be thought of only in relation to both the paternal interdiction and the loss of the genital organ, even if the latter is prefigured by birth or weaning. A castration at birth, he explains, could only be a castration of the mother. It is this proposition that Helene Deutsch, in her analysis of mothers, is trying to elaborate clinically.

But are we really dealing here, as Freud claims, with the girl's phallic activity and identification with her father? The phallic activity in question is surely that of the mother, or the woman when she becomes a mother, since it ultimately involves the phallicism of breast-feeding, in which the breast, as a "male" organ, contravenes the equation of femininity with passivity. For Deutsch, the woman's "genitality," and her femininity as such, cannot be conceptualized in terms of pure passivity, since the very model of loving satisfaction, the child fulfilled by the breast, entails two poles, activity as well as passivity.

Although we may observe a certain theoretical impatience in Deutsch, as shown in her borrowings from concurrent analytic writings—from Ferenczi, as we have seen, and from Otto Rank, but also from Abraham for the equation mouth = anus and the idea of a preambivalent sucking or a postambivalent love object—this does not invalidate her undertaking. On the one hand, her later work (1944–1945) retains her original notion of a conflict between activity and passivity. On the other, the fact that a paper by another analyst enabled her, as I have proposed, to symbolize in retrospect a "real" that she herself perhaps could not name, and in any event to metaphorize questions that arose in her own clinical practice, highlights what is at stake in analytic theorization: I would say that, more than any other, a construction of Ferenczi's served as an interpretation for her.

Moreover, beyond the influence of Ferenczi, we find the issue of fantasy (here, a fantasy of the phallic mother giving the breast) that could support the woman's consent to castration insofar as she is a mother. This is what Deutsch will later call the masochistic desire for castration, beyond pleasure. As she writes this paper, she has not yet read Freud (1924c) on masochism, or that text had not yet made an impression on her. This no doubt accounts for the distance between her 1925 and 1930 papers. For if we consider that, even more than the concern to find an equality of the sexes, it is masochism that preoccupies Deutsch in the earlier text, then "The significance of masochism in the mental life of women" (1930a) is not very different in its aim of accounting for frigidity and sexual inhibition in women. What is different is the fulcrum of masochism in each of these papers: in 1925, the pain of childbirth, in 1930 the idea of rape by the father. Motherhood is thus always conceptualized masochistically, except that, in the later text, it is based on infantile theories of coitus and parturition rather than on the reality of actual experience.

9   Motherhood, Frigidity, Masochism

Helene Deutsch's (1930a) postulate of a masochism inherent in femininity is not so different as it might at first seem from Freud's (1924c) considerations, when he studies "feminine masochism" in men and thus immediately dissociates femininity and masochism. What Freud does is to describe masochistic *manifestations* found in particular arrangements or fantasies (being gagged, whipped, forced into obedience, dirtied, debased), and, in more subtle elaborations, the *meaning* of fantasies of this sort that place the subject in a characteristically feminine position of being castrated, submitting to coitus, or giving birth.

Deutsch sets out very specifically from this meaning, and in so doing is faithful to Freud, when she proposes the triad castration-rape-childbirth, a "feminine masochistic" fantasy borrowed from men, in order to understand the girl's Oedipus, that is, the girl's turn to the father. Where does she depart from Freud? For her, it is not the difference of genital organs (the primacy of the phallus) that governs castration and symbolizes lack, but the shifting of a libido that was first invested in the clitoral-phallic organ and then, at a certain point in development, is no longer fixed (there is, according to Deutsch, no vaginal phase). The regression to the prior pregenital stages, especially to the anal phase, and the reversal of the drive—of sadism into masochism—come about only because the aggressivity or activity associated with the phallic phase no longer has an outlet.

Seen from this perspective, the girl's libidinal masochism accounts both for the idea of punishment attached to infantile masturbation and for the fantasy of castration and the transition to the father. It is the concentration of libido on the "male" clitoris that enables the girl at first to deny and then to accept castration. Deutsch specifies two periods in the phallic phase. The rape fantasies that accompany the possible second, "postphallic," phase, the phase in which castration by the father is not only acknowledged but desired, arise because of the excitabliity of this same erogenous zone:

> When we designate this masochistic experience by the name of the wish for castration, we are not thinking merely of the biological meaning—the surrender of an organ of pleasure (the clitoris)— but we are also taking into account the fact that the whole of this deflection of the libido still centres on that organ. The onanism belonging to this phase and the masochistic phantasy of being castrated (raped) employ the same organ as the former active tendencies. [p. 50]

Like Freud, Deutsch maintains that there is an entire period in which the vagina remains undiscovered. In contrast to Freud, however, she makes this a phase, one that she calls "postphallic" and that defines the difficulties or the refusal of the oedipal detour, since, as Freud will note in 1931 and 1932–1933, certain women never achieve it. For Deutsch, it is neither anatomy nor biological evolution that makes a woman, not the passage from one zone to another, but the oedipal fantasy, or the position taken in relation to that fantasy. For the passage to the father to occur, there must first be phallicism and impasse:

> [T]he hitherto active-sadistic libido attached to the clitoris rebounds from the barricade of the subject's inner recognition of her lack of the penis and, on the one hand, regressively cathects points in the pregenital development which it had already abandoned, while, on the other hand, and most frequently of all, it is deflected in a regressive direction towards masochism. In place of the active urge of the phallic tendencies, there arises the masochistic phan-

tasy: "I want to be castrated," and this forms the erotogenic masochistic base of the feminine libido. [p. 49]

There is thus a regression, a reversal, of the drive and the corresponding fantasy. This fantasy reveals Deutsch's neglect of the underlying wish, for what the girl seeks in the second object—the father—is what she did not find in the first, the mother. This is so, it seems to me, because Deutsch stands by Freud's account of masochism (1924c), an account that is based on the feminine position in the man and thus does not place the emphasis on object choice, on what is sought or desired in him. What is desirable in the father, and lacking in the mother, is not investigated by Deutsch.[1] The awaited child is a rationalization: this should logically follow rape, as an end that justifies the means.

In this paper Deutsch has little to say about the mother. There is nothing desirable or enviable in her, for she is, from the outset, a castrated mother. If, faithful to Freud, Deutsch mentions that the little girl can blame her mother for her missing organ, she is unlike Freud in that she does not see here the girl's specific recrimination but merely one of the ways in which the child tries to explain the loss she has undergone. Above all, what Deutsch establishes before Freud is that imputing castration to the father signals the entry into the Oedipus:

It is interesting to note that, when the father is blamed for the little girl's lack of a penis, castration by him has already acquired the libidinal significance attaching to this idea in the form of the rape phantasy. Rejection of the wish that the father should have been the aggressor generally betokens, even at this early stage, [the] rejection of the infantile feminine attitude. [p. 48]

Thus it is not repressed love for the father that produces the fantasy, but the fantasy that conditions love—or fear.

Why this displacement with regard to Freud (1919a), for whom the infantile beating fantasy in its unconscious phase (being loved by the father) is a mark of the traversal of the Oedipus, a residue and not a cause? Are we not to understand that what Deutsch is looking for, and tries to reconstruct, is an explanation going back to childhood for the essentially masochistic *jouissance* of maternity, accepted by some women and refused by others, the resisting ones being frigid or sterile? Putting the masochistic infantile fantasy at the beginning, as the cause of oedipal love, enables Deutsch to account for masochism as an infantile derivative that presides over all the stages of "fulfilled" femininity (coitus, chidlbirth, mothering):

> At that period there is a close connection between the masochistic phantasies and the wish for a child, so that the whole subsequent attitude of the woman towards her child (or towards the reproductive function) is permeated by pleasure-tendencies of a masochistic nature. . . . [A]ll the active birth-phantasies, whose roots lie in this identification [with the always masochistic mother] are of a bloody, painful character, which they retain throughout the subject's life. [pp. 50–51]

Let us return to the basic argument of the text. Deutsch announces it: "the discussion will concern itself with theoretical premises rather than with the clinical significance of frigidity" (p. 48). And there will be an opportunity, in explaining the relation between female sexuality and the reproductive function, to understand sexual inhibition in women. The model of the masochistic-passive position that is supposed to define femininity is, for Deutsch, that of maternity. She defines the maternal position as feminine-passive-masochistic and persists in seeking its origin, the same preoccupation as in 1925.

Though Deutsch had said that the clinical treatment of sexual inhibition was her point of departure in the earlier text, it is not discussed there. In her concern to find its causes and final meaning in a reconstruction of "normal" female development, she ignored both the symptomatology and the indications for analysis. The later text, in this sense, extends the 1925 paper and corrects its lacunae. The entire second part of the paper, after some theoretical reminders, is devoted to what might be called a typology of frigidity and female sterility. Here Deutsch mentions her clinical experience and at the same time assesses her responsibility. An awareness of the power and the limits of analysis and a concern to know where it is leading—where one wants to go—are an explicit part of her reflections and reveal her ethics as a clinician in engaging the treatment or the transference. "In far the largest number of case," she explains, "feminine sexual inhibition arises out of the vicissitudes of that infantile-masochistic libidinal development which I have postulated. These vicissitudes are manifold, and every form they assume may lead to frigidity" (p. 51). What is called female narcissism finds its source here, as an ego defense after the repression of dangerous masochistic tendencies. Likewise, the masculinity complex, in which we see the impossible renunciation of the male organ, is justified by the avoidance of masochistic dangers threatening the ego, dangers associated by Deutsch, as by Karen Horney, whom she cites, with the relation to the incestuous paternal object. The masculinity complex is all the more marked, for Deutsch, if the primary phallic tendencies were strong. She thus distinguishes two phases of penis envy: one reactive, the other primary, a distinction that anticipates the one Freud would make in 1932–1933, when he emphasizes the initial phase of phallic activity addressed to the mother (primary penis envy) as necessary for the passage to the wish to have a child by the father.

Another effect of the repression of masochism presupposed by the love of the father is confirmed, Deutsch says, by a particular type of object choice that we observe in certain women. Such a woman takes as a partner an affectionate and passive man at the cost of remaining "misunderstood" and unsatisfied in her desires, these desires being "bound up with conditions whose fulfillment is highly offensive to her ego" (p. 51). Or she may fall victim to a passion for a man who will mistreat her, in accordance with her unconscious wish for castration or rape.

In other women, splitting is foremost and presents the analyst with a problem in directing the treatment. Such women have adopted a mode of masculine sublimation in social life even as they remain masochistic in their sexual experiences. The success of analytic treatment in such cases is highly uncertain: "It is particularly difficult to detach these patients from the said [masochistic] conditions and, when analysis has given them the necessary insight, they have consciously to choose between finding bliss in suffering or peace in renunciation" (p. 53).

The best evidence that Helene Deutsch is far from making a virtue of masochism, that she is not advocating it but simply ascertains it in her clinical work, is the problem of conscience that such cases pose for her:

> The analyst's most important task is, of course, the abolition of the sexual inhibition in his patients, and the attainment of instinctual gratification. But sometimes, when the patient's instincts are so unfortunately fixed and yet there are good capacities for sublimation, the analyst must have the courage to smooth the path in the so-called "masculine" direction and thus make it easier for the patient to renounce sexual gratification. [p. 54]

Better masculinity than masochism.

Deutsch reveals the same concern when she describes other configurations derived from the vicissitudes of the Oedipus, cases, for example, of strong sexual inhibition and feelings of inferiority. Two paths are open to the analyst: either to try to convert penis envy into desire for a child, or to encourage these women to realize themselves in the direction of their masculine tendencies. The result is the same: "[W]e often find that . . . the capacity for feminine sexual sensibility develops automatically in a striking manner" (p. 54). Whether one pushes for a child or for sublimation, the residue of penis envy is calmed and no longer impedes femininity, that change of sex of which Freud speaks in 1931.

Where Deutsch simply communicates without theoretical proselytizing is in emphasizing that a certain number of women can be frigid without experiencing any suffering from this or having any other symptoms. Here, analysis cannot be effective. Deutsch notes that, in such cases, it is never the woman who seeks help, but her narcissistic husband. Frigidity and neurosis must be dissociated. It is possible for some women to be frigid without being in the least neurotic, while others are neurotic without being frigid. Moreover, we find that the symptoms of the various neurotic structures of such women can be resolved while the frigidity persists. Conversely, frigidity sometimes resolves where there is no progress with regard to the other symptoms.

According to Deutsch, there are two forms of frigidity in hysteria. A sexually uninhibited woman may remain frigid while having a love life involving a long series of romances. Or a woman may be attached to only one love object but on condition of the exclusion of the genitals. Any other part of the female body but the organ destined for sex may be the site of the sexual investment found in conversion symptoms. As far as obsessional neurosis is concerned, if frigidity is resolved this may have to do with the ambivalence proper to that psychic structure, as is clearly seen in cases "in which the most violent orgasm may result from hostile masculine identifications. The vagina behaves like an active organ, and the particularly brisk secretion is designed to imitate ejaculation" (p. 56).

The clinical evidence Deutsch cites calls for a more nuanced critique of her premises, such as the claim that there is a masochism intrinsic to femininity. She formulated these terms on the basis of what she encountered in experience, and, first of all, on the basis of an actual refusal of masochism. Why do we find a masculinity complex or sexual anesthesia in women? Because "being a woman," for the unconscious, implies castration (an imaginary infantile representation of the feminine position), which can be felt as a *real privation* if it is not understood as a *symbolic lack* (cf. Lacan 1956–1957, lesson of March 6). Do some women accept castration as a symbolic lack? It seems to be so in the "sublimation" in maternity, that transformation of one part of the masochistic libido attached to the functions of motherhood: "If it is true that men derive the principal forces which make for sublimation from their sadistic tendencies, then it is equally true that women draw on the masochistic tendencies with their imprint of maternity." Further: "In the deepest experience of the relation of mother to child, it is masochism in its strongest form which finds gratification in the bliss of motherhood" (p. 57).

Thus Deutsch affirms the kourotrophy of every woman, the care and protection of children: "Long before she is a mother, long after the possibility of becoming one has ended, the woman has ready within her the maternal principle, which bids her take to herself and guard the real child or some substitute for it" (p. 57). Isn't she pointing here to a "maternal instinct"? In other words, the way in which a woman can recuperate something of her phallic value is through identification with a preoedipal mother, the very mother with whom, as Freud says in 1932–1933, men fall in love.

Beyond the conflict between sexuality and the reproductive function, a conflict that can take the form of wholly emphasizing

the one or the other—the masochistic prostitute in her relationship with her pimp, the *mater dolorosa* who places all her masochism in her relationship to her child—Deutsch notes an additional
form of feminine passivity that she associates with masochism: an
altruistic *jouissance*, in which the woman takes pleasure in being
the object of her partner's *jouissance*. She gives an example that
she believes to be historically situated and in the process of disap-
pearing, the example of women who, out of ignorance and unen-
lightened upbringing, have never thought of finding any satisfaction in intercourse other than what they can give to their partner:
"what they feel is a happy and tender sense that they are giving keen
pleasure [to someone else]" (p. 57).

The reason why frigidity is better tolerated by women than
impotence is by men is, according to Deutsch, that some women
are able to do without a localized *jouissance* and make no demands
in this regard. Thus we can better understand her concern, in the
1925 paper, to note that, if the *jouissance* experienced in the functions of motherhood, from coitus to breast-feeding, is active and
passive at the same time, this activity with passive aims compensates
the woman for her nonpossession of the male organ, the one that
is active par excellence. In the same way, Deutsch says, the girl is
aware of the benefit she can derive from castration:

> In coitus and parturition the masochistic pleasure of the sexual
> instinct is very closely bound up with the mental experience of
> conception and giving birth; just so does the little girl see in the
> father, and the loving woman in her beloved—a child. . . . When
> does the female child begin to be a woman and when a mother?
> Analytic experience has yielded the answer: *Simultaneously*, in that
> phase when she turns toward masochism. . . . [p. 56]

In this construction, desire seems to be evaded. This is so because Deutsch is more interested in the identification with a masochistic mother than in the devaluation of a mother deprived of
the phallus. The result is that, if the masochistic mother is a
mother castrated by the father, in accordance with the sadistic
infantile conception of intercourse, the emphasis on the *real*
(menstruation, defloration, bloody childbirth) of this *imaginary*
castration conceals the *symbolic* value of what, in the moment of

the child's perception of sexual difference, the mother lost that might be desirable.

In contrast to Freud, but also because he does not always explicitly formulate it, Deutsch does not show that the identification with the mother loved genitally by the father (and thereby castrated) is at first refused, by the girl as by the boy. Nor does she show that the love for the father comes about by way of an identification with him that is a refusal of the castration presupposed by the "feminine" position. She jumps over the stages that Freud will articulate in 1932–1933: from identification with the father to love for him, from the wish for a child by the mother to the wish for a child by the father. And she does not indicate that what she is attempting is a reconstruction, one that starts out from the erotic problems of certain women and also from the girl's "oedipal" position, the love for the father that implies the recognition and acceptance of castration. This is so clear that we have the impression that Deutsch is speaking of the unconscious phase of the beating fantasy (to be loved = to be castrated by the father) as if this were a conscious wish on the part of the child. Hence we do not understand the triad borrowed from Freud (to be castrated, to undergo coitus, to give birth) in the appropriate register, which is always the unconscious. Just as Freud (1919a) shows that the anal regressive form of the fantasy (being beaten oneself by the father) is a reconstruction and can in no case be remembered, likewise a child by the father is the only element that can emerge; the rest is deduction.

The postulating of a "feminine" masochism (pain marked by pleasure) in women, and the investigation of what gratification can be found or refused in motherhood, originates in Deutsch's inferences about the unconscious phase of the beating fantasy. If, following her, we assume that the woman—unconsciously—derives pleasure from her suffering and her "castration," in other words, from her "feminine passive" position with regard to the father, when she becomes a mother the woman is not entirely in masochistic *jouissance* because of the clinical fact of the split between a masochistic motherhood that excludes sexuality and a masochistic sexuality in which the "sublimation" that should pertain to motherhood is referred to intellectual or "masculine" activities that are nevertheless, Deutsch says, compromised by the maternal.

The contradiction between the masochistic conditions of sexual gratification and the aims, themselves masochistic, of procreation increases the gap between a prescribed femininity and an original masculinity. The girl is divided between her femininity (identification with the oedipal mother) and her masculinity (identification with the phallic father or mother), between passivity and activity whose origin Deutsch tried to describe and to which she returns in her third study, "On female homosexuality" (1932). Starting from the result, a mother fixation, she works back to the history of her women patients through the vicissitudes of the transference that, she says, repeat developmental stages. In none of the cases that she has encountered, she says, has the preoedipal fixation excluded the appeal to the father. Homosexuality in the mother–child mode was never a continuation of the first relationship but a return following the failure of the oedipal approach to the father.

Note

1. The paragraphs added in the German version of this paper (Deutsch 1930b) come much closer to this question. There Deutsch notes the reorganization of object relations in the little girl, who passes from phallic activity addressed to her mother to great rage when she perceives two things: that her mother has not endowed her with the desirable attribute, and that she has been dethroned by others, especially her father, in regard to her mother's love.

10   Deutsch on Female Homosexuality

Helene Deutsch retains fear of the father and of masochism in this 1932 paper, but the emphasis has changed. What prevents the passage to the father, or the establishment of the Oedipus, is the attachment to the mother (the forbidden kind and the appropriate kind) and, at the same time, the inadequacy of the father, however the child may perceive it: too little or too much power. Deutsch tells us that she is basing her argument on the analyses of twelve women, two of whom provide the material for detailed observations. As with Freud, the effect of retrospection, of seeing what one had been unable to see before, is all the more obvious in this paper because more than a decade separates the two major observations that Deutsch reports.

The first analysis and the conclusions she drew from it date from the time when Freud published the case of the young lesbian (1920a), thus well before he himself began to place the accent on the relation to the mother. The second case, an analysis conducted between 1928 and 1931, bears the stamp of Freud's 1925 paper, "Some psychical consequences of the anatomical difference between the sexes." What Deutsch had designated as the preoedipal in the first observation, though without generalizing it, has not been confirmed. But, what is most important, Deutsch can now show the effect of a reflexive return to her own clinical work. The impasse that she had signaled in the first case, the frustration of her attempt with regard to the manifestations of the castration complex of her patient, can now be explained: "I was very much tempted to assume that the patient was living out her masculinity in her homosexuality. But in this very point she failed to fulfill my analytic expectations and presented me with a problem at the time which I could understand only years later" (p. 489). And the central point of her contribution is just this: contrary to the remarks of Freud (1920a) and even Jones (1927), she describes an origin of female homosexuality in which the inversion is explained by a return to the first fixation to the mother after the failure of the appeal to the father. Far from being an identification with the father, this is a flight from him in order to seek refuge in a regressive relation, not in the male–female mode but in the active-passive, mother–child mode, in which the two roles are exchanged.

So it is in this third paper, published in 1932 but conceptualized, she tells us, before 1931, that Deutsch mentions preoedipal hate and desire for the mother in connection with the first analysis, conducted twelve years earlier: "I should like to emphasize the fact that even at that time it was clear to me that the hate against her mother and the libidinal desire for her were much older than the Oedipus complex" (p. 487). We have proof, if proof is needed, that Deutsch had seen the preoedipal nature of this relationship: at the point in the treatment when she noticed the emergence of the Oedipus, the reappearance of the paternal relation, she referred the patient to a fatherly male analyst. The result was unexpected. The patient broke off her analysis but realized her homosexuality, which up to then had been latent. Some time later, Deutsch met the patient, who was now "a vivid, radiant person," having formed a lesbian relationship that was "quite consciously acted out as if it were a mother-child situation, in which sometimes one, sometimes the other played the mother" (p. 487).

Is this acting out? It is a transference effect, Deutsch says. What had arisen in the transference had become detached from the woman analyst and carried over to other women. Frustrated in the treatment, the patient's wishes had found satisfaction in life: "It was evident that the overcoming of her hostility toward the analyst had brought with it the overcoming of her anxiety, and, consequently, a positive libidinal relationship to women could appear in place of the anxiety and hostility which had caused the neurotic symptoms" (p. 488).

Symptoms, anamnesis, analysis of transference and transference dreams, orientation toward the primal fantasy: the case report offers a valuable reflection on the management of the treatment (including what was missing) and on the interpretation of symptoms contrary to the initial expectation, since at that time the hypothesis of a castration complex in women was not yet accepted. Deutsch's attention was drawn so strongly to this material in the patient (who dreamed of the castration of her sons) that she came to consider this complex to be the core of the woman's perversion. In addition to her latest suicide attempt, the neurotic distress that had brought the patient to analysis was the anxiety that overcame her when she had to give orders to other women or criticize them, especially when she had to hire new servants. Her husband, she reported, did not protect her enough, was not active enough, and she reproached him for this.

The perversion was her exclusive and entirely conscious attraction to people of her own sex, though she was unable to explain, except as a fear of enslavement, why she had never acted on it. Instead, she felt anxious when she experienced arousal in embracing certain other women. Her conscious anamnesis traced her choice of female objects back to puberty, when she fell in love with women teachers who ordered her about, making her feel both protected and afraid. Her original attraction toward her husband had to do with the activity and virility that she thought she saw in him before he disappointed her on this score and failed to be supportive enough.

Deutsch underlines the initially positive tonality of the transference. The analyst seemed to be a kind and understanding mother, in contrast to the patient's own severe, cold, and consciously hated mother. It was through the analysis of typical dreams of returning to the womb (here Deutsch notes that she had given a paper on this topic at the time)—transference dreams that involved the patient's being swaddled or bandaged and that came at a point in the treatment when she was once again experiencing depressive crises and suicidal impulses—that Deutsch was quickly able to elicit two screen memories. One had to do with the patient's awakening after one of her suicide attempts; saved by a man (the doctor), she thought that he nonetheless could not truly help her. The other, which involved a dangerous operation undergone by her mother, rekindled the murderous hatred toward her and, via a dream, led to memories of infantile masturbation. In a further scene, she saw herself bound hand and foot to her bed as her mother defied her to continue her forbidden games. She felt both anger and, in spite of everything, the sexual excitement of those times, but the most painful memory was of the passivity of her father, who just stood by.

The patient's renunciation of onanism, her repression of sexuality, and also her repression of her hatred for her mother dated from this scenario that Deutsch quite rightly believed was more a fantasy, the prototype of later events, than a trauma, and that, in the patient's history, marked the connection between desire and maternal prohibition. Aggressivity, hate for the mother, reactive guilt, and transformation of the hate into masochism: thus, when the patient said that she feared the enslavement of a homosexual relationship, what she really feared was a masochistic attachment to her mother. The oedipal material that Deutsch found in the reproaches that the patient addressed to her father because he was not active enough in his love for her arose, she tells us, only after the elaboration of this older, repressed phase relating to the mother, the phase that, ten years later, Freud would call "preoedipal." Deutsch understands this emergence of the father complex as an appeal to the father to which a father substitute, a male analyst, would be more likely to respond, this time more appropriately, in a transference in which he would be able to offer a corrective for the original relationship.

Among the later cases, analyzed between 1928 and 1931, what Deutsch found each time was an overt homosexuality modeled on the mother–child relationship. She privileges one of these, in which the woman patient was divided between two love objets, a young girl toward whom she played the maternal role and an older woman, active and authoritative. Four dreams are reported: a miscarriage, a homosexual seduction, a dream of Anna Freud disguised as a man and the analyst herself (Deutsch) smoking a cigar like Freud, and a dream of the death of the patient's younger sister. The transferential aspect of the first three is clear and enables Deutsch to make a transference interpretation of homosexuality as mother fixation, reinforced by the failure on the part of the father: "the patient's turning to the woman corresponds also to a flight from the man" (p. 496).

The reconstruction of the patient's history is thus interwoven with her dreams and confirmed by them: justifiable oral envy of the mother when she weaned the 9-month-old patient in favor of a younger sister; jealousy of her mother's new pregnancy, followed by a miscarriage, when the patient was 3 (the dream of the miscarriage shows that she wanted to take the place of the child); and finally a memory from a later period, when, identified with the oedipal mother, she herself wanted a child. For us, this memory is a fine example of the "hysterization" of the little girl, then aged 12, at the very moment when her father's weakness, due to cardiac problems and financial difficulties, made him more accessible to the child; he was no longer the threatening Other. She identified with him in fantasies in which she imagined herself supporting the family, which, Deutsch notes, she was able to do later on through her work. Her reaction to the birth of her last sister during this period was thus different from her earlier reactions. She had gotten beyond the Oedipus and perhaps would have stayed at that level if oedipal guilt, as manifested in another dream (her sister is dead; the patient is about to set forth happily to have a good time with her father, but the mother looks at her disapprovingly) had not reactivated the older guilt vis-à-vis her mother. This is a withdrawal: she has no right to remain attached to her father.

The passage to the father is thus impeded by the revival, in oedipal competition, of a former guilt, itself a reaction formation to the hatred stemming from frustration by the primary object, the mother. And this guilt accounts for the turning of the aggressive impulses of each phase of sexuality addressed to the mother into masochism libidinally linked, as in the first case, to maternal prohibition.

The definitive choice of a homosexual object is possible only on condition of the approval of a mother substitute, approval of the activity, such as the masturbation left over from the phallic phase, that Deutsch sees as characteristic of female homosexuality. She notes it, in the second case report, in connection with one of the transference dreams in which the patient, unclothed by a woman, awoke crying, "My God, Frau Doktor!" What she was asking for, Deutsch says, was to be saved by the analyst from the fear of punishment, either by the analyst's preventing her from masturbating or by her approval and even her participation. Likewise, it seems that the passage from latent to overt homosexuality in the first case could be explained by the sole fact of the positive maternal transference, the analyst's benevolence being taken for approval and facilitating the overriding of the maternal prohibition.

This maternal interdiction of *jouissance*, at whatever phase it appears—oral, if there was a painful loss of the breast, phallic in the forced renunciation of onanism—is important for Deutsch: "the form which this active behaviour of the girl toward the maternal object takes depends on the developmental stage at which the homosexual object relationship is taking place. . . . Usually the most urgent tendencies are the phallic ones, and they cause the relationship of one female to another to assume a male character, whereby the absence of a penis is denied" (p. 509). It is of little importance that, as in the most common forms described by Freud (1920a) or Fenichel (1931), it is the recognition of masculinity that is demanded of the partner or femininity that is sought in the other: this "male" form is often just a façade concealing more infantile tendencies. And, although phallic activity is involved, this is in fact addressed to the mother, a demand for compensation for the humiliation she imposed in the phase of clitoral masturbation.

In contrast to the earlier papers, the emphasis here is on the attachment to the mother. Yet Deutsch does not give up her former ideas about the female Oedipus. The reversal of sadism into masochism has already occurred in the relation to the mother and has prepared the way for the push toward passivity that leads to the father. But she maintains her definition of the oedipal position as a masochistic passive attitude. It is because of the strength of the girl-child's libidinal drives, derived from the primal relation to the mother, that she will fear the realization of her wishes with regard to the father. Fear of the father is as much a fear of a sadistic castrator as it is a fear, sensed by the child at the least shortcoming on his part, of the disappointment that might follow the child's demand for his love. The tilt toward passivity, Deutsch explains, comes about only with the hope of a child from the father, but the tilt is really a regression to a phase preceding phallic organization. The little girl who had to renounce possession of the male organ, convinced of her inferiority, first regresses to the anal stage, which enables her to symbolize sexual difference and what she can expect from the father, namely an anal child.

Closer to the Freud of "The disposition to obsessional neurosis" (1913a) than to the Freud of "A child is being beaten" (1919a), Deutsch is simply illustrating, from the perspective of female homosexuality, the series of regressions that result in a little girl's devaluation of her genitality. First there is phallicism, then anal regression in which the contrast between activity and passivity predominates. From there we may a posit a regression to the earlier stage, that of the oral phase in which Abraham (1916, 1924) distinguished two periods, a preambivalent phase of sucking and a sadistic-ambivalent phase of biting. The oral envy of the second patient, her death wishes toward her mother and the children she is carrying, are analyzed in these terms by Deutsch. Abraham and Ferenczi provided her with the theoretical framework that enabled her to conceptualize her clinical treatment of women. Jones' 1927 paper, "The early development of female sexuality," which was itself based on five cases of female homosexuals, together with the child cases analyzed by Melanie Klein, confirmed what Deutsch had assumed concerning the role of orality in the development toward femininity. And, of course, her own 1925 model of the relation to the breast as the first sexual relation had included the reversability of opposite roles of activity and passivity.

The apparent contradiction in the theorization of fully achieved femininity is resolved by the exchange, in female homosexuality, of the roles of mother and child. The identification with the mother can even be reinforced, as in the case of the second patient. With one of her love objects, the girl, this patient was simultaneously the preoedipal mother who actively suckles the child and the oedipal mother who possesses the child, a substitute for her next younger sister. In her relationship with the other woman, where, in contrast, she was identified with the child who is given the breast, she was able to convert into activity her aggressive impulses toward her mother. Thus the best refuge against the fear of losing the love of a father whose power to give is uncertain, who gives no assurance that he will be able to respond to an appeal, is abandonment of the father and of masculinity and the forming of a revised maternal relationship in which *jouissance* is authorized: nothing is lacking.

There can be no doubt that, in analyzing the first patient's dreams of return to the womb, Deutsch was the first to call attention to the deep desire, followed by hate, for the mother. And Freud's emphasis in 1931 on the hatred that accompanies the separation from the mother is in no way alien to the clinical material that Deutsch adduces in her 1932 paper on female homosexuality. Freud knew this paper in advance of its publication, since he mentions its content indirectly in 1931. And, conflating it with the 1930 paper on masochism, he anticipates it and muddles the issue.

In the following year Freud does pay homage to Deutsch's contribution. We may recall that his 1925 paper on "Some psychical consequences of the anatomical distinction between the sexes" mentioned only a loosening of the tender relation to the mother when the girl discovers her inferior organ. Where hate is concerned, Deutsch and Otto Fenichel (1931)—whose contribution on this subject is also not mentioned by Freud—are surely those who, even more than Melanie Klein or Ruth Mack Brunswick, presented case material that enabled him to reach definite conclusions about this phenomenon independently of the way each of them analyzed it. We may also consider that, between 1925 and 1931–1933, other views of Deutsch's were taken up by Freud. Thus her emphasis in the third paper on the father as being able or unable to grant the girl what the mother deprived her of is repeated by Freud in 1932–1933. To be sure, he mentions the mother's lack, a meaning of her castration that Deutsch did not stress, but he himself had waited before making it the explicit reason for the turn to the phallus-bearing father.

The same is true of the internalization of the mother's prohibition of phallic activity, the role of dethroned mother that, in Freud's version, the child takes on in her own struggle against masturbation. Though he thereby points out the relation to the castrated mother, devalued and deprived of her rights when she is deprived of the phallus, it is Deutsch who anticipated the implacable superego dimension of this internalized prohibition: apart from the identification with the phallic mother in homosexuality, this can end only in a renunciation of all sexuality or in a masochistic attachment to the mother. Freud's 1931 formulation of a transition to the father that occurs with the help of passive tendencies in so far as these have escaped catastrophe, seems like a direct echo of Deutsch's remarks, or at least an agreement with her position.

Deutsch drew on the work of others, especially Freud's. There can be no doubt that Freud took a lot from her and, to an extent, acknowledges this. He cites her as early as 1925 (1925a) and in his two papers on femininity. He does not criticize in her what he criticizes in Karen Horney, namely the notion of the masculinity complex as a defense against incestuous wishes. Finally, he ascribes to the maternal transference the richness of the material produced by women analysts, material that he, as "father," would not be able to evoke in his women patients. But he does not acknowledge her fully, certainly not her priority in appreciating the hatred for the mother and the unnaturalness of the Oedipus.

11 Regressions and Fixations

Fenichel's paper, "The pregenital antecedents of the Oedipus complex," cited by Freud in "Female sexuality" (1931) dates from 1930 and claims no priority or originality. Its aim is epistemological, and this, interestingly, is what Freud derives from it. According to Fenichel, it is important to avoid confusion, not only because the presentation of so-called pregenital material can be confusing in itself, but, he says firmly, because it is necessary to adhere to doctrinal certainties in distinguishing between regressions and fixations, and between what has remained unchanged from the preoedipal phase and what is a regressive deformation, as in the case of obsessional neurosis, where the subject, seeking to avoid the Oedipus, returns to earlier modes of satisfaction, making regressive use of pregenitality.

Pregenital antecedents are to be found in all cases, since "[a]ll neurotics suffer from having fended off the Oedipus complex by some inappropriate method, and so having failed to master it" (1930, p. 141). But at least for the time being, he says, they can be reconstructed in a way that is accurate and generalizable only through the study of cases in which there is no regression. Only by finding in such cases the traces and features of earlier organizations can one retroactively postulate its existence and see it confirmed by anamnesis, associations, or the forms of the patient's transference.

Fenichel therefore offers clinical observations to illustrate the pregenital stages that come before the Oedipus complex and, with supporting empirical evidence, to resolve to his own satisfaction the debate on female sexuality, a debate centering on the woman's change of object and her change of erogenous zone. He sets out three cases, an atypical one of a male patient, he tells us, but an interesting example of pregenital factors, and two cases of neurotic women, whom he considers to be hysterical and hence without regression, and who were both very attached to their fathers. Their history, however, reveals something quite different that preceded and determined the modalities of this attachment. Fenichel notes that each of these female patients, though not in the same way, belongs to that category of women described by Abraham, in whom the castration complex is expressed as revenge against men. They demand reparation (and sometimes provide it themselves) for what they were deprived of. Yet the complaint about having suffered damage does not preclude the other form of the complex noted by Abraham, the form in which desire is fulfilled, namely the fantasy of possessing the male organ.

The first patient, whose love life was subject to the same limitations as in the case of the neurotic man (the condition that there had to be an injured third party and disparagement of the partner), came for treatment because her self-image was impaired by sudden irruptions of sexuality (compulsive masturbation) and prostitute fantasies in stark contrast to the ideal of reserve and self-control that, she said, came from her father. The case is an excellent illustration of the normalizing nature of the girl's Oedipus; as with the boy, the father is the one who enables the child to separate from the all-consuming, incestuous relation to the mother. The patient's childhood history quickly revealed the split in the parental images. On the mother's side, there was a *jouissance* at first recalled in connection with anality, the mother's intimate encouragement of and attention to the child's well-formed stools. On the father's side, there was an extreme reserve in this regard, one that the little girl, following a reprimand by her father when he caught her masturbating, understood as a disapproval of all sexuality.

The demand for a penis, the analyst tells us, had its source not, as he had expected, in the patient's disadvantageous comparison with her brother's organ, but in another connection relevant to the same complex: the capacity to evacuate or retain associated with the male organ. The patient recalled, as the trauma of sexual difference, a memory of the humiliation she suffered in early childhood when, in her brother's presence, she had an accidental evacuation after an enema; the fact that she could not "hold herself in" was clear proof that she had been castrated. An intestinal illness at age three marked this imaginary castration for which Fenichel finds the unconscious formula: being sick = being incontinent = being castrated, all these evils attributed to the mother on account of an intervention of her father's that she never forgot:

> "Whatever did you give the child to eat?" he had asked, whereupon the little girl came to the conclusion that her mother had made her ill—i.e., sensual enjoyment with the mother made her ill, incontinent, castrated her: "It would have been better to obey my father, who always disapproved of it." The mother was the witch who seduced one and gave pleasure, but the pleasure was fatal. [p. 152]

In this infantile imaginary, where the mother's poisoning causes the intestinal disaster, we clearly see what Freud, in 1931, says he personally never encountered in women: the fear of being killed, devoured, and poisoned by the mother. Fenichel, it seems to me, and this is the primary interest of his comments, suggests that this is a reconstruction, a retroactive rationalization at the oral level, of castration, not a prefiguration of it. The mother who poisons you with urine or some other purulent liquid (associated, in a screen memory, with the mastitis that led to weaning) can drain you of all your contents, suck you dry: this is a reinterpretation, Fenichel emphasizes, of the overly erotized gratification perceived in this mother during toilet training, when the child gave in to the mother's demand for her narcissistically invested bodily products.

Paradoxically, the patient refound this figure of a castrating mother in men who forced her to have intercourse in her prostitution fantasies, in accordance with her infantile theory of the sex act, in which the prostitute is emptied out by men. Her vengeful behavior toward her lovers—fantasies of oral-sadistic fellatio— are, says Fenichel, the equivalent of a partial incorporation of the father via identification with the archaic devouring mother. A fantasy of rape by her father's hand, his five fingers representing five rapists, confirmed the interpretation in terms of incorporation, anal this time, of masturbatory practices displaced from the anus to the vagina. The patient associated these with the pleasure of enemas administered by her father in childhood and with what she expected to get from them, namely well-formed stools, an anal child, and not the emptying out imposed by the mother. The father was endowed with the ability to restore to her what the mother had stolen in different phases. What the patient interpreted as his refusal, his disapproval of his daughter's sexuality and her other desires (including her literary ambitions in adolescence), triggered aggression in the form of vehement reproaches expressed in the course of her treatment and unconscious fantasies reconstructed by the analyst as evidence of an earlier oral-sadistic model in which she had cannibalistically appropriated the male organ as well as the father's whole body and the child stolen from him.

What Fenichel highlights, I think in a very Freudian way, is that this patient's complaint—the feeling of having something dead inside her body—combines punishment and wish. On the one hand, there is the guilt for the destruction of the object implied in oral incorporation; on the other hand, there is wish fulfillment in what seems to me to be an ongoing fantasy of holding and concealing the coveted object, even if is dead: she imagines that she has a hidden penis that the analyst could authorize her to use by bringing it back to life (as Fenichel notes explicitly), in the same way that the father grants what one has been deprived of by one's mother. Fenichel observes that we have here a twofold figure of the father as avenger and savior. There is the father who forbids incest, clearly, but also, as we see by what emerges in the transference even if the analyst does not formulate it this way, the father who is supposed to *unite desire and the law* (cf. Lacan 1966, p. 824). His prohibition of *jouissance* detaches the child from the mother and protects the child from her.

But this prohibition must not extend to all of sexuality; in other words, the father himself must have desire. If this is not the case, the girl has no opportunity for the masculine identification with the father by which she poses the question of his desire (cf. Lacan's analysis of the Dora case [1955–1956, pp. 197–199 and 1956–1957, lessons of January 16 and 23]). This is not, it should be noted, an identification with the father's organ—and his *jouissance*—as in the case analyzed by van Ophuijsen or later observations by Fenichel himself (1936), but a superego identification with the father's ideals.

A similar lethal *jouissance* on the part of the mother is found in the second woman patient Fenichel describes in the 1930 paper. Here the father actually died (of a mental disorder) when the child was born, and the little girl could not help suspecting that her mother had killed him with a venereal disease. This is, in other words, a rationalization of the first handicap she felt, the lack of a father. Fenichel suggests that the paranoid interpretation of her mother's wish for her is not without a basis in reality. This unloving, or at least ambivalent, mother let her daughter know that she had been an unwanted child for whom the worst was feared: ugliness and stupidity. These fears were perceived as death wishes and, according to the law of the talion, tormented this rejected and thus hateful child, the patient, in her later relationship with her own daughter.

The dead father was idealized, if not deified. No one could equal him, and in the transference the patient tried to show the analyst's impotence, his inadequacy compared to the ideal father, a challenge that Fenichel nevertheless hears as an appeal: the only right man would be "the father of her phantasy, the fairy-prince coming from the beyond. She had endless phantasies of 'salvation,' and anxiety about her Christianity constituted the most powerful resistance in her analysis" (p. 160). No man was good enough, and so she kept on humiliating the men with whom she had affairs, taking pleasure only in their weaknesses, which she worked hard to provoke: their tears, premature ejaculation, and potential impotence. Her compulsive debasement of the partner, and her scorn of the real organ, did not keep her from greatly fearing the loss of love that could be the logical result of her behavior. She thus became furious at the men who dropped her.

Oral symptoms (alternation of bulimia and anorexia), elective dietary restrictions (fish was forbidden, since it represented her father's soul), dreams and fantasies (devouring fragments of dead bodies, absorption of feces, oral impregnation) are interpreted by Fenichel as mystical union with the dead father, a Christian communion that did not preclude blasphemous thoughts about Christ's penis. These obsessional features do not modify his diagnosis of anxiety hysteria. The patient's sacrilege is placed on the same level as her scorn for the real organ in her relationships with men: she accepts sexuality, the father's body or that of his substitute, on condition that the genital organs are excluded, as in Abraham's (1924) characterization of hysteria.

Two traumas triggered this patient's neurosis. The first of these was the birth of her daughter, whom she found ugly, not (Fenichel says) the child she wanted from her father. She feared retribution in which her daughter would harm her the way she had wished to harm her own mother. The second trauma was the birth of a daughter to her lover and another woman, which she experienced as a personal injury: the other woman had what she did not have.

It is important to note that, in regarding these events as traumatic disappointment and harm coming from the father, Fenichel locates his patient's demand on the oedipal level, even though he points to the prototype of these traumas in earlier, pregenital experience. The reproaches addressed to the father and the lover have the same form as those the patient could have addressed to her mother. On the one hand, the postulated pregenital antecedents have a basis in actual history, but they are also a child's rationalization of the first privation, that of the father: "the further the analysis advanced, and the more completely the infantile amnesias were dispelled, the clearer did it become that her real experiences with men were relatively unimportant and that the chief object which influenced her real character-formation was the one parent whom she knew—her mother" (p. 161). Men "were only screen-figures for the latter. It was to her mother that her longing for tenderness, and also her hatred, her aggressive impulses and her active castration-tendency were directed" (p. 162).

Her demand for love, and her fear of losing it, primarily concerned the living parent, the mother, who accordingly bore the responsibility for the two forms of damage the patient had undergone: being a girl, and hence castrated (not the ideal child) and being fatherless (not having what others have). Through the fantasy of mystical union she made up for her mother's crime, restoring the father who had been murdered by the mother and who, moreover, possessed the desired organ. In her anxiety attacks she ascribed her castration to her mother. Fenichel remarks that, implicitly or explicitly, she demonstrated through these crises that she was impotent, and castrated, and that her mother was to blame. At the same time, her anxiety enabled her to assume a masochistic position of suffering in the face of someone who wanted her dead. She both took revenge against her mother by exhibiting her impotence and also demanded to be desired as such, as castrated. According to Fenichel, this obsessional feature of ambivalence, already manifested in her relations with men (debasement, but fear of abandonment) originated in the pregenital anal phase. As in the preceding case, the girl continued the mother's overpreoccupation with intestinal functions. The fantasy of a castrating mother presupposed a prior idea of the mother as stealing the child's stools. Retroactive fear and *jouissance* are combined in this phase: "[e]ven when she was grown up, she could imagine no greater proof of love than that her lover should empty the bedpan when she was ill" (p. 162).

Whatever the patient's expectation, Fenichel stays with the material he is given in the treatment. When a construction is not made by the subject herself, it is deduced from her symptoms. But that is not enough for him. What he needs in addition, in the absence of conscious anamnesis, is validation by unconscious material (fantasies, dreams, or associations) of what can be inferred from the phenomenology of the symptoms. Thus, if nothing is "recalled" by the patient herself with regard to the oral phase that might be presupposed on the basis of her symptoms, one must hold back, acknowledging the barriers set up by repression to the archeological part of analytic work: "The symptom-picture which I have described makes it abundantly clear that an oral phase preceded this anal ambivalence, but I am not able to give exact particulars about the time when she was an infant at the breast" (p. 163). This reserve, it is clear, indicates his prejudice in favor of reminiscence but also his caution in interpretation.

In my opinion, the primary interest in Fenichel's approach is that he does not put in question the oedipal position of these two women even as he is eager to show how the modalities of their attachment to the father, or the vicissitudes of their love life, bear the mark of prior phases of sexual development. These are pregenital phases in which the object is above all the mother, and in which castration can be retroactively figured in the frustrations inflicted by this object at each stage—and yet we must not be deceived. In other words, the imaginary formulation that corresponds to the mother must not lead us to ignore the symbolic value of the male organ as the *gift* of the father. It seems to me that Fenichel notes this very subtly in suggesting that what the first patient is asking for is absolution in regard to her desire, the restitution of the internalized phallic object that is none other than the signifier of the father's lack of desire (something dead). The deification of the father and the mystical effusion in the second case highlight the unimportance of the real organ, derided by the patient, in comparison with the phallus that she herself could *be* even if she does not *have* it, as is shown in her demand that her mother love her as a girl, as castrated.

Fenichel states that the pregenital (anal or oral) material, whether revealed from the beginning in the treatment or evoked by the analyst, is evidence of stages of sexual development in which demands and frustrations involve the mother. Like Helene Deutsch (1932) he recognizes in anality the passage necessary in order for the girl to symbolize what she can expect from the father: the anal child. Like Deutsch faithful to Abraham (1920), he agrees that the girl conceives this child through defecation, active as well as passive, the father's gift consisting in allowing her to imagine the organ or the desired child as a product of his body.

The preeminent status Fenichel accords to orality is explained by the theoretical point he is attempting to establish clinically on the basis of the masculinity complex he has discerned, namely the identification with the father. In connection with cases of hysteria, he paradoxically retains, from among the three modes of identification that Freud had noted (1921b, Chapter 7), only the first, the oral incorporation of the father. This is undoubtedly the case, he announces, because his research bears on what precedes the Oedipus—namely the early ways of symbolizing castration—and because, given this aim, he is supported by Abraham. The notion of partial incorporation, that is, incorporation of a part of the object's body, that he mentions in each of these cases is largely inspired by the second part of the latter's 1924 paper and closely corresponds to it.

But Fenichel holds back when it comes to the phallicism of the girl, and this is where he disagrees with Lampl-de Groot. He personally, he says, has not encountered this kind of active male desire (the masculinizing identification with the father) in the cases he has analyzed. The fact that he focuses on the chronological coincidence between the phallic phase of development and the oedipal detour is probably the reason for this. What is phallic is not, in his view, pregenital (cf. Fenichel 1934). It is likely that this resistance is in part determined by his anatomical prejudice, in which the possession of the mother presupposes an act of penetration into a hollow organ that the anatomical configuration of the girl does not allow one to imagine. But his obstinacy on this point, his unwillingness to grant it credence, is nevertheless of interest. They are evidence of his caution, but also of what he does not take into account, namely that the phallus is first a maternal one. The mother, for him, is more castrating than phallic. And she does not appear as a castrated mother. This is connected with his investigations of the two female cases in his 1930 paper: the question of the mother's desire (what does she want from me?) is raised there as being the first enigma for the child. The devouring *jouissance* that is ascribed to her (the anal or vampire mother) is one answer.

This is a lethal *jouissance* from which the father offers protection by forbidding incest and offering himself as desiring. The approval or "blessing" awaited from him can thus be understood as the pacifying, regulated aspect of desire, in contrast to the obscene and lawless nature of *jouissance*.

It remains the case that the transference onto the father of the hate felt toward the mother, on account of the restrictions she imposes in the course of tending to the child and on account of the fear of being devoured by her, are mentioned by Freud in 1931 with awareness of the observations of Fenichel and also of Helene Deutsch, Melanie Klein, and Ruth Mack Brunswick.

12   Castration and Love for the Father

If the equivalence of castration and love for the father was seen in the case of the boy (who can no longer be in a feminine position once he has recognized the possibility of castration), it appeared only in a comment added to Freud's paper on "The dissolution of the Oedipus complex" (1924a), though with no reminder of why the identification with the father occurs, namely the refusal of the mother's castration.

Moreover, although Freud later (1932–1933) states that, for the girl as well, it is the mother's castration that devalues her in the child's eyes, the imaginary event (cf. the Wolf Man's primal scene) that makes the mother a castrated woman is not mentioned in this text as it was, albeit indirectly, in the case of the boy in 1924. With regard to the girl, where can we find a reference in Freud to the role of the father in the mother's castration? Is it when he regretted that he did not know enough about girls and could speak only about the boy, yet asserted the primacy of the phallus for both sexes (1923a)? What is it that he discovered or rediscovered between 1923–1925 and 1931–1933 that could have led him to take these developments for granted in the early 1930s? And what led him to presuppose, in connection with the little girl's masculine identification (an identification, he explains, with the phallic mother or with the father), a fact that we may, I think, assume from now on without forcing the text, namely that neither the boy nor the girl can at first agree to be identified with the castrated being that one becomes if one is loved by the father?

This seems to me to be the best way to understand how, even if their conclusions are different, the statements and intuitions—and also the objections—of other analysts are useful to Freud, if only because they sometimes place the accent on something he himself had at one time pointed out but without seeing its implications: a retroactive effect, one that, as we have seen, he directly correlated with the advance of knowledge. He is sometimes stimulated by an element of his own work that has been picked up by one or the other of his colleagues, whatever he himself has done with it.

The father's role in the mother's castration is mentioned by Freud, but I did not see its significance until I read Karen Horney's 1922 paper, "On the genesis of the castration complex in women." Discussing a woman patient's compulsion to eat large amounts of salt, as her mother had had to do on account of hemoptysis in her own childhood, Horney notes that what is at issue in this identification is the patient's unconscious belief that, on account of her father, she had suffered in the same way as her mother had. Horney then reports that the associations of another woman patient constantly revealed her feeling that she had been *beaten down* with illness because of her father; when her hypochondriac symptoms subsided, *beating* fantasies emerged and became the dominant feature in her neurosis.

This reference to beating fantasies is especially valuable because it explains what could not be seen in Freud's "A child is being beaten" (1919a), though it was there if one only knew how to read it. This is the equation, for the girl, of castration and the father's love that is found in the incestuous, and therefore unconscious, phase of this masochistic fantasy: she herself is being beaten by her father, in a combination of guilt and erotism that is both the crime of incestuous genital intercourse and also its punishment.[1] Being beaten = being loved = being castrated by the father; though the incestuous love is repressed, we may conclude that it is so because castration is involved, even if this means seeing here a formulation of the law of the father or the prohibition of incest.

Note

1. Compare "The economical problem of masochism" (Freud 1924c) and the discussion of Hoffmann's story "The Sandman" in "The uncanny" (Freud 1919b).

13 The Origin of Hatred for the Mother

Though this had not been indicated in "Some psychical conse-quences of the anatomical distinctions between the sexes" (1925a), what Freud describes in 1931 and 1932–1933 as the indices of the girl's entry into the Oedipus are the girl's hate for her mother—the first sign of a turn toward the father—and her imputing both seduction and castration no longer to the mother but to the fa-ther. The first point to be noted here is that the Oedipus is thus the recognition of the father as castrator. In this elliptical way Freud is announcing what he had been saying for a long time in connec-tion with the infantile sadistic theory of coitus: being loved by the father, for both girl and boy, is equivalent to being castrated by him. The second point is that the hate for the mother is hate for a castrated mother. Hate as a reversal, a converse of love: isn't this what Freud is trying to say when he invites the reader to reconsider what had not been noticed up to this point, namely the exclusive tie of the girl to her mother in the early phases, with complete neglect of the paternal object?

If, he says, in 1931, the girl's later reproach for having been endowed with an inadequate organ is directed to the mother, this is a rationalization of the same sort as the other reasons the girl gives for the change of feeling that she does not understand. What really matters is this change of feeling. It has a cause, but one that is not perceived as such and must be reconstructed. This can happen only through psychoanalysis, that is, in the retroaction of unconscious recollection, not on the basis of some memory or of direct observation. And, according to Freud, this cause is the trauma of sexual difference that, because it is governed by the alternation of presence and absence of the male organ, requires the devaluation of the mother when absence is observed in her. This strict deduction follows from Freud's remarks: the appeal to the father, at this point, in no way indicates the girl's recognition of her castration. On the contrary, her demand remains entirely phallic, since she wants to get from him what the mother cannot give her, the object that has become eminently desirable through the certainty of its lack in the mother.

The decisive fact that forces the girl into the Oedipus, for Freud in 1931 and 1932–1933, is the mother's castration. All the prior reasons for hatred that originate in the constraints of childrearing can be added on, but not inevitably so and not before this time. We can therefore understand why he does not pick up the pre-oedipal hate, connected with oral or anal frustrations, that Fenichel sought in the anamnesis of his women patients. For Freud, this is not where to locate either the hatred or the ambivalence that may follow it and may be considered a legacy of the mother complex in the woman's relation to her father or to men. If it seems to appear, it is always retroactive. In other words, hate arises only when the representation of sexual difference becomes relevant, that is, when it becomes necessary to renounce the phallus of the first love object.

The girl's reproach to her mother upon finding herself castrated, the reproach that Freud (1925a) had said he did not quite understand, has found its basis and its logic between then and 1932–1933. Earlier frustrations do not explain it, because what is important is not that the mother is imagined to have "castrated" the child by thwarting it in one phase or another, but that she herself, at a particular moment, has been recognized as castrated. The castrated mother, not the castrating one: Freud's counterargument to Fenichel (and to Klein, as we shall see) is no doubt motivated primarily by the confusion these other theorists introduce. By 1932–1933 we understand that the mother herself is lacking. The fact that she may later be perceived to have deprived the child of the breast or of some other satisfactions is secondary, in all senses of the word.

The mother's lack is decisive for the way in which each sex will resolve the Oedipus and hence decisive for neurosis. This lack is all the more crucial to understand in the case of the girl, because, if clinical experience leads Freud to revise his views on femininity, he does so on the basis of having ascertained, first, that at the end of the indirect course of development leading to femininity the oedipal position is in no way obvious or certain, and, second, that maintaining this position once it has been reached does not seem to be a corollary of neurosis in women.

What is the meaning of this asymmetry—that the irresolution of the Oedipus does not lead to neurosis in women the way it does in men—if not that the root of neurosis is to be found elsewhere and is common to both sexes: the acknowledgment or nonacknowledgment of the mother's castration? Is this not how to understand what Freud designated as the prehistory of the Oedipus complex (1925a) or the preoedipal period (1931) in the girl? As he says, he had not sufficiently taken into account the duration and strength of the initial attachment to the mother, because he had not realized the power and the unique meaning of the presence or absence of the phallus that makes it the exclusive object of either love or hate. Like identification, love has to do with castration. This idea was already present in "The ego and the id" (1923a), if we recall that identification, before or after object choice, always came down in the end to a refusal of castration, the first identification (to the parents) dating from before the recognition of this possibility. What makes the object valuable, so that one will want to have it or to be it, is nothing but the presence of a term whose absence one has foreseen as a possibility. The infantile belief in the woman's penis is thus always to be situated in the aftermath of the recognition of sexual difference.

Thus the phallus as condition of love and identification was there in 1923, but the concept was not spelled out until 1931 with the theory of the girl's change of object and the hate that replaces her love for her mother. Freud's criticism of Jeanne Lampl-de Groot for not having noted this in her 1928 paper on the evolution of the Oedipus complex, a criticism that seemed rather unjust, is explained by the discovery he had made in the meantime (between 1925 and 1931), a discovery whose steps he retraces in "Female sexuality" (1931), ending with the observation that the girl's love for the phallic mother changes to hate, bringing to the fore all the prior resentments, when she recognizes the mother's castration.

What Freud calls the girl's "preoedipal phase" has been misunderstood. It can be understood correctly only by attention to his papers, in which it is presented as the time before the recognition of the negative feature, structural and not accidental, that is the lot of all women: their castration. Likewise, the twofold orientation of the boy's Oedipus (involving the phase of passive love for the father) normally ceases with the certainty of the division of the sexes as a function of castration.

Although the preoedipal phase precedes the Oedipus and is deduced from its failures and obstacles, it does not, as some have said, lead into or prefigure it, either by revealing the earliest stages, as Melanie Klein says, or by collapsing *pregenital* and *preoedipal* as Fenichel does. Klein and Fenichel may well have been led to their conclusions by Freud, either by reading him cursorily or by the ambiguity of the term *preoedipal* itself. The two terms, *pregenital* and *preoedipal*, are both to be found in Freud. But, for him, all oral, anal, or phallic drives are pregenital. The discovery of the full Oedipus complex is proof that pregenitality does not coincide with the orientation or nonorientation toward the oedipal object: these drives can be addressed either to the father or to the mother. Heterosexuality, even if Freud makes this clear relatively late, is an acquired limitation in object choice (cf. 1920a).

The hate toward the mother signals the girl's Oedipus and indicates the passage to the father. When we find its traces in the woman, whatever elements or events may later turn up as causes in her analysis, we find that the separation from the mother was made only insofar as the mother was experienced as defective, as lacking the phallus, that is, the object of the demand for love at this time in childhood that is therefore called the phallic stage, a stage in which interest is focused on the genital organs and sexual difference.

If Freud insists on the girl's penis envy and her hate for her mother, this is because paying attention to that hate is what enabled him to confirm the primacy of the phallus for the girl—a single representative of sexual difference for the unconscious—and also, more generally, to recognize that what is sought in the love object is the phallus. Freud will cling to this "discovery," this causal connection, in proportion to the long time he took to arrive at it, even to the point of doing an injustice to other developments that he did not take the trouble to retain or to revise. Thus we can explain what seemed to be an ambiguous position with regard to Helene Deutsch: an absence of criticism, however far from Freud's views her own could sometimes seem to be (especially in her 1925 paper on femininity), and confusion about the exact content of the papers of hers that he cites.

Viewed from the perspective of the time needed for a discovery, and the perspective of the part that others played in it, it now seems to me that Deutsch's mention of the hatred for the mother is less important for Freud than what she states in her paper on masochism (1930): the love for the father is equivalent to castration. If Freud ascribes to the 1930 paper what in fact is to be found in the 1932 paper on homosexuality, we can see his motive as being Deutsch's retrospective logic, namely that castration, which she emphasizes in the first text and that, for her, is tantamount to passivity, is the reason for the hate that she describes in the second one.

14   The Disagreement
       with Abraham

Given Freud's enigmatic attributions (for Deutsch), impasse on the content of the contribution (for Fenichel), or unqualified rejection (for Horney, Klein, and Jones), is it an accident that these authors, in the works that Freud mentions, all refer to Abraham, specifically to a page-long clinical vignette from his 1924 paper on the history of libidinal development, the part entitled "Origins and growth of object-love"? What Abraham proposes there, and is accepted as fact by all (though, to be sure, with modifications or slight distortions), is the identification with the father as cannabalistic incorporation of the penile organ, partial love as the first step toward object love, and oral sadism as the cause of penis envy. On this Freud says nothing, even if this means that he may ignore material that might tally with his own ideas, or that he may fail to acknowledge another theorist's priority.

Freud cites Abraham primarily for the 1920 paper, "Manifestations of the female castration complex." But his praise is ambiguous, since, at the same time that he emphasizes its excellence, he notes its limitation with regard to what, in his opinion, overturns all previous conceptualizations: the hitherto neglected relation of the girl to her mother. Considering his absolute silence on the 1924 paper to which his colleagues refer, I therefore see a dividing line and suggest that, even on female sexuality, the debate is not so much between Freud and Jones (as might appear to be the case) as between Freud and Abraham.

Whatever prevented him from making this explicit, it is as though, from 1931 on, Freud saw what might separate the two of them, and this despite the fact that he could not have found a more rigorous clinician, one closer to himself in terms of caution and respect for empirical fact, than Abraham. The distance between them, hardly noticeable in Abraham's 1924 paper on the development of the libido, nonetheless seems to me to be the heart of this matter. We can thereby understand Freud's errors and prejudices in his 1931 paper, but also, more generally, what sets him apart from his pupils, and not only when it comes to femininity.

What is Abraham trying to say in this section of his 1924 paper, this quasi-appendix, just a few pages in a long discussion, that he presents as the second part of his text? He tells us that he wants to complete what he feels he had explained insufficiently in the section on manic-depressive states, namely the patient's relation to the love object, now to be explored in the context of a fuller discussion of libidinal object development. Could we not suggest that what escapes him is the uniqueness of Freud's construction, that the aporetic nature of Freud's statements (no synthesis, no truth presented in its entirety) appears to him not as an epistemological necessity but rather as a fault to be rectified or a totality to be restored?

What Abraham is trying to do is, above all, to specify the status of the object that he discerned in a clinical comparison of melancholia and obsessional neurosis, and hence, on the basis of these fictive stages imposed by pathology, to establish a kind of genesis, a progressive object love. Freud called Abraham an incorrigible optimist, perhaps because, with regard to the seamless passage from hate to love, Abraham had noted that analysis can transform melancholia into obsessional neurosis. Reconstruction (internal differentiation of stages in each phase, oral, anal, or genital) is thus responsive to clinical observation, but also to Abraham's preconceptions about a progression from narcissism to the object love that is the hallmark of psychic health. The belief in love as endpoint is what guides Abraham's thinking, and what leads him, though he does not succumb to premature optimism, to define the therapeutic ideal for melancholia as reversing the regressive tendency of the libido and opening the way toward object love and genital organization.

Is this concept of object love as a maturational goal accorded to genitality a prejudice on Abraham's part? It is, in any case, a disagreement with Freud's views of love, if we consider the disparity between men's and women's types of object choice or the fundamentally narcissistic nature of all love. There is no more passionate overflowing of ego libido onto the object than a woman's love for her child, loved first as a part of herself, or for her partner, who is nothing but her masculine ego ideal. Even parents' love for their offspring is a reflection of their own narcissism (cf. Freud 1914c). What is it, then, about Abraham's approach or conclusions that, as we know, his colleagues responded to with such great enthusiasm? And how could his conceptualization of phases of sexual organization in terms of development and progression, based on a single case of a woman patient, have been seen as a solution to the riddle of feminine sexuality in the eyes of a generation of analysts? And what, moreover, can explain the paradox that an authoritative account of femininity was ascribed to a page's worth of material taken from a text on an entirely different subject?

For it is odd that, if Abraham deplores a limitation in regard to his material on melancholia, this is because he had analyzed only male subjects intensively. The only female case that he mentions as a counterpoint in the second section does not, as he notes, belong to this clinical category. However, what he inferred from melancholia, the existence of an oral-sadistic stage, seems to him to be confirmed by some phenomena that he had formerly noted as pertaining to the castration complex. The symptoms of this young woman, in his brief report of it—kleptomania, mythomania, depressive crises—could therefore be subsumed under the masculinity complex whose manifestations had been inventoried in his 1920 paper. He notes that the patient's tearful despair was determined in part by her castration complex and the entailments of her damaged masculinity. And yet he finds something else here: her tears, which he sees as having the phallic signification of a wish to urinate like a man, concerned the patient's relation to her father. She was mourning not his actual death but the psychological loss that had marked the beginnings of her neurosis.

Having announced the unusual nature of this mourning independent of the actual loss of the object, Abraham returns to the patient's history. The abrupt break in her relationship with her father came at a precise point in her childhood (she was 6 at the time) and was connected to her observation of parental intercourse. To this primal-scene trauma Abraham attributes the loss of all contact with her father—which is how she described it—and an exclusive and compulsive interest in his genitals. Voyeurism and kleptomania (stealing the envied penis, castrating the father), but also mythomania (affirming that she had the penis and thereby feeling sexual arousal, the impression that something was swelling and growing in her lower abdomen) are said to have their source in an identification with the father, or, Abraham specifies, with the coveted genitals; the patient used an enema syringe, stolen from her father, for anal masturbation.

Two phases of this text must be distinguished. First there is Abraham's brief page that is the only mention in this paper of a female case and is the basis on which the other analysts claim the prevalence of orality in women. Then we have to reckon both with Abraham's commentary and the use he makes of this case in a broader context, and with the use the borrowers make of both the case report and certain aspects of the commentary.

In the brief case report itself, it is not apparent at this point how the mechanism of identification with the father or with his organ differs from what was noted in 1920 under the heading of castration complex: revenge or wish fulfillment (maintenance of the fantasy of possessing the male organ) on the basis of a sexual difference that is not, or not easily, accepted. It is another feature of the complex, one that Abraham also mentions in 1920, that establishes the origin of this penis envy, namely castration by biting.

At this point in his elaboration of the phases of development, the appropriation of the male organ in a sadistic fantasy of castration by biting has an entirely different meaning from that of a reaction to the trauma of sexual difference. The partial identification of which Freud (1921b) speaks, the symbolic incorporation of a trait, is, Abraham says, homologous with his partial incorporation. We are to understand this as incorporation not of the whole object but of part of the object's body, with which the patient then identifies. Abraham thus understands the cannibalistic nature of identification on the imaginary level, without seeing what is electively desirable in this feature removed from the person. He refers to Freud (at the outset, identification with and investment of the object are indistinguishable) in order to equate partial identification and what he calls partial love. The woman's penis envy, which we may encounter in the form of a wish to castrate the father or the partner who is his substitute, is, at least in the perspective of the analysts, only a manifestation of love. The contradiction that some of them, like Karen Horney, found in the clinical fact that penis envy and love for the father can coexist, is thereby resolved; this partial love, though imperfect, is still the first step toward true, complete object love (cf. Horney 1926).

Even though this is not Abraham's intention, seeing the archaism of such manifestations of the castration complex in terms of fixation at the earliest stage of development enables us to sidestep the phallic dimension of the claim. Yet Abraham sees progress in the fact that the object is not entirely destroyed in this cannibalistic incorporation, and this protection of the object is the beginning of the transition from narcissism to object love. It is important to note that he adds, by way of confirmation, the fact that the mothers of his two women patients were also represented by a single body part, the breasts, or, in their place, the buttocks. The fragmentation of the body and the early sadism of the oral phase mean more to him than the representation of sexual difference in the unconscious, to the point where he seems blind to his own theory when he says that the mother's breasts are to be identified with a female penis. Moreover, the connections he establishes between disgust for the mother, identified with feces, and her representation by the buttocks, have little to do with the equations penis = baby = excrement = gift = child, whose symbolic and linguistic functioning Freud (1916a) set out to demonstrate and that Abraham himself highlighted in his 1920 paper. The rationalization (the contiguity of the buttocks and feces) actually avoids what he nevertheless indicates: the mother too, regardless of the anatomical difference of the sexes, is conceived as phallic, identified with a body part that she does not have. The affect of disgust is not thereby situated as it might be in the later Freud, since the simple series breast-penis-feces, all detachable parts of the body, reveals something of the process of recognition of castration, in other words, of the moment of disappointment or separation with regard to a demand, first addressed to the mother, that she be a phallic mother.

According to Abraham, a trace of the limited interest in one part of the object, as a more or less distant effect of the primitive mechanism of incorporation, is to be found in child development and in the observation of children. Clinical experience testifies to such a reduction of the whole to the part, in which feces represent for the paranoiac the love object that he cannot expel, the fetishist devalues women in favor of one of their body parts or garments, or dreams occur in which the death of someone close is represented by the loss of a tooth, sometimes painlessly. As disparate as these examples are, Abraham maintains, in the list of parts standing for the whole of the person we find the equation penis = breasts, and other body parts acquire this phallic value secondarily. He notes this, but he does not stop to examine what it is that confers unique value on this body part taken from the object.

Because he is concerned with the preservation of the rest of the body, with the progress in love that he sees here, he misses the issue that, in retrospect, we see to be the crucial one, where castration and the common phallic denominator can find their place. This is the question, in other words, of what causes love, the question that Freud (1916a, 1918) does not hesitate to ask even before he clearly discerns the primacy of the phallus, if only when he notes the reduction of the man to his appendage, a transient regression and one that can be observed in women as evidence of their castration complex. But this fragment of narcissistic virility (the wish for the male organ) paradoxically enables women to achieve femininity (the wish for a man) and hence object love.

Let us recognize what Freud is saying. If, by cross-checking texts and projecting later ones onto those that came earlier, we can find already present in Freud the symbolic value of the male organ even before he formulated this explicitly, it is noteworthy that he needed so much time both to point it out as such and to relate it, for the boy and the girl, to object choice and identification. For it is only the issue of the girl's change of object that will lead Freud, in 1932–

1933, to assess the full scope of what he at first noted as the primacy of the phallus in the boy: a single organ to determine sexual difference.

The oral penis envy that Abraham observes in 1924, and that he sees as a regression or fixation at the stage of partial love, is in fact not considered in terms of this symbolic value, decisive for the female Oedipus, that Freud himself did not at first perceive. On the contrary, Abraham stops at its pathological dimension, an accident or fixation of development. This observation serves above all to confirm for him what he had said about the tendency in melancholic aggression to preserve all but one part of the object. This is proof that the destructive cannibalistic incorporation of primary identification is transformed, in the course of development, into partial incorporation; there is an ambivalent appropriation of one part, but preservation of the remainder.

The prevalence of oral symptoms found in many women is perhaps what guides Abraham. Anorexia, bulimia, nausea, vomiting, disgust: he noted these in his 1916 paper as referring to the earliest stage of the libido, without, Freud remarks, seeing the connection to hysteria. Is it the prevalence of orality in the imaginary efflorescence of the symptoms or fantasies of such women patients that prevents Abraham from seeing what Freud is beginning to specify at the same time (1923a): the difference between primary and secondary identification? According to Freud, primary (cannibalistic) identification, deduced from melancholia, comes before object love and sexual difference. He is careful to note that, for the sake of simplification, he calls this an identification with the father, although, since the lack of a penis has not been recognized and the lacking parent devalued, it is really an identification with both parents. The second identification, at the exit from the Oedipus, substitutes for the loss of the love object. Thus, abandoning his first object, the mother, the boy can either identify with her or reinforce his identification with the father, that first identification prior to the recognition of castration. Similarly, for the girl, the loss of the love object (the father) leads either to a stronger identification with the mother or to an identification with the father as lost object, a substitution of identification for object love, as in melancholia, via setting up the abandoned object in the ego. This regressive mechanism (a reversion to the oral phase) is more easily observed in the girl than in the boy.

Just as the masculinity in the boy's character is consolidated, when he leaves the Oedipus, by the strengthening of his identification with the father, it is the strengthening of her identification with the mother that, according to Freud, leads the girl to femininity. There is, however, a contradiction, or at least a logical difficulty, here. If what is involved for the girl, in this identification with the mother, is a reinforcement—which, if we follow Freud exactly in this text, we understand as a reinforcement of primary identification—how can this phallic identification be the path to femininity? Freud agrees at this time that the matter of identifications is quite confusing. The outcome of object choice, at the exit from the Oedipus, can, as identification with gender ideals, confirm primary identification, even if it does not obey the same mechanism. And we must also reckon with the mechanism of a regressive identification resulting from the Oedipus, one that, Freud says, can overlap with the mechanism of so-called primary identification.

Could this be the explanation of the role confusion in Abraham? The confusion is between primary identification—the kind he found in melancholia, a process of incorporation corresponding to the regression of the libido to the cannibalistic stage (this, as Freud always granted, was his discovery)—and the second, oedipal identification that comes about not at the same time but, precisely, as a result of the refusal of castration by both the boy and the girl. But this is neither said nor taken into account by Freud at first. Thus, though *The Ego and the Id* (1923a) is contemporaneous with "The dissolution of the Oedipus complex" (1924a), there is no question of the event that induces the dissolution of the Oedipus, driving the boy from the relation to his mother into the identification with his father.

Once again: what is the meaning of the massive rallying of the analytic community, between 1925 and 1932, behind the idea of the origin of penis envy suggested in Abraham's paper? We may recall that Freud (1925a) explicitly solicited responses when he raised the question of the girl's love for her father as the legacy of her love for her mother. On the basis of Abraham's 1924 paper, analysts contemporary with Freud believed that they had heard his question and found ways to answer it.

Understanding penis envy in terms of fixation at the oral stage, as we see even if Abraham does not dwell on this, makes it possible to derive penis envy from the oral envy of the breast, that earliest phase that Abraham finds in melancholics prior to ambivalence and that, for him, echoes Stärcke's views on weaning as the first castration. None of the analysts deny the identification with the father or the masculinity complex in women. They even agree on the term "castration complex" as a fact of clinical experience, a set of phenomena, extravagant as they may seem, for which it would be difficult to find and justify another name (cf. the efforts of Jones in his 1927 paper on this subject). But what disturbed the analysts, as can be seen in the very title of Karen Horney's paper, "On the genesis of the castration complex in women" (1922), is the explanation that Freud had been giving of what he found to be the equivalent of the boy's castration anxiety: the penis envy that is the girl's expression of her narcissistic claim on the male organ. The difference is that for Freud (1925a)—and Abraham had said this in 1920—instead of the fear of losing it, what we find in the girl is the lament for having lost it, having gotten it in damaged form, or not yet having gotten it. According to Freud, she saw it, noted the difference with her own genital, and wanted it. It is the recognition of sexual difference that causes penis envy in the girl and castration anxiety in the boy, and even, Freud notes, for the girl it is certainly not so much the problem of where babies come from that awakens sexual interest as it is this apperception of difference: she has seen on the body of the other what she lacks.

The awakening of sexual interest is thus an awakening of interest in the genital, and in the male genital exclusively; only the male aspect of her own sexuality interests the girl, either in the hope of one day getting the desired organ or in the denial of her lack. This, says Freud, is the origin of the woman's masculinity complex, which is not just an accident, one possible reaction to the discovery of castration that, if not overcome, will thwart development towards femininity. It is a necessary stage, an obligatory passage, however dangerous, that, though Freud (1925a) does not describe all the motivations, will lead her to change her object, renouncing the wish for a penis in favor of the wish for a child and taking the father as her love object. Envy, in the form of penis envy, thus becomes part and parcel of femininity. Freud does not hold back from drawing the implications of what he has recognized as a structural fact: penis envy leaves its trace in the form of jealousy as a character trait in women.

We can therefore see the advantage in thinking of penis envy as an early stage of development. The ambivalence it reveals must owe something to the mechanism from which it proceeds, namely identification, the first stage of love. There is no need whatsoever to speak of the envious nature of women if penis envy can be explained as partial love, the first mode of relation to any object and thus to the paternal object. On the contrary, Horney remarks in 1926, we find here a reason for sexual attraction:

> [I]f penis envy were the first expression of that mysterious attraction of the sexes, there would be nothing to wonder at when analysis discloses its existence in a yet deeper layer than that in which the desire for a child and the tender attachment to the father occur. The way to this tender attachment toward the father would be prepared not simply by disappointment in regard to the penis but in another way as well. We should then instead have to conceive of the libidinal interest in the penis as a kind of "partial love," to use Abraham's term. Such love, he says, always forms a preliminary stage to true object-love. [p. 337]

The last advantage, but not the least, of recourse to orality as the origin of penis envy was immediately perceived by the analytic community. At the same time as orality accounted for the change of object, the passage from the mother to the father, the breast to the penis, it could also account for the other change, difficult to conceptualize, that Freud (1931) calls a change of sex, the change of erogenous zone that finally occurs in the girl. If this is understood as a displacement from one receptive organ, the mouth, to another, the vagina, the investment of the female genital zone is no longer necessarily subordinated to the abandonment by the child of a primary masculinity, indeed to the revolt against the phallic activity that was at first so gratifying, a rejection, Freud says, that is due to her narcissistic humiliation when she finds that she cannot sustain the rivalry with the boy.

We have already seen in Helene Deutsch's 1925 paper (she had read Abraham and cites him) a similar extension from orality as a pregenital stage to orality as metaphor for the *jouissance* of the properly female genital organ. In other theorists (Fenichel, Klein, and especially Jones) we see this extension functioning as a given, a consensus on an accepted fact, too operative to be put in question. Jones' certainty in his 1927 paper, "The early development of female sexuality," which challenges Freud, is significant in identifying the two alimentary orifices, mouth and anus, with the vagina.

It is this round trip from Abraham to Freud that, it seems to me, permits a synthesis such as Jones' where, in Freud as in Abraham, there is question, hypothesis, and reconstruction. Thus, in a letter to Freud on December 26, 1924 (Freud and Abraham 1907–1926), far from having the certainty of those who cite his authority, Abraham shows his perplexity and the fragility of his hypotheses on the displacement from the clitoris to the vagina and the existence of a vagino-anal stage. Does the little girl have vaginal sensations? In a letter to Abraham of December 12, 1924, Freud says that these are difficult to distinguish from vestibulary sensations but declares himself eager to hear Abraham's views on female sexuality. Pending further investigation, he stands by the suggestions of Lou Andreas-Salomé that he cited in his paper "On the transformation of instinct as exemplified in anal erotism" (1916a) but still wishes to hear Abraham's hypotheses.

Hypothesis and reconstruction: this is how it was with the conceptualization of stages and the passage from one to the other. This way of thinking cannot be attributed to Abraham unless we forget that Freud suggested the possibility of a transition between orality to anality when he himself attempted to trace the sexual development of the Wolf Man (1914a). Only Freud said clearly that he was testing what he had been able to deduce from the *fictive* stages of pregenital development; his reconstruction is indirect and hypothetical, and he does not claim certainty. To be sure, we do find in Freud the linking of one phase to another and the notion of a sequence of pregenital stages. But orality and anality are theorized solely in the context of castration: the Wolf Man's regression stems from a castration threat. Regression from one stage to another one, presumably earlier, occurs as an effect of castration but also as a retroactive effect. The chronological order is merely an artifact of the attempt at an overall synthesis. Only the genital phase (as Freud calls it at this point), in other words, castration, entails the disturbances that enable us to imagine pregenital phases of libidinal organization. If the refusal of castration discovered in the phallic phase is expressed by regression to a prior stage of development or by the displacement from above to below (as Freud [1905b] noted in connection with Dora's symptoms), it is not surprising that a refusal of castration can appear in the cannabalistic form that Abraham describes in 1924, a fantasy of incorporation of the male organ that is essentially oral (biting) or anal.

The diagnosis of hysteria that Abraham suggests in view of this woman patient's displacement of symptoms, namely the exclusion of the genital organs as condition of her love for her father or a male substitute, along with his judicious remarks in 1917 in connection with oral symptoms being a more acceptable way to express sexual wishes, do not indicate that he himself drew the same conclusions from his brief observation that others found, namely that he offered a better account of the female castration complex than women's envious nature.

It is unclear whether Abraham considers the oral sadism that he emphasizes in this case to be the cause of penis envy. The fact that he uses it for his demonstration of the initially cannibalistic and destructive form of what will later be love does not prevent him from simultaneously believing that it is an effect or a reactivation of the castration trauma in the form of an older stage of development. We may also assume that he has recourse to the oral phase in order to explain the regressive aspect of this young woman's symptoms, just as Freud (1914a) discovered the trace of the Wolf Man's castration anxiety in his anorexia and fear of being devoured by his father. Thus, although he was the first to describe oral sadism with regard to the outcome of the Oedipus, Abraham does not draw either the conclusions of Jones, who refers to him to make it the cause of female homosexuality, nor those of Klein, who sees in it the origin of the oedipal conflict.

It seems to me that the best way to approach Abraham's clinical report is to posit reactivation of the first loss, the oral loss of the breast, at the moment of the discovery of castration, and to posit the equation of the penis and the breast, or of the sequence of losses (breast, feces, penis), on condition that we include the retroactive effect of castration. But it is important to note that these specifications as to the inverse order of the sequence—inverse in relation to development—are expressly denied by Freud at the same time as this paper by Abraham (cf. Freud 1923b, 1924a, and the note added to 1909a). Indeed, Freud's discreet but insistent remarks are a warning: the placing in sequence of equivalent objects must not disregard the special status of one of them. That one, the male organ, though last in the series breast = feces = penis, is originary and independent of chronology, and it retrospectively governs the series. Are we not entitled to see, in this play of notes and restrictions, sometimes too subtle to be immediately legible, a kind of admonition against the temptation to synthesis or to linear development that Abraham's paper, culminating in a table of stages, seemed to advocate?

In 1932–1933, Freud adds two major modifications to his 1925 paper. These concern the modalities of the girl's change of object (the manifestation of hate for her mother) and the exact role of penis envy and masculine identification. It seems to me that this is a way of responding not so much to Abraham's propositions as to the ways others might develop them. He felt the need to put matters in order and, beyond that, to correct what had not been understood—not understood by others, but also by himself. This is because the emphasis was not immediately placed where it belonged, in such a way as to draw attention to points that had been present for a long time but without their entailments being seen. Freud's reservations, his rejection of this or that opinion (especially notable in the 1931 paper) never amount to the imputation of ignorance to others. If he regrets a lacuna or argues with a construction in Jones, say, or Klein, he does so primarily in accordance with the results or impressions of his own clinical experience. He is forced to return to his clinical material and the conclusions to which it led him as much by the imprecisions, errors, and overhastiness of other theorists as by their clinical intuitions or skill. In this way, and first of all for himself, he comes to focus in closely on what is at stake, so that he can gradually correct his own statements.

It is from the responses he got that Freud perceived what it was that could lead to misunderstanding of his pronouncements (1925a) on the girl's relation to the first, maternal, object. I believe that this perception on his part is to be found in his criticism of the brief case report in Abraham that all the others cite, criticism that, I suggest, offers the best explanation for the errors and omissions that were so surprising in his references at the end of the 1931 paper. It is not accidental that Freud forgot Abraham's piece. For how could he note the distance between them or express reservations toward someone who could no longer reply? Abraham, one of the few privileged addressees whose advice was sought, whose suggestions were often taken up and referred to, had died in 1925. And how could Freud determine what he owed to each colleague, when what others made of his work revealed misunderstanding? What Freud recognized, in my opinion, is the ambiguity of his own formulations as well as Abraham's. He clarified his own first, those that had caused confusion between a necessarily *incomplete* theory of development, aimed at highlighting the infantile aspect of sexuality in the broad sense, and, on the other hand, a *complete* theory of development as a finality, interested more in the sequence of stages than in what can go wrong with them or in the trauma that enables us to infer them.

15 Melanie Klein and the Early Oedipus

The role of the mother is central for Melanie Klein; the father receives little attention. The prominence Klein accords the mother may be relevant to the reproaches later addressed to Freud for having neglected her.

Concerning Klein, two points arise right away. The first is Freud's rejection (as it was understood in the 1931 paper) of the theses she summed up in "Early stages of the Oedipus complex" (1928). The second is her clear loyalty to Abraham's work, as seen in her own adaptations of it: loyalty because the indebtedness she shows throughout, and her often unquestioning adoption of Abraham's concepts, provide the basic postulates with which she works, and adaptation because, as we shall see, she sometimes slightly distorts what she borrows from Abraham, in displacements that are not without consequence. From these two points we may set out to reconsider what her own contributions are. What she added to psychoanalysis comes from her having adapted Abraham's concepts, thereby transforming them. And she had an immediate impact, not just on Jones or Horney but also, I would suggest, on Freud himself via the intermediation of Ruth Mack Brunswick, who, in a 1940 paper, says that she is just repeating notes prepared and edited under Freud's supervision ten years earlier. Now, this text, without signaling that it is doing so, clearly echoes Kleinian ideas.

Though it places them in a different context, it integrates them to a large extent, especially when it comes to the primary identification with the mother.

I shall eventually show that the contradiction of Freud is not so great as might be thought. Freud may well have wanted to avoid confrontation in his criticisms of 1931 and may have overlooked the polemical nature of Klein's 1928 contribution, but for the moment I want to emphasize that challenge, if only with regard to what she calls the feminine phase in the boy, not just the girl, in contrast to the girl's masculinity complex. I see this as a polemic because it rather directly refutes what Freud, following van Ophuijsen or Abraham, places at the center of his construction when he approaches the issue of female sexuality, namely the masculinity complex and the existence of a phallic phase in the girl. This polemic is easier to discern in Freud's disciples, as is often the case in view of the fact that positions lose their complexity and become caricatured or more schematic. We see this in Jones, where it is even more pronounced in "The phallic phase" (1932) than in "The early development of female sexuality" (1927), and in Horney when she adopts Kleinian concepts, perceptibly in "The flight from womanhood" (1926) and definitively in "The dread of woman" (1932).

What is clear above all is the upset Klein provokes—it is irrelevant whether we see this as revolution or disorder—by taking up concepts from Freud (Oedipus, superego, pregenital phases), Abraham (oral sadism, partial love), or Ferenczi (introjection, symbolization). By serving not two, but three masters, she ends up serving none of them. She uses what she needs without regard for the hierarchy that Freud was establishing among his concepts or for the way in one of these is necessary for the understanding of another: castration anxiety to explain the exit from the Oedipus and the superego, penis envy as the reason for the separation from the mother, the trauma of sexual difference for conceptualizing the pregenital and re-ordering it. Thus we must be attentive to her use of terms and to the confusion that this can introduce and that Freud refutes, but also attentive to what she is trying to describe and is the first to define in such a radical way.

Klein does not use the term "preoedipal," at least not in 1928 and to my knowledge not later as well. Instead she speaks of the early

Oedipus complex, in other words, of a moving back of the Oedipus. Far from thinking that something precedes it, she places it at the beginning. And it is in terms of conflict that she speaks of the Oedipus, a conflict that has a genesis. The original trauma, she says, is directly represented (not just reconstructed as in adult analysis) in children's games and in the manifestations of their earliest anxieties in the course of their analysis. For example, she had noted in a 1926 paper, in connection with a little girl named Ruth, that when Ruth was an infant, her mother had not had enough milk to satisfy her hunger. At the age of 4 years and 3 months, in her analysis with Klein, she called a water faucet a milk faucet.

There is a traumatic series of deprivations inflicted by the mother in the course of weaning and bowel training, and to this is added the deprivation of the penis that the mother enjoys in possessing the father but thereby denies to the child. But the first trauma, the one that unleashes the child's aggression, is the loss of the breast, the prototypical good object when the child receives it, the prototypical bad object when the child lacks it. The child thus discovers the power of his objects to gratify or frustrate his needs. This sets up a conflict, Klein (1935) says, because from the time of the loss of the breast or the absence of the mother (which she interprets differently from Freud's *Inhibitions, Symptoms, and Anxiety* [1926a]), there is ambivalence between love and hate toward the presumed possessor of goodness. At this early stage of development, loving an object means devouring it, and so, when the mother disappears, the baby thinks it has eaten her up and destroyed her, and it is tormented by anxiety.

It does not matter whether we look at the papers that precede or follow the 1928 article in order to understand it, because Klein's perspective remains fixed, as does the way in which she bends to her own purposes the concepts she borrows. She takes them from Abraham's (1924) theorization of the passage from the oral sucking stage to the oral biting stage; in the latter, the loved object is destroyed cannibalistically. The twist that Klein gives to the concept of oral sadism is based on the causal sequence she introduces, one that is not found in Abraham, or at any rate not systematized in this way. It is true, however, that some of his remarks can be stretched to conform to this meaning, as when he speaks of a nostalgia for the breast, or highlights the problems that arise in the child's relation to the mother (in the course of which oral-sadistic impulses that have not faded away at the time of the Oedipus can create a lasting association between cannibalistic urges and the boy's disappointment in his mother), or when, citing Stärcke, he speaks of weaning as the originary castration.

Klein (1928) borrows from Abraham the notions of nostalgia for the breast, the Oedipus as introjection of the parental figures if a narcissistic wound occurs in the oral phase, and the revenge aimed at the mother as the first agent of castration at the time of weaning. She simply extends these observations, deduced from melancholia, to child development by interpreting what she encounters in child analyses as the symbolic representation of the earliest conflicts. In other words, Klein presupposes a melancholic phase in everyone, which she will later (1935) call the depressive position. There is no Oedipus, no relation to the maternal object, that is not conflictual from the moment the child loses the breast as a part of its own body and leaves the state of fusion with the mother. This is how I understand Klein's statement that "the Oedipal tendencies are released in consequence of the frustration which the child experiences at weaning, and . . . they make their appearance at the end of the first and the beginning of the second year; they receive reinforcement through the anal frustrations undergone during training in cleanliness. The next determining influence upon the mental processes is that of the anatomical difference between the sexes" (1928, p. 170).

There is a big difference, of course, between such a notion of the causes of the Oedipus or the "oedipal conflict" and what Freud has said up to now. For Freud, the oedipal position strictly speaking (despite the discovery of the complete Oedipus complex) determines each subject's mode of relating to the other sex: the son to the mother, the daughter to the father. This is why, in 1925, he contrasted the exit from the Oedipus in the first case and the entry into it in the other. In 1931, Freud (perhaps under Klein's influence?) agreed to call the first relation to the mother the boy's "positive Oedipus" and the girl's "negative Oedipus," instead of speaking of a "preoedipal" phase that would threaten the notion of the Oedipus as the kernel of neurosis. This first relation, for him, is not conflictual from the outset. Even when he emphasizes the child's state of vital dependence or original passivity and the distress that can result when child care and love are confused, he speaks in terms of primary narcissism, the fact that the sexual instincts are supported by the instinct for self-preservation. Moreover, he reveals the structuring effect of this distress, since it is a condition of the access to language. The cry is the first call for a return of the gratification that has been gotten and lost (cf. Freud 1926a). And the mother's absence, traumatic at first, is also what facilitates symbolization, thanks to the repetition of experiences of absence and presence as departure and return alternate (cf. Freud 1920b).

For Freud, the series of frustrations is not decisive. When oral, anal, or even phallic frustrations are attributed to the mother, they merely correspond retroactively to the phallic phase that arises later and ends the sequence of so-called pregenital stages: that is, they correspond to castration. This is what leads the boy to abandon his feminine position with regard to the father and his love for his mother (his positive Oedipus). The father, hitherto a rival as much as a model, is now assumed to have deprived the mother of her penis and now becomes only the rival who must be avoided because he has the power to castrate. Likewise, it is the recognition of castration that may cause the girl to leave her mother (her negative Oedipus) and enter the Oedipus proper.

At least up to the 1930s, when Klein speaks of the Oedipus she is clearly in a different domain from the one in which Freud situated matters, because she is trying to give priority to the child's highly ambivalent relation to the maternal object on whom he depends. He *introjects* the mother, she says, not only because he identifies with her and this is, according to Freud, a primitive or archaic form of love, but also because privation joins love with revenge and the will to destroy. At the same time, if we follow Klein (1932), it is through this imaginary incorporation of objects that the child becomes able to perceive his world and to symbolize it. Klein's use of the concept of introjection exemplifies the way she develops, and also belabors, notions she finds important as she describes the mirror phenomena that her practice of child analysis made it necessary to explain, phenomena that she later defined as the to-and-fro play between introjections and projections. It is not so much the mechanism of primitive identification that is the source of the cannibalistic fantasies found in analytic treatment, but rather the oral sadism that leads to identification in the sense of the incorporation of the parental objects. This incorporation has two aspects, destruction and love, first of all of the mother, but also of the father insofar as he is recognized as the mother's property, both being represented by part objects (breast or penis), a concept that Klein originates on the basis of Abraham's distinction of the total incorporation characteristic of melancholia, the partial incorporation that is a partial love of the object, and, finally, object love.

The withdrawal of the breast, Klein says, makes the child want to appropriate what he has lost: the breast, the milk, but also everything he imagines the mother enjoys: the products of his body that she demands of him, the children whom she is gestating and whose arrival threatens him, the father's penis. This jealous wish for possession and destruction in turn makes the child, boy or girl, fear the mother's vengeance if she were to turn on him with the same torment that he wants to inflict on her:

> The boy . . . fears that his body will be mutilated and dismembered, and amongst other things castrated. Here we have a direct contribution to the castration complex. In this early period of development the mother who takes away the child's faeces signifies also a mother who dismembers and castrates him. Not only by means of the anal frustrations which she inflicts does she pave the way for the castration complex: in terms of psychic reality she is already the *castrator.* [1928, p. 174, emphasis in original]

Such a view of castration by the mother has neither the meaning nor the role accorded to castration by Freud. For him, the perception of the threat and the ensuing anxiety, though to be sure they occur at an early age—whether rediscovered in adult analysis or observed more directly in child treatment, as with Little Hans (1909a)—have to do with the recognition of sexual difference. And this occurs only in the phallic stage, at the time when interest is focused on the genitals. There has to have been a representation of the possible loss of the male organ if we are to use the term *castration* in connection with the bodily losses that preceded it and, retroactively, prefigure it. Klein's formulation to the effect that the mother, too, is the castrating parent can be understood in the Freudian sense only through the retroactive effects of analytic treatment. Either the mother may appear as the one who has robbed the child of his first treasures, or she is the castrator only because one wanted to castrate or rob her oneself.

Nevertheless, with this displacement of castration from the father to the mother, Klein shows better than any of her colleagues the effects of unbridled maternal omnipotence in the child's experience. The mother is the one who gives or withholds everything at her whim. Weaning and bowel training no longer have the value of yielding a part of one's own body in exchange for love; instead they are imperatives, without recourse and without meaning, that trigger rage when the child realizes his impotence and the love object's omnipotence. The loss that is imposed on him subserves the *jouissance* of the maternal Other, because the mother is considered to enjoy[1] everything, or because she deprives the child in order to give to others, the rival children or the father contained in her body.

The idea that what Klein discovers or somehow finds in the material of her child patients is this fear of being the object of the *jouissance* of the Other (the combined maternal and paternal figure) is confirmed by what she says about the "most bitter grievances" formulated retroactively in analysis by those who suffered beyond endurance because their many and urgent questions remained unanswered (1928, p. 172). Such questions were not conscious at the time, or the preverbal children were not able to express them. There was no answer, or, she says further on, no meaning they could find for what ruled their world, an ignorance that they continue to lament and to experience with a feeling of bitterness. Isn't this a way of describing what Lacan will later formulate as a structural fact, the *enigma of the desire of the Other* that can take the form of an absolute whim, in that there seems to be no law that would limit the mother's omnipotence?

Although he used different terms, Freud (1910) also mentioned this impotence of the child in the face of the enigma of sexual difference when he spoke of the failure of infantile sexual investigations; this failure later emerges in the transference in the form of feelings of abandonment or inadequacy, or the certainty that the patient will amount to nothing (cf. 1920b, Chapter 3). Freud connected this narcissistic wound with the Oedipus insofar as these unanswered questions, in his view, arise not from the trauma of weaning but from the trauma of sexual difference.

Be that as it may, what Freud and Klein have in common despite their differences is an equation of *jouissance* and knowledge on the part of the Other in contrast to ignorance on the part of the subject. This suggests to me that Klein's emphasis on the connection between early epistemophilia and sadism is her way of underlining the anguishing, indeed annihilating, aspect of an all-encompassing wish that is ascribed to the Other, a wish that the subject knows nothing about and has no way of deciphering or delimiting. If this Other removes your sources of pleasure (the breast that is offered or withheld without your having a chance to prepare yourself, the stools that are demanded), then it is easy to imagine that the Other must enjoy them, that they are taken away for the Other's advantage. Klein proposes an origin for these first conflicts, conflicts that are already oedipal, in that they have to do with the mother and the possessions, including the father, that one envies her. This theory of origin, which she was the first to suggest, is based on the excess of the child's anxieties in comparison with the reality of the dangers it faces or the actual strictness of the parents. She interprets this excess in the register of the purely dual relation in which the child first finds itself, that is, in the imaginary confrontation with the object on which it depends and whom it conceives as a mortal double.

This view of maternal omnipotence clearly implies an uncastrated mother who, in the child's fantasy, contains within her the paternal penis that is the source of the castration fear. Similarly, Klein's emphasis on the fantasy of the phallic mother is radically different from the Freudian perspective. Although she explains the retroactive mechanism of this fantasy, she places the accent on its secondary nature: it is a defense against earlier fantasies and later anxieties. In the fantasy of the mother's imaginary penis, when it appears in analysis, Klein sees the sign of an attenuation of the primal fear of the penis retained by the mother, a much stronger fear because it is the reaction to the twofold and terrifying power of the combined parent figure representing the threatening part objects, the penis and the breast: "Thus the femininity phase is characterized by anxiety relating to the womb and the father's penis, and this anxiety subjects the boy to the tyranny of a super-ego which devours, dismembers and castrates and is formed from the image of father and mother alike" (1928, p. 175).

The phallic attributes attached externally to the mother's body, and not internal objects, seem to represent an intermediate stage thanks to a process of displacement that is the very process of sym-bolization. This process, one that Klein sees at work in the child, is essentially phobic, an indefinite postponement, in a less threat-ening context, of the anxiety aroused by the primal objects. But, in these early stages that she describes, the male organ is above all that of the father incorporated by the mother, which the latter enjoys in the same way as she enjoys other objects. And the passive fantasy of possession or castration by the father through identifi-cation with the mother in coitus (cf. Freud 1914a, Horney 1922) is less important here than the feelings of hatred and fear with regard to the all-encompassing *jouissance* ascribed to the mother or to the fantasmatic parental objects who withhold gratification.

These reconstructions contradict Freud's, in my opinion, only if we insist on keeping the two sets of descriptions on the same level. Klein, it seems to me, is seeing and clarifying something different on the basis of her experience, both when she puts to the test the substance of Freud's notions, their power to describe the phenom-ena that she has observed and is trying to integrate, and also when she seems to put in question Freud's linking of the Oedipus, cas-tration, and the superego and the logical ordering he proposes for them. The incompatibility diminishes or disappears once we agree on the fact that the mother described by Klein as the cause of all good and all evil is the mother before the recognition of castra-tion, in the sense that castration is precisely what puts an end to the mother's omnipotence. It is the law under which she falls and to which she, too, must submit. Freud connects this law with the father, characterizing his function. For the child at a certain point in development, the father is, in imagination, presumed to have what the mother does not have, the male organ of which he must have deprived her. If she does not have everything, this is because

she does not have all power, and especially not the power of rein-
tegrating her product, the child.

Freud confessed to Abraham that he found it difficult to know
what to make of the obstacles to the fantasy of the maternal breast;
in analysis, he says, it is always the father who appears as the one
who prohibits incest (1907–1926, letter of February 15, 1924). It
therefore seems all the more valuable that Klein was able to describe
the lethal, uncontrollable nature of the primitive imagos associated
with the archaic mother in the individual history of the subject,
the mother before the prohibition of incest. She enables us to see
the "primitive paranoia" that may arise at one or the other point
in analysis (cf. Klein 1935, 1940) as one of the modes in which
castration presents itself or is repeated. There is a choice between,
on the one hand, the presumed *jouissance* of the mother, which is
also that of the subject himself, whatever form it may take and
however much he may fail to recognize it, and, on the other hand,
castration, which must be accepted in the mother before it is
assumed for oneself.

Let me put this another way. There is *jouissance* of the mother in
the sense that one takes pleasure in her, in the primary narcissistic
fusion or undifferentiation of bodies, a *jouissance* the masochistic
reverse of which (perhaps erotized or sublimated) is her *jouissance*
of you, the possibility that she will appear not only as the one to whom
you respond adequately by becoming her object, but also as the one
who rejects you, takes vengeance on you, castrates or dismembers
you, and the like, according to Kleinian terminology.

Castration, however, is what causes her to fail, both in her power
and in the love one bears toward her, insofar as she was loved as
infallible and endowed with all possible desirable attributes. Castration, in this view, implies a loss, not only in the mother who is
lacking something but in the subject himself: the loss of that illusion that completed her, up to that point, by serving and satisfying
her *jouissance*. To recognize that the mother lacks something (a
lack that, for Freud, is signified imaginarily as the lack of the male
organ) is to recognize at the same time that she can seek to fill in
this gap. There is an empty place where the child may offer what
he has and where, because he is turned away, he experiences his
inadequacy. This feeling of inadequacy with regard to the gratifi-

cation expected by the mother, noted by Freud in connection with Little Hans (1909a), is very precisely described by Karen Horney (1932) in regard to the boy. Jeanne Lampl-de Groot (1928) and Ruth Mack Brunswick (1928a, 1940) point out that the girl, too, experiences this disappointment when she finds that she can no longer hide from her inability to respond to the desire that is attributed to the mother. Preserving the phallic dimension of the mother is thus a way to protect oneself from the question of desire and from one's own lack, first signified by the mother's desire.

I spoke of a choice between *jouissance* and castration, instead of using the stronger terms in which Freud describes the emotional storm that overcomes the boy when he discovers this lack in the Other that dislodges him from his place, and the hatred felt by the girl that is sometimes not understood or developed until much later, especially in analysis. Before Freud, van Ophuijsen (1924, originally given as a lecture in 1917) had summed up this distress as the child's knowing that she is asking the mother for something the mother cannot give. A striking formulation, this condenses into one sentence what appears in various forms in analytic treatment, namely the unconscious phallic claim addressed to the mother. The phrase is also noteworthy in that, beyond its exemplary description of penis envy, it precisely describes the juncture between the abandonment of the belief in the mother's omnipotence and the realization of the lack in the subject—here, the girl. The mother is hated because of what she cannot give (for the unconscious: refuses to give), and because her perceived lack not only forces one to look elsewhere for what might be desirable but also raises the question of her desire, the place one occupies in it, and what she expects of one.

Thus we understand how there can arise the destructive figure of a mother who is feared in proportion to the child's ignorance of what might satisfy her. In other words, it is the enigma of the mother's desire from the moment she is castrated—and hence lacking—that will retroactively revive the dimension of a ferocious maternal *jouissance*. The question of her desire (of what she is lacking) will be reduced to the question of her *jouissance* (of what she denies the child). All the reproaches addressed to her, as listed by Freud (1931), are indications of this reduction. They are rationalizations for what she deprives one of, though the deprivation is not known as such but is ascribed to the series of frustrations that she imposed and that, later on, are experienced as restrictions of one's *jouissance* with a view to her own. These rationalizations are those of castration, which is unthinkable, from the perspective of the *jouissance* of an Other, which can be imagined.

Why does Melanie Klein present this figure of the mother, a fierce mother whose *jouissance* has more in common with the father of the primal horde (Freud 1929) than with the mother who is desirous, because castrated, and whose function and meaning Freud gradually comes to understand? In my opinion, this has to do with the logic of Klein's clinical experience. She does not stress what the mother might lack, because what she is concerned with at the outset, and what is repeated, barely disguised, in the analysis of children, is the lethal aspect of the omnipotence of the first object for the child, which can be another version, a maternal one, of the need for the primal murder.

Even if the child, at the early age at which Klein observes him in analysis, has already had the experience of sexual difference (cf. her emphasis, in the 1928 paper and elsewhere, on the role of the primal scene and its repercussions), the major trauma, in her view, is not the castration represented by the possible privation of the male organ but rather the omnipotence of the first objects to whom one feels given over, for better or for worse, once they have escaped one, once one has experienced, in losing them even for a moment, the risk of death or annihilation that they made one incur. The inaugural drama whose ravages she describes lies here, in this absolute dependence, this submission to the first Other—the mother, in this case—whose fragmenting image is presented to the child in the mirror as a response to aggressivity, aggressivity that is, to be sure, his own, but provoked by the mother's power of refusal, for which the paradigm remains the refusal of the breast.

Note

1. Translator's note: In accordance with the author's Lacanian approach, "enjoy" has the double meaning "enjoy a legal right" and "have sexual pleasure."

16   The Theoretical Shift

Freud thus rejects Klein's proposal to move the Oedipus back in time. According to him, this runs counter both to the results obtained in adult analysis and to his discovery of the girl's long preoedipal attachment to the mother preceding the passage to the father. Although Freud does not mention this rejection explicitly, it must have to do with the fact that Klein's 1928 paper is abrupt, condensed, confusing, and insufficiently supported by clinical evidence. The paper is legible or decodable only in the context of her work as a whole, the preceding contributions as well as those to follow. It is only in this way that we can assess the scope of the discoveries that she wants to describe and mark the theoretical shift she makes between 1925–1926 and 1928.

For indeed, a shift is what this is. It is clear that what guided her up to 1926 (and she adduces this at the end of the 1928 paper in support of the early onset of the Oedipus) was the role she assigned to the primal scene and the associated castration anxiety. In papers Klein wrote in 1923 ("Infant analysis") and 1925 ("A contribution to the psychogenesis of tics"), the regression to oral or anal pregenital stages is conceptualized in the basis of castration. And it is evident, in the light of her earlier articles and the clinical examples they offer, that what she formulates in 1928 in terms of development is a reconstruction, in reverse order to its emergence in the analysis, even in the case of very young child patients. This foregrounding of the *jouissance* of the parents and the envy of their attributes, in which Klein sees the precocity of the oedipal conflict, is not what comes first in the material presented by children. In the beginning, she says (1926), castration alone is involved, and only after a long period of analysis do pregenital experiences and fantasies emerge. In the clinical vignette from the analysis of a little girl, Rita, Klein shows how the child's castration anxiety and her obsessional bedtime ritual reveal the connection she made between the role of her parents in coitus and sexual difference; thus, at the age of 2, Rita feared that she would be robbed of her genital. The influence of the Oedipus complex is measured by the later effects of the primal scene: children's night terrors, common as they may be, are its first neurotic manifestations. This is how Klein accounts for the traumatization of Rita, who had slept in her parent's bedroom, "and the effects of the primal scene showed plainly in her analysis. . . . There can be no doubt that there is a close connection between neurosis and such profound effects of the Oedipus complex experienced at so early an age" (p. 170).

Until 1926, Klein's description of the infantile interpretation of coitus remains very close to Freud's, child analysis confirming that parental intercourse is always understood as a sadistic act (cf. 1927a). And the identification with the feminine position that she finds in a boy patient's tics (1925) undoubtedly entails castration. It is on this point of sadism that we can perhaps best grasp the shift in Klein's later formulations: the traumatic sadism of coitus is less the sadism of the parents, the child's impression of their relations, than it is the sadism of the child himself. He attributes it to his parents because of the *jouissance* he presumes them to have, a *jouissance* from which he is excluded. It might be argued that Klein continues to understand sadism and the resulting fear of retaliation in their retroactive dimension, that is, as regression to earlier levels of organization because of castration anxiety. This anxiety is always there, but it is not recognizable beneath the disguises (repression as well as regression) that serve as defenses against it (cf. Freud 1926a in connection with Hans or the Wolf Man). For Klein notes very precisely, after as well as before 1928, how the child

reacts to early genital stimulation with a recrudescence of pregenital drives, along with sadistic fantasies directed toward the parents who are engaging in intercourse.

From the point of view of castration, what surprises Klein
(1927a) is the intensity of this aggression toward the oedipal objects
as revealed, to the knowing observer, in the playing of children in
analysis. She explains their excessive anxiety and their burden of
guilt as projections of infantile sadism onto the parental objects.
In addition to emasculation, the subject feels threatened by dismemberment, fragmentation, and the emptying of his bodily contents in reaction to his wish to appropriate and destroy all his
mother's possessions.

We must note that what Klein states as a postulate in 1928, sum-
ming up the conclusions she had drawn in her 1926 paper, namely
that the frustration of weaning gives rise to oedipal tendencies in
the child, was in fact only a marginal observation in that paper.
Thus it seems to me that, without forcing the texts, we can see a
hardening or a radicalization on certain points, and a reversal on
others, that take place in a relatively short time. It is not inappropriate to suggest that they are the effect of two major events for
Melanie Klein, and perhaps the result of these events.

The first is the appearance, in 1926, of Anna Freud's *The Psycho-
Analytic Treatment of Children*, a book very critical of Klein, especially
with regard to the play technique that she had set forth and that
was warmly praised by Abraham (1924). Klein responded to this
criticism in a symposium on child analysis organized by Jones
(1927b), and it is beyond doubt that the changes in her theorization of her clinical experience are part of this polemic, since, forced
to give an account of her technique and its aims, she in turn vigor-
ously challenges Anna Freud's principles. It is because Klein radically opposes Anna Freud's presumption of guilt in child analysis
that she finds it necessary to highlight what she had felt and what
had governed her practice, namely the striking presence of guilt
and anxiety in the child. Thus she reports that she tries above all
to separate the roles of parent, educator, and analyst and to adopt,
just as in the analysis of adults, a position of benevolent neutrality
without critically judging the child or mothering him; this, she
says, is the only way in which to let the child have free rein for his

aggressive fantasies with regard to the parental imagos that are still active and that he finds it hard to distinguish from his real oedipal objects.

Up to now, Klein had been able to content herself with the intuition that guided her empirically and, in her communications, to mention only the material she had obtained and deciphered in her analysis of children's play and their reactions to her interpretations, but the debate with Anna Freud impelled her to specify her ends and her means, as much for herself as in order to respond to the objections that were addressed to her. She had to supply the theoretical foundation for the positions she defended, either by constructing her own theory based on her practice or by finding in another analyst the conceptualization closest to her clinical experience. She does not claim originality; we see this in her constant concern to reaffirm her agreement with Freud on essential points. As for finding theoretical support elsewhere, this is not something new for her, although she does not fully express it before the quarrel with Anna Freud, because the colleague in question is Abraham, who had encouraged her and invited her to practice in Berlin, and who continued with her, for several months, the personal analysis she had begun with Ferenczi. It is not surprising that she adopted his hypotheses: as early as 1924, in a lecture to the Würzburg Congress that was not published but was included in *The Psycho-Analysis of Children* (Klein 1932), some elements of her analysis of obsessional neurosis in a little girl of 6, Erna, are taken directly from Abraham.

What is new after 1926 and clearly legible in the 1928 paper, "Early stages of the Oedipus conflict," is the way Klein now works with Abraham's suggestions on early development, bending them or giving them an additional turn so as to end up with the primacy of orality. It is no longer so much a question of interpreting the pregenital on the basis of castration, as she had done up to now, as of reordering development as a function of the archaic fantasies that she finds in the child.

It is certainly possible to suppose that, when she draws up the list of objects contained by the mother and stolen from the deprived child, she is proposing a reconstruction, and to suppose that this genesis of oedipal wishes relative to frustrations is by nature a fiction, as Abraham and Freud emphasized when, on the basis of fixations or regressions deduced from the contrast between one form of neurosis and another, they hypothesized equivalent phases of development. And we may suppose that Klein merely neglects to specify, in 1927–1928, that the presentation of libidinal development in terms of passage and progress from one phase to another is just a deduction, unthinkable without the retroactive dimension of the Oedipus. But this neglect is not, I think, an insignificant matter. It is, rather, a sign of what had happened in a very short time, a reversal of perspective that, although it is formulated elliptically in 1928, is entirely explicit in Klein's later work, where we find the primitively infantile theory of coitus (cf. Freud 1908c) used to justify what she now places in the foreground: the importance of the breast as lost object, sadism as an effect of oral identification, and the passage from the mother to the father (from the breast to the male organ) on account of a privation.

Though Klein follows Abraham, she uses his ideas in her own way. But whatever variations she may introduce, the second decisive event in her theoretical shift between 1926 and 1928 is Abraham's death at the end of 1925. As we have seen, she had other reasons to find in him the confirmation of the arguments she advanced in the 1926–1927 debate on child analysis. Abraham's remarks on oral identification in melancholia enabled her to define the cause of her own observation of children. The child's harsh superego and that of the melancholic have the same origin; their mode of identification, cannibalistic incorporation, is what determines its cruelty. And what she takes from Abraham and systematizes (partial love as incorporation of a part of the object) seems to constitute her reply to Freud's question on the girl's Oedipus: oedipal identification, in this view, is indistinguishable from the oral incorporation of a part of the object's body. In this way Klein refers to the same mechanism, the introjection of the oedipal love objects, in explaining the precocity of the superego and the male identification of the girl.

The reference to Abraham is overdetermined for Klein. Nevertheless, her constant citation of him as the unquestionable authority suggests that, after his death, she felt an obligation to carry on as his successor, to continue his work and draw out its implications further than he himself had been able to—in short, to be more Abrahamian than Abraham. It seems to me that she did this to such an extent that she often takes her reading of him for his own work. The concept of the loss of the breast illustrates this misunderstanding. Abraham speaks of a wish for castration or revenge aimed at the mother rather than the father, and he notes that, apart from this hatred, there is a nostalgia for the maternal breast that points to a still earlier, preambivalent, stage, but this is not the same as making the loss of the breast the cause of melancholia. In other words, the step Klein takes goes beyond Abraham and, a fortiori, beyond Freud.

Klein's reliance on Abraham is decisive in regard to the displacement we find in her theorizing. But, I insist, this does not mean that she adheres strictly to his utterances in their original context. On the contrary, it is obvious that she extends them in a way that he did not have in mind. We can see this in her emphasis on the part object, a notion derived from Abraham's contrast between partial object love (the ambivalent love for one part of the object, which he calls partial identification) and true, that is, genital, object love, which he makes the endpoint of development. Another example is the concept of the total introjection of the object, which, according to Klein, is a stage later than that of partial identification. Abraham, however, saw this as the most primitive (cannibalistic) stage, in relation to which partial identification represents developmental progress. Klein's (1940) notion of the recognition of the object in the depressive position as a whole object that one is afraid to lose seems to me to come from another context, that of the symbolization of the object. And although, as Klein says, this symbolization obeys the primitive mechanism of identification found in mourning, she assigns it a broader and more radical explanatory scope than what we find in Abraham.

17   The Phase of Femininity

Melanie Klein makes the greatest use of Abraham through her own contributions to theory (the loss of the breast at the onset of oral-sadistic identification, the importance of orality in the girl, the identification with the mother or phase of femininity for both sexes): all these themes of 1928 are extensions of the concept of partial identification that Abraham had proposed in 1924. But it is precisely this free usage of hers that enables us to understand and situate her contribution, to assess both what she offers and the charges, on Freud's part, to which she leaves herself open.

For example, we see that, although she takes a position on the girl's Oedipus in 1928, it is neither her feminism nor the fact that she herself is a woman that brings her into this territory. Implicit in her concept of the femininity phase is a challenge to Freud's notion of the phallic phase, but this is due less to the masculinist prejudice that she finds there (the superiority of the male organ in representing sexual difference in the unconscious), or to the misogyny she denounces in the concept of penis envy (women's jealous nature), than to her own discovery, one that never ceases to amaze her in her analyses of children, of the intense aggressivity and cruelty of imaginary attacks against the first object, the mother's body, along with the excessiveness of the punishments awaited in return.

If she envisages a different hierarchy from Freud's, it is because (as we know from her other work) what she is primarily concerned with is the violent aspect of the child's superego, the mirror image of terrifying parental imagos in which fragmentation and dismemberment are merely the archaic sadistic form taken by the reprisals, on one or the other side, for a lack that was not understood or symbolized as such. Likewise, though she speaks of a displacement of oral greed from the breast to the penis (from the maternal to the paternal part object), the male quality of the coveted object is less important than the limitless nature of the demand: from the first maternal object, the child expects everything.

Moreover, when she speaks of an oedipal conflict set in motion by an original frustration, Klein—as no one had done before her—calls attention to an oedipal meaning of privation. This is important if we consider what she is suggesting about the purpose of the Oedipus. Klein is the first to show that it is the oedipal myth that, in retrospect, serves to make sense of the structural fact that there is always a *third* in competition with the child (boy or girl), in that an other is presumed to reap the benefit of what the mother is depriving the child of. And this third is presumed to bring her the gratifying object that the child is unable to offer; the mother's separation from the child is experienced as evidence of this, and as a punishment.

In order to see exactly what the controversy is about, let us recall the two relevant points about Freud's post-1925 view of femininity: the girl's Oedipus (her passage from the mother to the father) and the male identification that she cannot escape. Klein (1928) replies with the concept of orality (the oral envy of the father's organ) and that of a femininity phase for both sexes.

Her theory of an orality inherent in femininity is stated right at the beginning of the paper: "In the girl . . . , the receptive aim is carried over from the oral to the genital position: she changes her libido position but retains its aim, which has already led to disappointment in relation to her mother. In this way receptivity of the penis is induced in the girl, who turns to the father as her love-object" (p. 170). Female sexuality is not Klein's major preoccupation, as it may have been for analysts like Karen Horney or Helene

Deutsch. Nevertheless, though she reaches the same conclusions, she sets out from other issues, such as the early superego, that lead her to apply them to the oedipal development of the girl and the boy alike.

The first point is the role Klein accords to oral frustration, which she sees as the cause of both primitive and oedipal identification. This concept avoids the problem Freud had noted with regard to the girl's access to femininity, her change of zone (from clitoris to vagina) accompanying her change of object. For Klein, although the object changes as a result of the original frustration, the aim of the drive stays constant: it is in a single mode, oral and receptive, that the girl naturally passes from the mother to the father. In the case of receptivity, because of the intrinsic similarity of the mouth and the vagina Klein emphasizes her agreement with Deutsch that the displacement of oral onto genital libido "begins with the first stirrings of the genital impulses, and that the oral, receptive aim of the genital exercises a determining influence in the girl's turning to the father" (p. 175).

In 1925, when he was investigating what could separate the girl from her mother and make her turn to the father, Freud (1925a) left the question open. Despite clear signs of a castration complex and a phallic phase in the girl, he found nothing that corresponded exactly to the castration anxiety that causes the boy to leave the Oedipus. And he had not yet connected the symbolic equation penis = child, which retroactively explains the passage to the father, with the lack of the mother herself, as he would do in 1931 and 1932–1933. The phallus had not yet been defined as the desirable object in the father because of its lack in the mother. Still, we can understand why, in 1931, he cannot accept Klein's postulate of an anatomical preformation, the receptivity of the genital organs. First, this contradicts what he had maintained ever since his first observations on hysteria, namely the masculinity of the little girl and the misrecognition of the vagina for both sexes, and, second, it is based on a prejudice that he himself has slowly discarded, that of a mutual attraction of the sexes.

We may add that the fact that Klein offers so many arguments weakens her point instead of strengthening it; a single argument would have sufficed. She first describes the oral incorporation of the father as the maintaining of the original drive. She goes on to state that the early awakening of the little girl's genital sensations is associated with the oral gratification of sucking. To these two motives she adds a third, which to my mind as (I cannot help thinking) to hers indicates the inadequacy of the others: the privation of the breast, she says, is what gives the child the idea of the parents' mutual gratification, in which the mother enjoys taking in the father's penis.

Despite Klein's warning that the pregenital and genital phases are mixed in together, surely the idea of a paternal organ in the oral phase implies that the child has already had an experience of sexual difference. In any case, it is problematical to locate this experience in the same chronological time as weaning. Moreover, it is difficult to reconcile this notion of an innate femininity in the girl, which presupposes the unconscious representation of a specific female organ and an innate recognition of the sexual aim, with two facts of analytic experience.

The first, it is universally agreed, is confirmed over and over again in the analysis of neurotic women as a masculinity complex, either the denial of the lack of the male organ or the expectation of having it; a feeling of inferiority; and the wish, disguised or not, for revenge against the man—father, son, or partner. The second fact, for which Klein gives the most convincing demonstration, is that every demand, of the boy as well as the girl, is at first addressed to the mother. Klein gives the same description for each sex of aggressive drives directed against the mother's body and its contents; it is the mother and her possessions that one must appropriate. From this perspective, it is noteworthy that she speaks (1940) of the girl's masculine identification in terms of a sadistic father. The deprivation of the father's organ, she says, is added to the deprivation of the breast that had given rise to the primitive sadistic identification with the mother (which, however, does not preclude the girl's modeling herself on the mother in her expectation that, like the mother, she will be fulfilled by the paternal organ). Thus, paradoxically, hatred for the mother is reinforced.

The second point I want to note in the 1928 paper is the identification with the mother, in the limited sense of a femininity phase, to my knowledge described only here in Klein. It may be an exception with regard to her work as a whole, yet, in this text, it is the basis for global formulations; the principle of the excluded middle is not operative here. Let me explain. After mentioning the superego as an effect of the child's contradictory early identifications, and its harshness as a consequence of its origination at the height of sadism, between the oral-sadistic and anal-sadistic phases, Klein recalls the link between early epistemophilia and sadism (cf. Freud 1913a), another way of describing what she had earlier (1923) called the geography of the maternal body. The epistemophilic instinct, she says, "at first mainly concerns itself with the mother's womb, which is assumed to be the scene of all sexual processes and developments. The child is still dominated by the anal-sadistic libido-position which impels him to wish to appropriate the contents of the womb" (p. 172).

Why does Klein feel it necessary to connect this identification with the mother, which she goes on to call the femininity phase, with a developmental stage on the border between the anal-sadistic stage and the nascent genital positions? If we are to follow her, this is because the femininity phase gives a new meaning to the anal-sadistic stage: the feces retained by the mother, which she commanded the child to relinquish, "are now equated with the child that is longed for, and the desire to rob the mother now applies to the child" as well as to feces (p. 174). Two aims are combined: destruction (Abraham's first anal-sadistic stage) because of jealousy of future rivals, and appropriation (the second stage) stemming from the wish to have children oneself.[1] Both the boy and the girl envy their mother this power.

There is another point to be made in connection with Klein's theory of maternal identification in 1928. In order to show their relevance to the exclusive tie to the mother insofar as the mother is not castrated, she shifts onto an imaginary level the equations whose symbolic motive Freud had shown, and the way in which she views the series feces–child–penis shows that she does not integrate it into the context of castration. For, in addition to feces and potential sibling rivals, the third object that may be aimed at by the child in the same ambivalent way (destruction and appropriation) is the father's penis contained by the mother. There is no primacy of the phallus. The male organ is just one object among others that the mother enjoys—as one enjoys the right to property—just like children, feces, or the breast.

From the perspective of the anal-sadistic maternal identification (wanting to get children from the mother or to have them as she does), Klein is above all concerned to give an account of a femininity complex in the boy comparable to the girl's masculinity complex, thereby concurring with Karen Horney (1922, 1926). What is enviable in the mother for the boy, as in the father for the girl, has to do not only with the anatomical advantages of each parent, only one of whose parts a given child will share by virtue of its sex. The boy's disadvantage with regard to having children is masked and overcompensated, Klein says, by a "masculine protest"—in other words by the overvaluation of the organ he possesses, and this partially overlaps with the protest against the feminine role, the passive attitude toward the father, that Freud mentions. The boy's phallic phase is thus a defense against his castration fears, which he experiences toward the mother as well (the mother who removes his feces is also a castrating mother): "This dread of the mother is so overwhelming because there is combined with it an intense dread of castration by the father. The destructive tendencies whose object is the womb are also directed with their full oral- and anal-sadistic intensity against the father's penis, which is supposed to be located there. It is upon his penis that the dread of castration by the father is focused in this phase" (p. 174).

The boy's male identification is always seen as incorporation of one part believed to represent the object. If this is a secondary process, the same must be true of the girl. First there is envy and coveting of what the mother enjoys; the girl's first identification, like the boy's, is maternal and comes from the same anal-sadistic tendencies as his. She wants to rob and destroy the mother, envy and hate toward her increasing, more than in the case of the boy, because of the *jouissance* of the father's organ that she imputes to the mother; this is another reason why the girl turns to her father. So it is with Erna (1932), in connection with whom Klein reports two cases of women patients mentioned by Abraham in the vignette of 1924.

However matters may stand with this additional motive for separation from the mother, in which the coveting of the male organ expected from the father places the girl-child in rivalry with her from the beginning, that wish is subordinated to the first sadistic wish for the orally gratifying incorporation of the paternal penis. The identification with the father is secondary here too, since it is above all the fear of the maternal superego that forces the girl to abandon her first identification. The disappointment that sets in later, in the oedipal position (cf. Deutsch 1932, Horney 1922 and later) is not analyzed by Klein in the 1928 paper, although she refers to it elsewhere. The disappointment mentioned here in connection with the mother explains the possible hostility toward the opposite sex. The woman's positive relation to men is, according to Klein, essentially determined by the intensity of the sadism toward the first object. Pregenital sadism that is directed toward the mother and, if it is excessive, weighs heavily on the tie to the father is also an obstacle to such a positive relation. Oedipal frustration thus no longer has its usual positive effect when the desired object is finally obtained, but it confirms hate that is now addressed to whoever reactivates the initial privation.

Is it feminine or masculine, this phase of identification with a mother who possesses all goods things and all power, a phase in which the boy and the girl seek to appropriate the paternal organ as well as the ability to bear children? Klein sets forth the paradoxes of identification, and perhaps does so unknowingly, in the same way as Abraham. The identification with the mother is masculinizing when the mother is one who lacks nothing, in other words, a phallic mother, or so we may conclude from the so-called feminine phase, which is one in which the child's sole interest is to provide the mother with the gratification that she refuses him. In contrast, as Abraham had shown, the identification with the father is feminizing when the fantasy of an oral castration inflicted on the father by the girl is interpreted both as access to femininity (the beginnings of love for the father) and in the register of penis envy, that bit of male narcissism, according to Freud (1916a), that enables the girl to pass over to the side of femininity.

The limited meaning of this maternal identification, the reference to anality that is surprising in relation to the more general meaning Klein assigns to identification, may be understood as her attempt to resolve a theoretical problem inherited from Abraham. Anal identification is a bridge that enables her to connect the primitive mechanism of incorporation or introjection with oedipal choice proper. I therefore believe that a kind of perplexity is to be found in the 1928 paper, where Klein is trying to correlate primitive identification, where, for Freud, the least manageable part of the superego is constituted, and oedipal identification with the gender ideal.

Her giving the name of "femininity phase" to the process of conjoining the two is justified from another point of view. There are, of course, the objections she raised against Freud's notions of the primacy of the phallus and the existence of a phallic phase in the girl. But the opposition here is not one of principle. Her contribution to the debate, and the question that calls for a reply from Freud, is this: by what process does the male organ become the desirable organ par excellence, the organ of which the mother has been robbed, in contrast to what fantasy seeks to maintain?

In this way Klein spots the weak point in Freud's "Some psychical consequences of the anatomical distinctions between the sexes" (1925a), in which the passage to the father is just an assertion (some women manage it) and remains unexplained in that neither the mother's castration nor the father's function as castrator is invoked.

Note

1. Klein's approach to this "maternal" identification, based on the bipolarity of the anal-sadistic stage (getting a child from the mother, by force if necessary, and having one as she does) will be put to a different use by Freud in 1931–1932. He will make it the basis of his belief in the similarity of the sexes up to the phallic phase. The expectation of a child from the mother, whether by impregnating her or receiving it from her, will be ascribed to the active and passive phallic wishes of each sex toward the mother, whatever the infantile rationalization—recourse, for example, to the anal imaginary (the cloacal theory of birth).

18   Between Klein and Freud

Freud's corrections in 1931 and 1932–1933 had no effect on Klein. It may be that she did not understand the ways in which Freud was responding to her, but the more important reason lies elsewhere. It is that, even when he points out the girl's hate-filled separation from her mother and her turn to her father, in these papers of the 1930s Freud does not indicate all the elements that could definitively explain his conclusion about the mother's castration.

What does he say? The child's love is addressed to a phallic mother, but the discovery that even she is castrated devalues her absolutely in the child's eyes. And the resulting hatred on the part of the girl is a retroactive sign of the turn toward the father and the access to the oedipal position that is appropriate for her. Is there a teleology in Freud's reasoning? The fact that some women arrive at the Oedipus—indeed find refuge there, as we see in their attachment to the real father—explains why all of the girl's hostility is directed toward the mother. If, when all is said and done, her destiny is to choose the father as her love object, she cannot, Freud says, transfer to him the aggressivity associated with the disadvantage she has recognized (the absence of the organ she feels she is lacking). For the boy, the hostility accompanying the scorn for or horror of a mutilated mother can be mitigated by being transferred onto the father, thereby confirming the properly oedipal rivalry;

at the same time, he is supposed to abandon his feminine position with regard to the father once he has made the connection between this and the woman's castration. The girl does not have the same recourse to start out with, namely the imputation to a rivalrous father of the castration that has been inflicted on her. It is the mother who is blamed at first, and the appeal to the father is an appeal for compensation. The mother is the one who is reproached for the harm the girl experiences. Abraham had also said this, in 1920, but in a way different from Freud's: "The retaliation [against the husband after defloration] is found to refer ultimately to the injustice suffered at the hands of the father. The unconscious of the adult daughter takes a late revenge for the father's omission to bestow on her a penis" (p. 8) and symbolically returns castration for castration.

Another formulation is that of Helene Deutsch (1925): castration must be libidinized and an eventual profit (a child) awaited before castration can be recognized and accepted as the function of the father. The figure of a castrating father, or the connection between love for him and castration, is secondary, in the sense that it is initially rejected. Hence the girl's reaction when she notices the mother's castration; like the boy, she refuses identification with this castrated being.

These formulations that we have been using in the context of Freud's earlier work are relatively elliptical when he comes to focus on femininity in the early 1930s. If they have no decisive effect on Klein, in no way modifying the position she took in 1926–1927, this is because what he says here about love or hate for the mother, depending on whether she is phallic or castrated, is somewhat consistent with the ambivalent love for a mother who contains the father's organ. But, to put the matter more precisely, what is neither clearly articulated nor sufficiently emphasized, even in Freud's 1932–1933 paper, is the fact that the castration of the mother implies the function of the father as castrator.

Is it entirely accidental that it took a particular effort of attention to read in "The dissolution of the Oedipus complex" (Freud 1924a) that the boy's certainty of the mother's castration, which lowers her to the level of all women, stems from his equating castration with the feminine-passive position in intercourse? We may also recall that to find in the girl this same meaning of castration (as equivalent to the father's love), we needed the contribution of another analyst, Karen Horney (1922), who, reporting the rape and beating fantasies of some of her women patients, brought us back to Freud's paper on beating fantasies (1919a), where that point had been made. Freud had thus already indicated the castrative function of the father's love, and precisely in the repressed phase, which must be reconstructed, of the girl's beating fantasy. But the return from the one paper to the other—what I call retroactive reading—was more necessary than ever if we were to discover the importance and the meaning of this function. In contrasting the mother's castration with what Klein emphasizes in 1928 (the child's sadism, his guilt, and his anxiety about the mother's retaliatory omnipotence), we have a better idea of what castration means when it is correlated with the paternal function: it is the limit set on the absolute power of the object as conceived by the child in its primitive distress and dependence.

The primacy of the phallus and castration enables us to understand the renunciation of the mother as love object as well as the refusal of the feminine position vis-à-vis the father, that refusal manifested by the subject of either sex in identifying with him. Moreover, the privation of the breast, in that it justifies the separation from the mother and the masculine claim (the possession of the male organ by way of compensation), does not account either for the aversion of some men, homosexual or not, for the castrated female sex, nor for the fixation on the fetish that is the condition for some other men to approach the woman as sexual object.

Though Freud defines castration, or sexual difference, as what determines the resolution of the Oedipus (its end for the boy, its beginning for the girl, separation from the mother in both cases), and though he gradually specifies that this castration is that of the mother, the fact that he took so much time to confirm this for both sexes—in 1923 for the boy, 1932–1933 for the girl—shows that we are not dealing with a presupposition here. There can be no doubt that this is a fact established on the basis of clinical experience, whatever difficulty or logical contradiction it may raise. Freud had said this as early as 1914 (1914b), criticizing Adler's "masculine protest": the child has no a priori scorn for women. The femininity that the boy or girl refuses is the kind that implies castration, according to the infantile interpretation of parental intercourse.

The devaluation of the mother on account of her castration cannot, therefore, be reconstructed unless we presuppose a phallic phase—the same organ for everyone—that ends with the recognition that every woman, including the mother, is castrated. Femininity = passivity with regard to the father = castration; masculinity = activity with regard to the mother = possession of the organ. Masculine identification is simply the effect of these infantile equations. But why, although we accept that the unconscious represents sexual difference this way, do we follow Freud in associating this infantile sexual theory to a primal scene, real of fantasied, in which the father regularly plays the role of a sadistic castrator? The analyses of the Wolf Man (1914a) and of Little Hans' phobia (1909a), in both of which Freud, as he tells us in *Inhibitions, Symptoms, and Anxiety* (1926a), uncovered a passive homosexual wish, led him to conclude that repression and regression merely disguised the anxiety of castration by the father. As he asserts in 1937, the refusal of femininity in both men and women is a refusal of the passive position vis-à-vis the father; the "masculine protest" is nothing but castration anxiety.

Taking these remarks from 1914 to 1937 together, we see that castration is feared as a punishment both for the love of the father and for the incestuous attachment to the mother, the rival father showing that he has exclusive right to her *jouissance.* Two formulations are explicit in Freud. The first is familiar: it is always the father who represents the prohibition of incest (cf. Freud and Abraham 1907–1926, letter of February 15, 1924). The second, which is harder to describe, is that the feminine position with regard to the father presupposes castration from the moment sexual difference is recognized. We can therefore deduce that, if the mother is presumed to be castrated, this is because the passive feminine position (love for the father) reveals a lack. The father is expected to give something that one does not have.

Prohibitor of incest, castrator of the one who asks for his love, possessor of the desirable object: what connections can we establish among these different paternal functions? It was in asking such questions that I was, paradoxically, helped by the fact that I found myself dissatisfied in retrospect, as though by a promise not kept, with these papers in comparison with the extremely relevant formulation of the meaning of castration in Ruth Mack Brunswick's 1940 paper on the preoedipal phase, a paper I have already mentioned and to which I shall return. What I find of interest in this paper is a definition of castration that emphasizes its *symbolic* nature, not just the *imaginary* one that we come up against in both Freud and Klein and that poses an obstacle to the understanding of castration as an unconscious process, even if we know that we are dealing with the pitfalls of reconstruction in analytic theorizing.

The recognition of the mother's castration, Brunswick says, is what puts an end to her omnipotence. This formulation enables us to see what Klein no longer takes into consideration after 1926–1927 (a lack of any sort in the mother), namely the phase of primitive and absolute dependence on the first object, with the accompanying effects of aggressivity and lethal identification. Calling this an "early Oedipus" or "oedipal conflict" involves a displacement, if not a reversal, of Freud's concept of the Oedipus at this time. In using the same term, the Oedipus, to refer to the child's ambivalent feelings, its fierce hatred along with the nostalgic wish to possess a maternal body that contains all good things, Klein is describing a period before castration, a time of an exclusive but in no way idyllic relation to the first object, in this case the mother.

Seeing castration from this point of view, as an end to maternal omnipotence, implicitly accounts for Klein's revelation of a set of savage infantile fantasies. And it echoes the figure of the father presented by Freud in the *Three Essays* (1905a) or in the study of Leonardo da Vinci (1910), a father who could put a stop both to the child's unrestrained sexual investigations and to the mother's whim (the arbitrary granting or refusing of satisfaction). The mother is imagined as castrated not only because of what the child pictures as coitus, but also because there was a father who turned her away from the attention she was paying to the child and who, though he took away the child's illusion that he could always be satisfied by her, at the same time relieved the anxiety (the simultaneous wish and fear) of being able to satisfy the mother, in other words, of being devoured by her; the unconscious, Freud says, does not distinguish between active and passive.

The father's castrative function, it becomes clear, is deduced from the fact that he occupies a place in the mother's life from which the child feels ousted. The mother's attention to the father, which arouses the child's displeasure, means that it is from him that she expects satisfaction. If she finds it there, this is proof that the father has something that she lacks and that he is able to offer her. By virtue of its alternating presence and absence, the male organ elevated to the rank of phallus represents both the father's power and the disqualification of the mother. This is because it is at the height of the phallic phase, inseparable, for Freud, from the Oedipus and the fantasies it entails, that the child takes an interest in what parental intercourse involves and thus realizes what, up to now, he had refused to believe: the threat of castration for the boy, the lack of the male organ for the girl.

The concept of the mother's castration that Brunswick presents, her falling from her position of omnipotence, has the advantage of linking and explaining the two aspects of the father as bearer of the phallus and as castrator. He is the one who possesses the phallus (*beatus possidens*, says Abraham in 1920) only because the mother turns to him in preference to the child. As bearer of the phallus he is also the castrator, since, diverting to his own profit the mother's request for love, he limits her demands regarding the child, thereby recalling the castration involved in any feminine position taken toward himself as love object.

Brunswick thus invites us to return to statements by Freud that we have forgotten, ones that were obscure but that we have tried to assess in the light of her contribution despite the fact that she does not mention it herself; this is nothing less than the function of the father as performing the castration of the mother. If we still remain unsatisfied, this is because she gives the meaning of castration in her 1940 paper but does not say how she arrived at it. To account for the child's aggression toward his mother and his gradual detachment from her, Brunswick looks at development in terms of a shift from an initial passivity to activity via identification with an active mother: the child leaves primitive dependence as he comes to do for himself and on his own behalf what at first he could only await from the mother.

But when all is said and done, by arranging the facts in the preoedipal perspective she is trying to illuminate, Brunswick, like Fenichel, Abraham, and Klein, succumbs to the lure of a genetic explanation. It is still possible to ascribe the chronological series of frustrations, up to and including the castration feared by the boy or already accomplished for the girl, to the power of the mother on which the child is dependent, to the obstacles she puts in his way, to the very fact of childrearing, to the active gratifications (oral, anal, or phallic) that the child claims because he first experienced them passively in being suckled, cared for—in short, seduced by his mother.

In contrast, what she says about the mother's castration, if we imagine that the mother was robbed by the act of an other, puts an end to the fantasy of maternal omnipotence, for the mother herself must obey the law of a third party. As a result, although the castration of the subject can be placed in the series of frustrating events that give rise to the aggression or ambivalence that will return later on in analytic treatment or in symptoms, the castration of the primary object is in another register, as we see from the devaluation of the mother and the end of her power and her mastery over the subject. So it remains to be explained why the passage from one register to the other, from the imaginary to the symbolic level of castration, comes about through the representation of a castrated mother.

It therefore seems to me that, if we want to retain Brunswick's formulation of a transfer of power from the mother to the father, we have to look to Freud for justification, if only because he is so insistent on the role of the father in prohibiting incest.

We may reproach Brunswick for the suspense in which she leaves us, but this is also a reason to be grateful to her. By echoing Freud, her formulation sends us back to the paper that, more than any other, explains the role of the father as obstacle to the mother's love, namely the essay on Leonardo da Vinci (1910), a study to which Freud was partial despite its paucity of documentation for the thesis of Leonardo's early fixation on his mother. This thesis is based on a memory of Leonardo's childhood and on a letter regarding burial expenses for a certain Caterina. In deciphering the childhood memory, Freud notes in connection with the origin of homosexuality something that had often struck him, namely the absence of a father in the family constellation of such subjects, who were abandoned to female influence. It seems, he says, that the presence of an active father is necessary in order for the boy to choose an object of the opposite sex. Here we see, as nowhere else in Freud, the two aspects of nostalgia for the mother. The first is the *jouissance* of possessing the maternal breast, which often leads to fellatio fantasies in the dreams of some women and passive homosexuals, and the second is the anxiety arising from the *jouissance* of the mother herself, which Freud emphasizes in analyzing the enigmatic fascination of the smile of the Mona Lisa: her devoted tenderness and her voracious seductiveness.

It is irrelevant for our purposes that Freud is in error from the point of view of art history, that some of his facts are based on the faulty translation into German of a text he cites as evidence, and that he relies on imprecise dating of two paintings—one the Mona Lisa and the other of St. Anne, the Virgin, and the Christ Child—in which he sees the two mothers of Leonardo's childhood. What concerns us in Freud's conclusions, and what remains significant regardless of its relevance to the appreciation of Leonardo, is that, in trying to account for the effect of the smile that is distinctive in this artist's portraits of women, he speaks of the agonizing enigma that the child faces regarding his mother's desire, however nostalgic he may be for it—and this in a text that has an autobiographical resonance in the similarity of Leonardo's fantasy of the vulture's beak to the visual content of a childhood anxiety dream of Freud's, in which his dead mother was surrounded by people with birds' beaks (cf. 1900, pp. 583–584). And we should note that he explicitly links the threat felt by the child to what he infers, in the case of Leonardo, from the absence of a father and the exposure of the child to maternal seductiveness.

If such absence can bring about the threatening aspect of the incest fantasy, we may conclude that the father's presence is what averts this by serving as the external obstacle that sets a limit to that excess of libido that Freud saw as the cause of anxiety in his first conceptualizations. In negative form, the father appears in the

Leonardo study as the one who, by fulfilling his role in satisfying the mother, saves the child from the emasculation he would undergo by being the passive object of the mother's *jouissance.*

The overlap of the two enigmas—the first, the question: Who impregnated my mother? being the source of Leonardo's vulture fantasy and the other represented by the twofold meaning of the Mona Lisa's smile—leads Freud to a surprising confession: the uncanniness of the primal nostalgia for the breast. He clearly presents the devouring aspect of maternal love in this text, and, to my knowledge, nowhere else in these terms nor correlated with the paternal function as it is here. Nevertheless, this element can escape our notice if we do not look for it, concealed as it is by the way in which Freud describes Leonardo's return to artistic inspiration as based on nostalgia for the time when he was the sole object of his mother's adoration. And Freud's interest in the alternation of artistic creativity and inhibition in Leonardo, as well as his own fascination with the smile that he attributes to the artist's real mother, mitigates this threatening aspect.

Anxiety is sublimated and inhibition overcome; in other words, the incestuous representation is bypassed. Freud analyzes the androgynous figures in Leonardo's later work as a sublimation of the incestuously combined male-female image reminiscent of the artist's blissful childhood relationship with his mother (though, as in the *Three Essays* [1905a] and the case of Little Hans [1909a], the mother is not held guilty for her expressions of devotion).

The fantasy of the phallic mother that Freud describes in connection with Leonardo's childhood memory repeats what he had said in the *Three Essays* and in the paper on the sexual theories of children (1908c) about the child's belief in the woman's penis, here brought into connection with the cult of the phallus in ancient times. An erect phallus, he tells us in the Leonardo study, is found on representations of Mut, the maternal deity with breasts and a vulture's head; the phallus and breasts are also found in depictions of Isis, Hathor, Neith of Sais (the Greek Athena), and Aphrodite. And the imaginary representation of the mother's phallus takes on another dimension in the case of Leonardo da Vinci, for Freud makes the presumed absence of a father the source of the intensity of the artist's infantile sexual investigations that will be transformed into intellectual curiosity about the flight of birds.

Is this representation of the mother with phallic attributes a primal fantasy or merely a retroactive one to be located in the aftermath of castration? What Freud goes on to interpret in connection with a minor lapse in Leonardo's journal strongly suggests the retroactive nature of the fantasy of suckling or of possession by a phallic mother. On the occasion of the death of Leonardo's father, the artist mentions the time of death twice in the space of a few lines but says nothing about the cause of death. The psychoanalyst, Freud says, has learned that such lapses reveal hidden emotions. What might these be in this case? Rivalry in identification, a wish to triumph over the father, and, finally, reproaches: nothing that is alien to the oedipal configuration. Here we see that the Oedipus is a retroactive effect. The figure of the father is called on to make sense of the limits placed on gratification as well as on the repression—which was not understood—of the first *jouissance* on account of the anxiety aroused by the excess of gratification.

The mother is phallic and remains so, or becomes so again, only on the basis of the refusal of castration. The father is the agent of this castration; his very presence robs the mother of the right to enjoy her product. Leonardo's own rationalization of his fantasy in terms of an early interest in the flight of birds has sexual meanings (the phallic prowess of flight, the burning desire to be capable of sexual acts) that Freud points out as signs of a nostalgia for incestuous *jouissance* without a rival that has endured despite the prohibition and because of it. Leonardo maintains the fantasy at the risk of being dispossessed himself, even sacrificed, as is suggested by his identification with Christ, who was also born from a virginal mother, this, according to Freud, being one of the motives for the childhood memory.

This 1910 study that mentions the imaginary maternal phallus and the devaluation of a castrated mother in the eyes of the homosexual does not yet refer to the circumstances, even imaginary ones, by which the castration of the mother is ascribed to the father. This emasculation experienced by the child who has served as the mother's *jouissance* is consistent with Klein's remarks on the fear of the castrating mother, except that—and what Freud says here is crucial—the emasculation could have been prevented by the presence of a father. Such a presence means not only the prohibition of incest by the threat of castration of the son (the *jouissance* of the father of the primal horde who alone possesses all the women and deprives the sons of them; cf. 1912–1913), but also the castration of the mother, in the sense that she is thereby separated from her product, that part of herself that she no longer has the right to reabsorb.

On the one hand, there is the infantile belief in the mother's penis, followed by the boy's horror or contempt for her castrated genital, or by the girl's hatred. On the other hand, there is the fear of a phallic mother. On the level of fantasy, this seeming paradox is in agreement with the essence of the representation of a phallic mother. At all events, the childhood nostalgia[1] persists despite the threat, while the abandonment of the fantasy, which at first is equivalent to a refusal by the Other (what the mother does not give, she refuses), implies consent to a loss of a part of oneself as well as a part of the object. One has either the fascination of a completeness regained at the cost of anxiety or else hatred, or at any rate separation, at the cost of renunciation.

Note

1. The ambivalence of the nostalgia for the maternal breast, this uncanniness (cf. 1919b) that Freud mentions in Leonardo's vulture fantasy, can escape notice because of the simultaneous emphasis on the joy of creativity, the triumph of a *jouissance* recovered via sublimation. Thus I, for one, did not understand what Lacan (1956–1957), at the end of his seminar on object relations, meant by the "desire of the mother" (a twofold dimension) in Freud's study of Leonardo. And it was as I was seeking something else, namely an understanding of Klein's concept of the hate of maternal *jouissance*, that Brunswick's allusion to the unlimited power of the uncastrated mother led me to this essay of Freud's, an essay that explains the threatening aspect of maternal desire (for Freud, feminine desire) and the role of the father as prohibitor of incest. While Freud (1914d) speaks of cryptomnesia, I would say that what guided me, perhaps erroneously, was Lacan's *translation* of a Freudian conceptualization whose emphasis is unclear because certain points are not repeated. Never-

theless, before understanding Lacan one has to have encountered the questions that his way of theorizing resolves. For, if it is precisely to the desire of the mother in Freud's 1910 study that Lacan refers, this is because his critique of "object relations" as a perversion of the principles and the conduct of analytic treatment involves, among other things, putting in question the role Melanie Klein assigns to the maternal object.

19   Objections, Fidelity, Disagreements

There is no doubt that Freud's way of proceeding by stages and doubling back has made it hard to understand him, to see the interest of a given point taken in isolation or, even more, to track the corrections he makes as he goes along bit by bit. This non-totalizing feature of Freud's theoretical exposition, the discrepancy between statements that were made at different times and that he did not reconcile with each other, is, in my view, the reason why his corrections made in 1931 and 1932–1933 on the issue of the girl's Oedipus had no effect on Melanie Klein. As I noted above, what might be seen as Klein's dispute with Freud in connection with the femininity phase or identification with the mother, is, in my opinion, a request that he give some further explanation of his concepts of the Oedipus, oedipal identification, and the function of the father.

Likewise, although Freud (1931) says that Klein's moving the "oedipal conflict" back in time changes the entire course of development and is inconsistent with the results of adult analyses, we must nonetheless recognize the legitimacy of the issues she raises, if only because of the arguments she advances in the 1928 paper and her caution in the papers that precede it.

Let us look at those arguments. Klein no longer reasons, or at any rate no longer reasons explicitly, in terms of retroaction when she makes chronology prevail over reconstruction by emphasizing the trauma of weaning, thereby ignoring the historiographic model that, according to Freud (1910), is to be applied to analysis, where the past is written for the future in terms of the present. But, as we have seen, Klein stresses the active presence in the child of fantasies that are merely reactivated in the adult, and in this way she notes the inextricable interweaving of the genital and the pregenital, this being one way in which she makes herself comfortable with an alleged sequence of phases. She no longer feels compelled to recall that she started out with the analysis of children who, though very young (3, 4, 6 years old or more) were struggling with the Oedipus, castration, and the primal scene, and this is undoubtedly because of the astounding repetition of pregenital fantasies that she uncovers during the sessions and because of the immediate reduction of anxiety brought about by her interpretations of this material to the children.

Inhibitions (as in Trude's absolute inability to play), the intensity of night terrors (as with Ruth), and sadistic fixations (in the case of Erna) always have to do with the mother, with the hate toward her, and with the repercussions that are feared. What Klein is concerned to demonstrate as independent of the trauma of castration (though she does not deny this trauma) is what she finds so striking and disconcerting: the paranoid projection she encounters in young children but gradually comes to describe in relation to an original melancholia, a return onto the self of the fault at first attributed to the Other.

The problem is a logical one, directly connected with the synthesis or coherence she is trying to achieve. We may sum it up by saying that, in approaching the primitive superego and oedipal choice through a single concept—cannibalistic identification—that covers both, she makes weaning, which is the cause of the superego, into the precursor and the model of castration, which is the cause of the oedipal "conflict." And she attributes to both the same effects of separation from and hate for the mother.

I have described the issues Klein discusses and the arguments she advances. As for her caution, before 1928 and even afterward, beyond the lapidary formulations of the paper that Freud challenges ("Early stages of the Oedipus complex"), caution is evident in what she says about the development of her thinking. She clearly states that what is problematical for her has to do with the vicissitudes of the drive; the aims and source of the drive remain pregenital, while the object is already oedipal, since fantasies of an oral- or anal-sadistic nature are aimed at the introjected parental figures (cf. Klein 1929). She is cautious in setting forth her motives, and cautious because the prevalence of harsh superego figures in young children, beyond Freud's definition of the superego as the outcome and successor of the Oedipus, is what leads her to speak of early stages of the Oedipus and is her way of accounting for the later ambivalence and identification of the oedipal stage proper. In his 1927 emendation to the English-language edition of *The Ego and the Id* (1923a), Freud seems to have allowed for this interpretation, noting that one factor in the formation of the superego is the long period of distress and dependence experienced by the child in addition to the Oedipus complex.

In 1926 Klein was still relating the Oedipus to parental intercourse and the resulting identification with one parent and competition for the other; nevertheless, even here she spoke of a mode of identification that was not associated only with the phallic stage. And if indeed she spoke of the oedipal process in terms of absorption and expulsion, the same concepts Freud had used in his paper on negation (1925b), she was just repeating his usage and at the same time defining the task that he had to undertake, as an analyst, in distinguishing the various identifications at work in the child. To be sure, when Klein in 1928 speaks of the excessive goodness side by side with the excessive harshness of the introjected superego objects, she is positing a split not so much of the subject, the way Freud does, as of the object (though she would not articulate this explicitly until 1935). But this is because the object is primarily conceived as a part of the self. This is the explanation for the mirror effects (introjection, projection, fear of retaliation) that she goes on to develop: the mother's body is not distinguished from that of the subject. It makes no difference whether it is the object or the subject that is split, insofar as what is not accepted is the distinction between the bodies, the fact that the loss of the breast brings the end of narcissistic fusion. The "oedipal conflict" set in motion by oral frustration is simply the moment when the child finds that he has lost a part of himself along with part of the object.

The child feels that he has been amputated and devalued by the mother. He is not enough for her; the privation of the breast that she inflicts on him is a sign, interpreted as a punishment. I suggest that, when the child turns to the father, represented by his organ, the incorporation of what is an object of satisfaction for the mother means that he is now the father's equal in this regard, hence the concept of identification. He seeks to refind the value that he himself once had for her, when, enjoying the breast, he could imagine himself the sole good object of the mother's *jouissance.*

Klein's conviction that she is just deepening and extending Freud's remarks is valid if we consider the observations that she solidly supports with the clinical examples missing in the 1928 paper, along with her emphasis, however mistaken it may be, on concepts that are scattered throughout Freud's work. In 1923 she refers to the Leonardo da Vinci essay (Freud 1910) to note the relation between inhibition and the incest fantasy; she also cites Freud's (1925b) paper on negation and the function of judgment as the first mode of symbolization; his references (1914c, 1917, 1923a), to the loss of the formerly loved object; and his work on the formation of the superego, so hard to define that he himself did not return to it until 1929, when, we may note, he gave great credit to Klein. Yet Freud had only criticism for her extension of the concept of identification, and, between 1925 and 1932–1933, he takes issue with her point by point.

He prefers to stay with a limited definition of the Oedipus, despite the revisions he himself has already introduced with the notion of the complete Oedipus, in which, even for the boy, loving the mother does not preclude loving the father at the same time. For each sex there are two aspects: the boy's negative Oedipus is his feminine-passive position vis-à-vis his father, his positive Oedipus his active wish to possess his mother; the girl's negative Oedipus is the active wish addressed to the mother at each phase, her positive Oedipus her love for her father, a "femininity" that presupposes castration. But, for both sexes, the positive Oedipus is never anything but the loving relation to the opposite-sex parent. The myth depends entirely on this asymmetry that Freud hypothesizes in 1925 (1925a). What comes first for each sex is the love for the mother, which ends under the pressure of similar circumstances. The reconstruction of the girl's bond to her mother in the 1931 paper, in which all phases, including the phallic, are said to concern her, serves to make the point that the phallic phase and the Oedipus (negative for the girl, positive for the boy) coincide. But in each case this is an *active* Oedipus vis-à-vis the mother.

Only castration, that is, the mother's castration, leads the boy or the girl to abandon the first love object, and it does so in the same manner for each sex. Klein speaks of weaning and the incorporation of the paternal organ contained by the mother as a substitute for the breast. But this does not account for what determines masculine identification for both sexes (the girl's masculinity complex, the boy's giving up the feminine position toward the father), nor does it account for the girl's hate, which, for Freud, is reserved for the mother, and her choice of the father as the locus of the demand for what he can give and the mother cannot.

The turn toward the father holds true for both sexes. The additional step for the girl is that she must pass from the male position, her identification with the father, to the female position, her love for him, as she accepts her lack, that is, her castration. Although he does not have to "change sex," the boy is not any luckier, since, if he is to avoid impotence, he must avoid the always threatening representation of incest with another woman, a substitute for his mother.

What makes the boy leave the Oedipus is the possibility of his own castration, and this is conceivable only in the phallic phase, at the moment when, having ascribed the same organ to everyone, he now becomes aware of its absence in others and ultimately in the mother. Likewise, the idea of a lack presupposes that the girl discovers sexual difference, a disadvantage that she could deny but that (in some way that Freud declared himself unable to understand fully) separated her from her mother. The girl, it turns out, raises the same charges against the mother as does the boy (cf. Freud 1931, 1932–1933). The additional step that Freud takes in 1932–1933, when he states that the girl's Oedipus, her passage from mother to father, is likewise determined by the mother's castration, makes it absolutely necessary to connect the terms *Oedipus, phallic phase,* and *castration* that Klein tries to unlink. The mother's castration is inseparable from the phallic phase. It is only because, at a certain phase, there is a concentration of interest and sexual activities on the genitals that it makes sense to speak of the threat of castration (that the parents issue in connection with masturbation and that the boy had not really taken seriously before), the perception of sexual difference (that the girl had been able to deny before this), and the combination of the two. This is demonstrated by the equations Freud had made earlier on in his analysis of the Wolf Man's phobia (1914a) and the beating fantasy (1919a): being loved by the father means being castrated. In this view of parental intercourse that is no longer oral or anal, nor merely sadistic, but phallic, the mother is castrated when she is loved as a woman by the father. Yet the process by which the subject comes to be aware of the mother's castration, if only by interpreting the division of roles in the primal scene, is not mentioned here. It hardly needs to be noted that castration, separation, and hate of the mother are not perceptible to the subject at the time they arise. They are unconscious phenomena whose origin can be deduced and constructed only retroactively, in analysis. Yet, though it is relatively clear in 1932–1933 that, for the unconscious, the absence of the male organ in one person relates to its presence in another, that the father becomes the bearer of the phallus solely because of the mother's lack, neither the function of the father as castrator of the mother nor the meaning of this function is spelled out in this paper. However we understand this, as a deliberately circumscribed aim or as an ellipse to be filled in by those he is addressing beyond the fictive audience of the lecture, it must be admitted that Freud does not supply all the elements that lead him to his conclusions. In contrast to Klein and Abraham, he is not seeking a synthesis but presents all his arguments gradually and separately. The emendations that mark each step in his theorizing are the culmination, each time, of reflection on a different matter (cf. Freud 1915b).

As we have seen, the primacy of the phallus, formulated (Freud 1923b) as the representation in which the infantile genital organization is specifically distinguished from its adult counterpart, is related to the mother's phallus only for the boy. The abandonment of the belief in the maternal phallus is firmly established for the girl only in the context of the change, at first not understood, in her feelings for her mother. The hate for the mother, when it reappears in the course of analysis, is a sign of the change of object that has occurred. But, like the castration complex, it can arise only after the choice of object, clearly an oedipal choice, has been made (cf. Freud 1918). If the primacy of the phallus and the mother's castration are overlapping concepts, their convergence is a retroactive effect. To place them in relation from the beginning would have required a concordance of elements from across a range of issues: fetishism, male homosexuality, the masculine symptoms of hysteria, infantile theories of sexuality, the repression of love for the father, and, finally, female homosexuality, in which the adoration of the beloved Lady (Freud 1920a) reveals, among other things, the adoration of a substitute for the phallic mother.

Freud constantly claimed that he did not have enough time to theorize the central role of the mother with regard to castration. I am stressing this in order to show his particular way of advancing in knowledge: by ceaseless returns, moving by fits and starts in a fragmentary way that does not pretend to offer a complete explanation.

As a final example, let us consider once again the terms in which, in 1932–1933, he indicates his disagreement with Melanie Klein's moving the Oedipus back in time: her suggestion is in accord neither with the results of adult analysis nor with his observation of the perseverance of the preoedipal attachment to the mother. We see two things here, a conceptual revolution that Freud resists, and a difference in clinical experience that he has neither the means, nor, undoubtedly, the intention of reconciling. In the first case, Klein's attempt to transform the entire pattern of development, we understand the logic of retroaction that, Freud had discovered, governed the way the analysand's history emerges in the course of treatment, in the opposite direction of chronological development. This unconscious logic is surely incompatible with the linear and teleological concept that Klein, following Abraham, is trying to assert. The second point, the attachment to the mother, involves a meaning of castration that Freud had come to see only gradually, one to which he will now grant major importance in the girl's development into a woman. The concept that he calls the feminine wish par excellence, penis envy, enables us to understand the symbolic value of the phallus, which causes love and attachment by its presence, hate by its absence. Symbolization comes into play through a grasp of pure difference.

Does Freud flatly refuse to accept Klein's hypotheses? In spite of the brevity of his conclusions in 1931, if we read him attentively we find that this is not the case, even if he finds it hard to integrate her ideas. He takes into account her theory that oral-aggressive or sadistic wishes found in women reflect an anxiety of being killed by the mother and an impulse to retaliate. What we find as oral- and anal-sadistic fantasies, even in the child, can only be understood as regressive, the result of repression brought on by castration. These primitive emotions or pregenital drives that are the basis of Klein's investigations do not appear as such in analysis but are transformed into anxiety on account of repression or are occasionally transferred to the paternal object, where they do not belong. Similarly, the notion of penis envy that Freud introduces in 1932–1933 as an intervening and decisive step between the first wish for a child, which is an active wish toward the mother, and the oedipal wish for a child passively awaited from the father, seems to me to be an inverted echo of Klein's formulation in 1928, in which penis envy follows the girl's wish to have a child. Freud reverses this; in contrast to Klein, who sees here evidence of the girl's early femininity, he retains what she says on the literal level, namely that this first demand is addressed to the mother, but does so in order to confirm his own finding that the girl needs penis envy, needs something enviable or desirable on the part of the father, if she is to pass to the wish for a child.

To repeat, Klein was aware of Freud's disagreement in the matter of the timing of the Oedipus but not of the attention he paid her or the replies he indirectly addressed to her on other points. This is not surprising if we recall the time it took us, even with our larger perspective, to see this dimension ourselves in Freud's two papers on femininity of 1931 and 1932–1933, a dimension of replies and adjustments that he could make only retroactively, in light of the developments his own work had inspired in others. Was Klein opposing Freud on principle or legitimately disagreeing with him?

Was she going off on a tangent or actually extending his work? Was her clinical experience unlike his, or did it present incompatible evidence? These questions we have been asking in connection with Klein no longer have the same meaning once we realize the extent to which difference and contradiction can turn out to be more fruitful, in calling for emendations and clarifications, than agreement or hasty clinical illustration.

It is perhaps in this way, by closely studying the issues involved in Freud's rejection of Klein, and precisely because I did not suspect that I would draw these conclusions, that I can confirm what was at first merely an intuition based on some omissions and errors that I found in Freud at the end of the 1931 paper. This intuition was that, in these final pages that seemed to be an homage to predecessors and collaborators, something much more fundamental seemed to be at issue for Freud, something that, as he said, had to do with conceptualizing development and the process of adult analysis. For this final gesture of authority it is Melanie Klein who has to pay the price more than others, even more than Jones or Horney, in place of someone who is no longer there, Abraham.

20   Freud and
        Ruth Mack Brunswick

It is easy to misunderstand the preoedipal and phallic phases in the girl, the latter implicating her in the problematics of castration. How else to explain that there was so little response to the work of Ruth Mack Brunswick, though she sheds considerable light on these issues? Though she published a paper partly under Freud's guidance in the 1930s, it was not until after Freud's death that the English version (Brunswick 1940) and the notes made under his supervision appeared.

It is not that Freud forgets Brunswick in his two papers on femininity of 1931 and 1932–1933. In a note to the first he refers to a case of delusional jealousy that she reported (Brunswick 1928a), in order to illustrate how, in his view, paranoia in a woman can be traced back to initial dependence on a mother or mother substitute. And in the same paper he notes their agreement on other points of feminine development, including the orgasmic rage some women recall having experienced during enemas administered by their mothers, which can be thought of as anal seduction. He again cites Brunswick in the 1932–1933 paper, along with Helene Deutsch and Jeanne Lampl-de Groot, as one of the women to whom the analytic investigation of feminine prehistory owes its notable contributions. She is, he says, the first to have described a case going back to a preoedipal fixation without achievement of the oedipal position.

Oddly enough, five years later, in "Analysis terminable and interminable" (Freud 1937), he fails to mention the appearance of another paper in 1928, one that is the best known of Brunswick's contributions, her account of the continued analysis of the Wolf Man, which Freud had handed over to her (Brunswick 1928b). Let us recall the context. Freud first reports the technical innovation he allowed himself in this treatment (1914a) when he set a termination date in order to mobilize an analysis that was getting bogged down. Later he refers to the correction he made in 1923 regarding the complete cure of this patient after 1914, for, when the Wolf man returned to Vienna after the war, Freud was called on to help him once again, to deal with unresolved transference issues. He finally has reservations about this judgment of 1923, the ensuing years having been troubled by some disturbing incidents. On each of these occasions, he says, his student Ruth Mack Brunswick was helpful to the patient, and, he adds, he looks forward to her publishing her own account of the case.

What, then, are we to make of the silence on the case report published in 1928 and dealing with the further analysis of the Wolf Man in 1926 and 1927? Freud may have been disappointed not to have an account of the treatment beyond this time or of the therapeutic procedures he himself had employed (cf. Freud 1937), but does this justify "forgetting" the publication of the initial report in which the diagnosis of paranoia had, around this time, been approved, if not suggested, by him? What is intended, annulled, or invalidated in a certain way by this ambiguous omission? In acting as though nothing had happened, is he showing that he would have preferred to see the case report postponed until the completion of the case might have modified the diagnosis that, though it was his, he had in the meantime come to rethink (cf. Freud 1937)? In his forgetting this account of an analysis conducted under his supervision, is there something else that he is trying to erase?

It would seem that Freud made a choice in 1937. To agree with Kleinian problematics as they are reflected in the work of Brunswick (cf. the paper that appeared in 1940), the work in which he himself had taken part a few years earlier, would be to disavow his daughter, Anna Freud, whose views on child analysis were diametrically opposed to Klein's. The fact that he cites Anna in the 1937 paper, where we would expect priority to be given to the mechanisms of introjection and projection developed by Klein, seems to me to be consistent with his ambiguity regarding the published or unpublished work of Ruth Mack Brunswick.

But whether he was dissatisfied or disappointed, Freud's 1937 paper does not reject Brunswick, whose closeness to him as a student and whose clinical skill he notes. But his obvious reserve has several motivations. One, consistent with his characteristic method of tirelessly returning to the same points to correct or refine them, might, as I mentioned, concern the diagnosis of paranoia that he had formulated and, in any case, confirmed with regard to the two cases Brunswick reported in 1928 (1928 a, b). Another motivation, less theoretical than strategic, would involve the positions he shared with Brunswick in the 1930s vis-à-vis Melanie Klein. I am referring to the attention that he and Brunswick paid to Klein's objections, however implicitly or indirectly, and that, as I have tried to show, influenced his positions on femininity in 1931 and 1932–1933.

The two papers of Brunswick's that interest us, "The analysis of a case of paranoia (delusions of jealousy)" (1928a) and "The preoedipal phase of the libido development" (1940) do not have the same status. The earlier one is a detailed clinical case report, session by session, that, beyond its fidelity to the Freudian spirit, is the first paper up to that time to relate the history and the morbid effects of a fixation to the maternal object. This fixation was revealed in an analysis that required a rethinking of the oedipal problematic and the relevance of the oedipal myth for female development. The 1940 paper is an attempt at synthesis concerning what is meant by "preoedipal," that concept used by Freud in 1931, no doubt (as she suggests) at Brunswick's instigation, and aimed primarily at correcting the initial bias in favor of the naturalness and symmetry of the Oedipus. In addition to the role played by Freud, the text is all the more interesting because, following the argument Freud (1925a) had begun to set out, in which illuminating the girl's prehistory would shed light on the oedipal prehistory of the boy, it enables us to assess the full measure of the reversal that is being proposed. It is no longer femininity that is being reconstructed or defined according to the masculine parameters that had been used up to that time. An entire stage of the boy's development, with all its vicissitudes, could be understood in the light of the discovery made about the girl, that of a preoedipal period that is as certain as it is repressed, obscure, and hard to reconstruct.

Reconsidering the issue of the preoedipal in the boy and the girl, Brunswick invites us to think in a new way about the relation between dependence on the mother and castration. She defines castration as the end of maternal omnipotence, which enables us to conceptualize that omnipotence in a register other than the purely imaginary. This is a translation of the Kleinian concept of primary identification with the mother, by means of a slight displacement. Brunswick does not see identification with the mother in imaginary terms of oral sadism or devouring; she restores the symbolic aspect of the mechanisms of introjection and incorporation that Freud, too, was describing (cf. 1917, 1923a). In other words, the deciphering and exact evaluation of Klein's contribution add another dimension to what Freud subsumed under the term "castration," a term that would be inadequate if it had not been newly explained or differently inflected by Ruth Mack Brunswick, in accordance, we may suppose, with the meaning that Freud gave it, though he himself did not manage to describe it in such a radical way.

21   A Case without an Oedipus

Fifty dense pages in the German edition, more than eighty in the English, for two and a half months of treatment; an attempt to reconstruct material as it arose spontaneously or was prompted by interpretations from one session to the next; transcription of the text of dreams followed by their partial deciphering: this is the case report on feminine paranoia that Ruth Mack Brunswick gives us in 1928 (1928a).

The paper is divided into six headings, four large sections in addition to the introduction and conclusion. Three pages of introduction are reserved for the patient's presenting symptoms and the aspects of her family history that she is willing to offer right in the first session. And ten pages of conclusion are devoted to differential diagnosis and the mechanisms of what Brunswick considers a psychosis. The third, fourth, and fifth chapters focus on the handling of the transference. There is nothing surprising here, if we consider that what is at stake is the conduct of a treatment that, apart from an initial psychiatric diagnosis of delusional jealousy, involves two elements: first, the intensity of a transference that Brunswick evoked as soon as she saw indications for it, and, second, a childhood history whose construction is suggested to the patient and is reported to the reader in the first of the long sections. This first part, on the analysis of infantile sexual tendencies, is longer than the three others together. It is divided into rubrics on the role of seduction, death fantasies, infantile masturbation, penis envy and castration anxiety, and homosexual jealousy and anal erotism. These rubrics give the impression of familiar ground, but this should not mislead us. The same is true of the three following sections, in which Brunswick speaks of three stages of paranoia: jealousy, the negative transference, and persecution and the completion of the analysis.

We shall return to this effect of reorganization of the periods of the treatment interwoven with or superimposed on its chronological sequence. For what is most interesting and original about this paper is its presentation of an analysis in the temporality of its development and the handling of a transference that Brunswick describes as risky. Brunswick set out with a wish to learn more about female paranoia, to get the patient to supply the missing piece of the puzzle, that is, to force her to confession, recognition, and working through of what she had not known. Brunswick thus shows us the extent to which one reveals one's ignorance more than one's knowledge in presenting a case. Reporting exactly, without evasion or conceit, she describes her interpretations as well as the precipitation of delusion or interruption of the treatment that she risked in giving such interpretations. She speaks of her confusion in her "forcing" of the transference that, she tells us several times, was somewhat arbitrary but necessary in view of her sense of the case. It was only afterwards, in the treatment itself and in the report she wrote up later, that she was able to confirm the appropriateness of what she had done.

If she made an initial wager about the possibility of a transference and its utilization in a case of psychosis, we may say that she made a second one as well, since, while there was still a lively controversy about the primal scene as proposed by Freud in the case of the Wolf Man (1914a), she undertook to show how this concept actually worked in analysis. If there is no spontaneous anamnesis in a patient, the analyst must use the evidence he has to attempt a construction whose validity he can prove only by the confirmation furnished by other dreams or by memories evoked by the initial suggestion. In fact, the symptoms of Brunswick's patient, her childhood history, even her delusional jealousy, cannot be separated from the way the analyst takes hold of them in the transference, and there alone. The repetition, in dreams, of past experience is the sole guarantee of their truth and of the analyst's inferences, the sole proof of the accuracy of the reconstruction she offers to the patient.

The role assigned to the analysis of dreams and to construction, to the conception and the "forcing" of the transference, as well as to the later thematic organization of childhood material that arose in the course of the sessions, invites us to establish a homology between Freud's case and Brunswick's. We would then have a sort of female Wolf Man (Sol Aparicio, personal communication; see also Aparicio 1985). But, without forgetting this first point, I must privilege another, and this because I was slow to realize what was going on in this paper from the theoretical point of view over and above what the author or Freud himself saw in it. For what I see here is the clinical evidence par excellence that provides an empirical foundation for Freud's theory of the Oedipus and the girl's castration. The strength of the ideas is confirmed in clinical practice. Conversely, Freud's conceptualization starts out from pathology and is inspired and sometimes validated by it.

Let us look at the case. The patient is a young woman who was hospitalized after a jealous outbreak accompanied by suicide threats and acting out. The intern who was treating her for mastoiditis, and to whom she described this recent psychiatric incident, referred her to Brunswick after she left the hospital. From the outset, Brunswick was struck by the patient's accessibility. Reserve and a defiant timidity quickly gave way in conversation, to the point where, to the analyst's surprise, the patient was perfectly willing to use the couch. The patient was concerned about several symptoms: her absence of emotion, attacks of buzzing in her head, and the sense that her eyes were popping out toward her temples, these phenomena being associated with sudden rages that she could not understand any more than she could the feeling of an electric current running through her head. In addition, there were marital difficulties: frigidity and dyspareunia, and a continuous menstruation brought on by sexual intercourse when it occurred.

She was the youngest of five brothers and sisters; her mother had died when the patient was 3 and the father had remarried. After her mother's death, she was given into the care of a sister, ten years older, before being sent to the country until the age of 11. This sister, intellectually and sexually abnormal, a prostitute even before puberty, enuretic and hence mistreated by the parents, died in an asylum at the age of 29, the same age at which, Brunswick notes, psychosis developed in the patient, who had married at 28, several months before the delusion and the beginning of the analysis.

The patient's initial complaint was that she had never received the maternal affection that her stepmother, her father's second wife, offered to her son-in-law, the patient's husband. The content of the delusion was directly related to the sexual relationship she imagined between her husband and stepmother. Her husband's infidelity, which was at first only a suspicion on her part, soon came to her as a rumor from the outside, magnified to the point where she felt that she was the object of universal mockery and conspiracy. Overwhelmed by the tone of triumph and scorn that she discerned in her stepmother's voice, she was soon convinced that the laughter and glances of her neighbors or strangers she passed in the street were aimed at her; at the same time, she was astonished at what she was feeling: how could she be observed by people who knew nothing about her, least of all that her husband was deceiving her?

On the basis of these preliminary data, Brunswick tells us that she decided to present the case by reporting the patient's material as it unfolded in the course of the treatment. In telling us that she is presenting material as it arose during the analytic work, she is nevertheless running the risk of relegating to a secondary role what is in fact decisive in this treatment and, in my opinion, allows for this linear exposition. Because she offers the patient a construction from the outset, based on the conscious elements of anamnesis related in the introduction and on the interpretation of two dreams from the following sessions, she solicits and obtains a certain type of material. The material is called upon to confirm or disconfirm the construction she had hazarded. If the case is atypical, as Brunswick says in her conclusion, in that it is a psychosis accessible to analysis, the construction itself is typical, since it bears on one of those events that, as Freud says, occur in all or almost all childhood histories of neurotics, namely observation of parental intercourse, seduction by an adult, or threat of castration (1916–1917, Lecture 23). Here we are dealing with a seduction. The two dreams that Brunswick uses as the basis of this construction occur as early as the second and third sessions. She incited both of them, in that she had suggested to the patient this way to compensate for her lack of memories when, in the second interview, the young woman revealed her problem: agitated and reticent at the same time, she claimed not to know anything.

The first of these dreams, experienced as a nightmare by the patient, was an anxiety dream that had recurred regularly since the onset of the psychosis. The other occurred during the night following the interpretation of the first one and was a transference dream, as the analyst announced right away.

In the anxiety dream, a man in black (the German term also has the sense of "bogyman") breaks into the patient's house and has sexual relations with her. She is very afraid but achieves orgasm. Her first association in connection with this man is an unusual detail of his clothing, inconsistent with his male features: he wore a hairnet, as the patient's sister had done. She also mentions that this man in the dream often wears a black coat. In trying to describe how she felt in the dream, she says, with some embarrassment, that it reminds her of how she feels while masturbating. Then, with great precision, she recalls a scene of masturbation in her childhood, when she was 9, with a girl who was a bit older. She had been very attached to this friend during the time of their sex play, which was interrupted by the scolding of an aunt and the accusation of the older girl that unjustly placed all the blame on the patient. She remembers what she felt, after that, toward this girl whom she had loved and who had betrayed her, namely a mixture of fear, guilt, and hatred. The resurgence, in analysis, of this forgotten episode makes a big impression on the patient, who states that she now understands what she was guilty of.

In explaining to the patient how common and relatively harmless childhood masturbation is, and in suggesting to her the possibility of an earlier seduction as origin of the compulsion to masturbate, the analyst is trying to relieve the patient's guilt but also to orient her toward an initial fault that was not hers or hers alone. Now, although her first supposition, according to which the man in black (or bogyman) is a substitute for the sister is accepted on account of the hairnet and the black coat that recalls the mourning for the dead sister, the relation Brunswick suggests between the masturbation and the original agent of seduction is less plausible to the patient. Brunswick's still discreet suggestion on this point leads only to a disguised confession of the persistence of onanism in the form of a question about whether it makes one ill as an adult. As we can see, interpretation up to this point is tolerated only with regard to matters that are isolated from one another.

It is after the second dream, the one whose transferential tonality is pointed out by the analyst, that we see how big a step it is from interpretation to construction. In that dream, a stranger asks the patient either for some unfamiliar bread or for information as to where he can get some. When he speaks, he has an accent that gives her a feeling of great pleasure. He gives her two pairs of pants and an overcoat to hold for him. She waits for him, but he does not come back. This, she says, is a pleasant dream; she always liked foreign accents, especially if they are light. Furthermore, this was what had led her to marry her husband, who, in his long military service, had taken on a light accent. When Brunswick points out that her, Brunswick's, German is accented, the patient confirms that, since the time of the first interview, the analyst's accent gave her the same voluptuous feelings as in the dream. The first phase of interpretation is simple: the analyst is the foreigner. The pants given to her in the dream are the equivalent of the black hairnet, in other words, the male organ of someone who is really female.

When the interpretation links the two dreams and the screen memory of masturbation, it becomes a construction. In the first dream, a man who represents the patient's older sister seduces her. This dream evokes the memory of a screen incident (the scene of masturbation). On that basis, we might posit a link between the sister and the childhood friend; in her first forceful interpretation Brunswick suggests that the patient had experienced something similar with her sister. The initial reaction is a violent rejection on the part of the patient, one that takes on the value of a denial when the patient goes on to say that, to be sure, she and her sister had slept in the same bed until she was sent to the country at the age of 4. Her sister, she hastens to add, was always affectionate with her, but never in an inappropriate way. At this point, the analyst once again feels that she has to relieve the patient of guilt. She reminds her of the sister's abnormality and suggests that the adolescent of the later sex play in the country is undoubtedly a substitute for the loved and missed sister. Because of the emphasis placed on the intensity of the longing for the sister, which would account for the transfer of love onto another object, the patient acknowledges the possibility of physical intimacy between herself and her sister. Brunswick sees here an admission that, for her, is the sign of accessibility to interpretation and hence to the analytic process, though the patient's overcoming of resistance entails her exchanging a paradoxically lesser guilt, the avowal of incestuous relations in early childhood, for the greater one of having been unfaithful to her sister.

At the end of this same session, in which the patient no longer refuses the analyst's construction, she also accepts the transference interpretation that Brunswick offers on the basis of the structural analogy between the two dreams: the bogyman is her sister, the foreigner whose voice arouses pleasure is the analyst. The analyst is thus the sister. The future of the treatment seems to be compromised by the fact that the patient fails to respond to the analyst's warnings about the mechanisms of the transference and the hostility that can arise there; her strong protest and her "deafness" are attributed to the intensity of the transference.

Having established a solid transference and a construction that is, at least in part, accepted or not contradicted, Brunswick pursues her project of trying to reproduce the material as it emerged, essentially in the form of dreams, some screen memories, and associations to these dreams and memories. The contrast between the phenomenology of the treatment, reproduced in the linear narrative of the paper, and the reconstruction of the patient's history is all the more apparent because, as Brunswick retrospectively describes the case, there are a number of discrepancies between what she is looking for (which we learn only at the end), what her aim is (modified by what she had not expected but, as the treatment progressed, gradually encountered), and the clinical findings that she had to account for theoretically. Thus the entire first section, in which she presents her construction and then the material that followed from it, is not explicitly theorized in terms either of supporting references or of points to be clarified. The only identifiable issues, in this initial phase, seem to be whether the patient would accept the construction and whether it is possible for analysis to shed light on delusional jealousy.

Once the hypothesis of the viability of analysis has been put forth, what Brunswick is aiming at is connected less with the Freudian assumption of the role of repressed homosexuality in paranoia than with material she had not expected to find. The "construction" can thus be understood as a modification of her technique as a result of the kind of resistance she faced from the time of the second session (the patient's avowed ignorance). What might it mean? She does not say, although her description of the first dream as a recurrent anxiety dream points to the aftermath of trauma, as with the Wolf Man's dream (Freud 1914a). Similarly, when she hears of the feelings the patient experienced in the recollected scene of masturbation, she shows that this is just a screen for an older event.

What is the effect of this construction on the patient? It must be admitted that, though the hostility that reappeared with the screen memory is legible in disguised form in the anxiety accompanying the first dream, no further hostility emerges in the dream of the stranger. Nor does it in the entire first phase of the treatment, at the end of which it appears that the patient does not envy men anything, and, above all, that she has nothing further to say about her husband and stepmother, in other words, about her delusion.

Brunswick is quick to notice that the transference dreams are the only ones that can be interpreted. More precisely, they indicate when interpretation can be heard by the patient; Brunswick has to wait for the situation repeated in ordinary dreams to be relived in transference dreams in order to be able to convince the patient that she is reproducing pieces of her history. The analyst's job is to show that these forgotten fragments shed light on some of her symptoms and her difficulties with her environment; a "translation" or symbolization of the repressed, Brunswick tells us, is possible only with this twofold repetition. Thus, because of the strong sense of reality that accompanied it, the patient's dream of solitary masturbation beside her sleeping husband is evidence of actual masturbation, past and present, a return Brunswick says, to the original situation. But another dream, this time transferential, follows it and reveals the fear of the consequences of masturbation: madness and the return to the asylum that she suspects the analyst is planning for her. Likewise, although the patient's dreams of hypertrophy of the male organ that will be returned to her correct her original theory of mutilation due to masturbation, the interpretation in terms of penis envy or castration anxiety is not possible right away. For, apart from a fleeting memory of castration anxiety following a threat by the sister, a threat that took effect only when it was associated with a prior screen memory in which the patient compared her genitals with those of an older brother, the remembered jealousy of the boy and the fear were immediately erased by a new denial of castration. This denial was supported by the conviction that the beloved sister was phallic, and it appeared in a series of transference dreams: a penis exhibition in which each woman received a man (hence a vagina) and a male organ; a dancing school where she learned feminine seduction while discovering that she had a penis; scenes of enuresis, in which the urine stood for a secretion similar to male ejaculate.

The dream that marked a turning point at the end of this first phase of analysis and a major change in the treatment is also a transference dream, one in which the patient is masturbating a female dog sitting in a chair, until her stepmother interrupts her. This dream reveals the patient's wish to be masturbated by the analyst, but here the analyst, identified with the patient who masturbates the dog, the anal animal of the stepmother who mistreats her, is also identified with the stepmother who refuses love, though the mistreatment is a form of attention in itself. This dream is a turning point for several reasons. First, it replays in the treatment what had been deciphered in a preceding dream (the patient stopped masturbating because she was coming to a session) but could be interpreted only after this repetition in a transference dream; there can be no renunciation of desire, Brunswick says, before this can be formulated and interpreted. At this time, then, the interpretation serves to improve the physical relationship of the patient and her husband. This dream is also important because it is the identification of the analyst with the stepmother that led Brunswick, in the analysis, to take the place of the persecutory object, the stepmother hated because she withheld love from the young woman.

What can we say about this first phase of the treatment? We found a confirmation, certain though indirect, of the initial "construction" in the dreams and screen memories dealing with masturbation, whether this was the result of seduction or a repetition of it. Moreover, Brunswick speaks of the patient's infantile sexual theories: the idea of castration as cutting off the male organ, or the idea that everyone has the phallus, especially the mother substitute—in other words, a refusal of the universality of women's castration. But what we do not find is the analyst's evidence for her inference of a connection between the fixation on phallic *jouissance* and the original seduction, a connection that the patient had hitherto been unwilling to grant. And the patient acknowledges neither her castration nor the connection between her delusional jealousy and her jealousy in the past, the latter having appeared in a screen memory from her third year, in which her sister, busy with the boys who surrounded her, threatened the little girl, who was trying to attract attention by masturbating. It is significant that, after the analyst explains why a child might be led to masturbate, the patient suddenly remembers her fascination, at the age of 2, with her older sister's pubic hair—black hair, though she had spoken of her admiration of the sister's beautiful blond hair, evidently a displaced admiration. Similarly, the dream of the man in black with the hairnet represented a male organ on a woman. If the patient is fascinated by pubic hair, the analyst says, this is because she thinks that a phallus is hidden behind it. Can we go further than Brunswick and infer that the belief in the phallic nature of the love object facilitates repression of both the threat of castration and the abandonment one experienced on the part of an Other?

If there is a discontinuity between this initial phase of the treatment and the three phases of paranoia, it can be located in the moment when Brunswick clearly realizes the extent to which one of the aspects of the transference (the love) could be an obstacle to the analysis and not a motivation for it. The "forcing" she then decides to implement in order to counter the resistance due to the positive transference is possible only because of her careful attention to the indications of this homosexual transference, whose risks she accepts. She knows, and tries from the beginning to warn the patient, that she can or must become the hated persecutory object, a substitute for the loved first object.

But, apart from this shift in the handling of the transference, we are actually more aware of the continuity in Brunswick's conduct of the treatment. There is continuity in technique, first of all, since, though she takes the risk of a transference psychosis, this is because she retains the model of the analysis of neurotics and the concept of the transference neurosis as repetition (cf. Freud 1914d). In "forcing" transference phenomena, she is following the same principles as in the analysis of neurosis in order to obtain the part of the material that she knows she is missing. And there is continuity with regard to the infantile material that emerges. Though there are qualitative changes (for example, the appearance of even earlier scenes in the patient's dreams and an increasing complexity), this only serves to confirm the relevance of the initial "construction." In this sense we can simplify her division of the paper by seeing not four but two phases of the treatment, if we consider that, with the "construction" and the first dreams that reply to it, we have the establishment of a puzzle, and if we consider that it is because Brunswick is looking for the missing piece that she takes note of the hate, the negative transference, and brings it onto the analytic stage. This enables her to interpret, the one by means of the other, both the repetition of the present conflict (the paranoia), which she must provoke, and the repetition of the infantile *jouissance* on which the patient is fixated.

If Brunswick acts so as to ensure that love will turn to hate, she does so because she has understood that the patient is repeating a privileged relationship to a feminine object whose sole concern she is (one of the patient's dreams involved her being the only one to come to the sessions), and that this prevents the reactivation of her past hostility and jealousy. When Brunswick risks the possibility of a repetition of delusional jealousy in the analysis, she does so on the basis of a theory of transference as repetition, but also because she was able to spot the indications, sometimes subtle, of ambivalence in the positive transference; if she has been assigned the role of the loved sister, she should also be able to take the place of the stepmother who stole the patient's husband from her. In calling the husband in for an interview, during which she asked the patient to wait for them, she assumed the role of the persecutory delusional object. Yet it is noteworthy that the initial reasons she gives for this act are rationalizations: she wanted to give the husband the opportunity to complain about his wife; in addition, in this case in which she emphasizes the patient's childishness, certain practical details had to be arranged with the husband, as in a child analysis. It is only after she states these pretexts that she characterizes her decision as a maneuver, a tactic whose essential motive is her feeling that the patient, gratified by reporting dreams in which she lacks nothing (possessing a male organ like everybody else, urinating standing up like a man), is preserving a delusional situation in the analysis.

The effects of the "forcing" are immediate. The patient forgets all her dreams in the first session following the maneuver and is late for the second, claiming that she had gone to the wrong street. In the third session, she overhears a telephone conversation in English that the analyst made before the session and is sure that the analyst wants to be rid of her, in complicity with enemies in her family. These family members are justified in their anger, since the patient had neglected her domestic duties, but she is convinced that she is surrounded by enemies, that everyone has it in for her. Here she reports a brief dream whose importance Brunswick stresses: a rooster is surrounded by hens and copulates with all of them in turn. The patient herself observes that her husband could be the rooster, though she says nothing further about his infidelities. At the same time, she stubbornly refuses to hear Brunswick's interpretation to the effect that the feelings ascribed to her are a projection of the patient's own anger onto the analyst. The patient asks to end the session early, to which, given the young woman's denial and inaccessibility, Brunswick agrees.

Only in the fourth session does the patient reveal some new feelings, to the astonishment of Brunswick, whose experience in the analysis of neurotics did not prepare her for the rapid changes found in psychosis. Now ready for analytic work, the patient says that the analyst's interview with the husband was what triggered her present crisis. Overcome by a wild jealousy, she had felt a panicky fear in which the outer world no longer existed; all she could hear was a terrible electric humming in her head, and she realized that she would have to kill herself. What surprises her the most, she now sees, is that it is not so much her husband as Brunswick who was the cause of her jealousy. Brunswick seizes on this remark to point out to the patient that her jealousy concerns her stepmother: she envies her husband the affection that she herself would like to have. Since the patient had suspected sexual relations between the analyst and the husband, as formerly between the stepmother and the husband, there is little difference between the transferential and delusional situations. Again we see that it is thanks to a double repetition (a new edition, in the transference, of old conflicts that had been repeated in the delusional jealousy) that the interpretation can have the effect it would not have had otherwise. This had been the case, up to now, with the interpretation the analyst had offered on the basis of the patient's declaration of hatred for men, who had robbed her of her sister. Brunswick's suggestion, that her stepmother had stolen her husband just as the boys deprived her of her sister, had gone unheeded.

The result of these interpretations is that the patient now understands the mechanism of projection that she had rejected in the preceding session, when she had attributed her own anger to the analyst, and she understands that her present feeling of relief makes possible the revelation of several transference fantasies whose similarity to early experiences she now recognizes.

Another effect of the "forcing" of jealousy in the transference is the appearance of hate for the husband who bears the phallus, possesses the penis that she does not have, with which he can seduce the woman she, the patient, loves. This hate is due to envy, as we see in a new dream of a masked ball, in which, as Brunswick interprets it, the patient reveals her rageful envy of the superior male genitals. As had happened earlier, the patient recognizes, and then denies, male privilege. After this clear revelation of penis envy, her material involves her masturbation with her sister, together with the *jouissance* she experienced each time, a *jouissance* that is refound as if in return to a situation in which she lacks nothing.

We may recall here how decisive for this treatment, based as it is on the analyst's reconstruction, are the confirmations or disconfirmations occurring in the material that the patient brings later on. The first confirmation that Brunswick gets at the beginning of the analysis has to do with the fixation on masturbation, as inferred from the presumed seduction. The second, whose implications she did not see right away but that she pointed out nonetheless, specified the phallic nature of the agent of seduction, the patient's dreams and associations pointing to a male organ on a female.

As we learn from this case, the threat of castration, insofar as it does not go beyond the patient's own castration (whether as an injury or, on the contrary, as hypertrophy of the male organ in dreams) does not seem to be crucial. And, I repeat, it is not coincidental that the "resistance" Brunswick saw in the first phase of the treatment was connected to the multiplication of dreams asserting the possession of male and female privileges at the same time. The screen memory concerning the little girl's fascination with her sister's pubic hair indicated that, though one may be castrated oneself, it is not necessary to accept the castration of the first love object. The sister remains phallic.

In this attempt to "force" repressed material that the patient was withholding, we can understand that the repression was mainly concerned with the castration of the primary object (who is also the real Other of the demand; cf. Lacan 1966, pp. 632, 824). The provoking of jealousy in the first phase of the paranoid transference also has the major effect of revealing the nature of the phallic value on which the patient is fixated. She envies her husband not so much because he is a man, equipped with male attributes, as because he has, or is, what is needed to suit the loved woman—indeed all women—as we see in the dream of the rooster possessing all the hens. Likewise, Brunswick tells us, the patient must have imagined that the boys who took her sister from her had something better to offer than what she could provide. She therefore fears that the analyst will prefer her husband, just like the stepmother who had always withheld her love from the patient, the daughter of the house.

The change in dream material that, in this phase, argues in favor of the reality of the original seduction stems from the new lifting of repression brought about by the interpretation of jealousy after it was reactivated in the transference. But what is especially evident in these dreams is the patient's wish to find or refind the lost *jouissance* and her own phallic value: in the sexual relations in these dreams, where the analyst, the husband, and the man in black substitute for the sister, the patient has what it takes to keep them, just as, since they are all bearers of the phallus, they have what it takes to satisfy her.

At the same time as the homosexual tonality of the transference is being confirmed in its two aspects of love and hate, the almost hallucinatory sense of reality that appears in a dream of masturbation with the sister, followed by a memory of a similar scene in actual experience, offers the first proof of the correctness of the construction Brunswick had suggested. There had really been an early seduction, the patient agrees, and the logical result of this, Brunswick says, is that the blame, instead of overwhelming the patient, was referred to the dead sister who had initiated the act. The sense of reality indicates that the content of the dream, in this case the seduction, is not a fantasy but a real event. And Brunswick adds, as a counterpoint to the vividness of the memory reflected in the dream and the patient's recollection of the sexual positions, that the older sister had seduced the younger one by masturbating her in order to teach the little girl how to masturbate her in return.

Though they are evident in the treatment, the patient cannot recognize the manifestations of hostility toward the analyst, whether because of the extreme defiance she shows Brunswick, or because of her blocking of associations, or her certainty that there is a conspiracy against her. Thus, when Brunswick speaks of the negative transference as the second turning point, I think she is describing not so much a new direction as the patient's resistance to surrendering material that, Brunswick will later say, was the most deeply repressed. At several points she calls it the homosexual nucleus that had not been touched up to that point, which seems problematical in view of the abundance of material that had already appeared and been interpreted in this sense. To be sure, it is hard to separate out what can be seen retroactively and what Brunswick describes as transferential signs of an increasing hostility in the course of the analysis. The patient, she tells us, can no longer avoid reacting to what she has now come to believe about the seduction. Proof of this is the failure of all of the analyst's later efforts to exculpate the sister by referring to her ignorance of appropriate behavior. These efforts were in vain on account of the patient's remorse for having approached the idea that the Other could be guilty and her feeling that, by acknowledging the sister's role in her current illness, she would be betraying her.

There are threats to the transference: a death wish on the part of the patient disguised in her uneasiness on the subject of the analyst's upcoming journey; the conviction of a plot being hatched against her by Brunswick and her staff, who are accused of suspecting her of theft (she states that *there could be something missing from its place* without the analyst's knowing it); an oversensitivity that makes the spacing of sessions necessary; absence or deterioration of dreams when the patient is not actually silent. The end of each session could be the end of the analysis. It is never certain that the patient will return, Brunswick says, and though her physical relationship with her husband has improved, this is partly because of the hostility toward the woman analyst. From this perspective, it is significant that, in the series of three dreams reported from this phase of negative transference, the first two can be seen as deceptive dreams and the third as a confession.

The first dream is about childbirth; the patient gives birth to a big blond child. Brunswick is the midwife and the husband is the father of the child. The analyst notes that the blond man (which the husband is in reality) is the successor to the blond sister. The child is thus the product of the phallic sister, now replaced by the husband. But, Brunswick says, we must not be deceived by the favorable appearance of a dream that suggests a possible cure—here, in the direction of heterosexuality. On the contrary, the deciphering of the latent content shows the persistence of the attachment to the first, female, object. The second dream is a heterosexual orgy to which the patient is invited by her sister. But here too a detailed examination shows that the ultimate meaning of this heterosexuality is the defiance of the traitor and revenge against her. In the third dream, the confession, the analyst appears as a phallic inquisitor who, threatening that she will withhold something promised, commands the patient to tell what she has kept hidden. The patient, in the session, then recalls something that, she says, she had almost forgotten: a time when, bereft of her sister and her childhood friend, she had gotten into the habit of masturbating female animals and was happy when, having introduced her finger into their vagina, she got the same quivering that she had observed in her sister.

Brunswick at first interprets this third dream as representing the double role, active and passive, assumed by every child, and especially by the little girl who is masturbating; such a child takes the active role of the father and the passive one of the mother with regard to herself. When the analyst explains this, the patient confesses the masturbatory episodes with animals, though, when asked, denies that she and her sister did such things with them, though the sister had taught her to masturbate in this fashion. To the question whether her sister had done the same thing with her, she replies in the affirmative: this had happened once, but she remembers that she then pushed her sister away, crying because of the pain she had felt. Noting the connection between the child's pain and the current sexual difficulties of the patient, Brunswick pursues her questioning—faithful, it seems to me, to the dream itself, which is a summons to a confession. How long has the patient recalled this form of masturbation, and why didn't she mention it before? As in the dream, the young woman recalls what she had never spoken of, namely that at the age of 5 she had come back home for a year, and it was at this time that the masturbation had taken this form. But she is not aware of her omission: she claims that she has indeed spoken of the year spent at home; as for the masturbation, not only did she always know about it, but she never denied it.

It is this transference dream that opens the way to a confession of the patient's experience, a confession reported as an association to the confessional dream. And the dream specifies two points that she has never mentioned before: the initiation into vaginal penetration, active and passive, but also the fact that, contrary to her initial claim that, against her will, she had been sent to the country between the ages of 4 and 11, she had in fact returned to spend a whole year at home. Though Brunswick does not say so, we may infer either an increased attachment, an attachment linked, if only in retrospect, to the gratification that the patient gave her sister even if she did not feel it herself, or an increased guilt that she could not confess. She again speaks of her great jealousy and her feeling that she could neither keep her sister, nor satisfy her, nor be satisfied by her.

Let us review the data. The intensity of the positive transference at the beginning of the treatment, had it not been countered in time, could have put a stop to the analytic investigation. When Brunswick brought the negative transference into play, the initial effect was the repetition of the jealousy and its eventual admission, preceded by manifestations of paranoia toward the analyst (certainty that the analyst had it in for her, was discussing her with others, and was trying to get rid of her). The analogy between the transferential situation and the delusional jealousy explains the nature of this jealousy. In Brunswick's admirable formulation, what causes the patient's hatred of men (rage against her husband in the dream of the masked ball, indifference to the death of the younger brother in a screen memory, hatred of the boys who monopolized her sister's attention) is that they have what it takes to seduce and retain the loved woman. This is certainly penis envy, but with a special feature: it pertains only to the wish to arouse and maintain the desire of the female object. The entire series of dreams in this phase, in which jealousy is reactivated, undoubtedly proved the reality of the seduction. But, I suggest, it also had the meaning of a return to the early situation of *jouissance* in which castration (of the sister, the analyst, the husband, the man in black) is once again denied together with the castration of the patient herself. The intensity of the transference was validated: Brunswick appeared regularly in these dreams as a substitute for the sister who had brought her to orgasm. We may conclude that it is this same transference, reduced to a mere repetition of the real of childhood *jouissance*, that caused the withdrawal from symbolization, the formulation of hostile feelings that the analyst had been expecting.

There are three points to keep in mind about the second of the phases in which paranoia, in the form of hostility, became more marked in the transference. The first point is the patient's persisting belief in the woman's phallus, a belief shown in the confession dream in which the analyst is a phallic woman. We may hypothesize that she believed and disbelieved at the same time, given her recriminations against Brunswick to the effect that she might be missing something. The second point is the assurance, in this confession dream, that she will be given what she was promised if she tells all. Note that this obedience to the fundamental rule of analysis (to say everything that comes to mind) is consistent with what Freud (1932–1933) says about the quest for the phallus, unconscious though it may be, in women who hope to be compensated by the analysis itself. The third point is the absence of protest when the patient is persuaded that she simply served the *jouissance* of the Other: her sister masturbated her only in order to be masturbated in return and later initiated her into vaginal penetration, despite the child's discomfort, only so that she herself could reach orgasm. The recollection and statement of these facts occurs without any anger whatsoever, either in the session in which they are discussed or the dream in which they are announced. We may infer that the patient thereby gained some value in the eyes of her sister.

The three dreams of this phase all have the same meaning: the impossibility of separation from the first object (feminine-phallic) and the repression of hate. Before the second dream (of the sister who draws her into the orgy) the patient believes herself to be to blame for her sister's syphilis, an illness she herself is afraid she has contracted. And although, at the end of the dream, she is angry at her sister for having contaminated her—made her "bad"—by forcing her to have sex with multiple unknown partners, the anger stays within the domain of the dream. The third dream (about perverse practices with animals) shows that her confession of abuses suffered or committed matters less than her having lost the attention of her sister when the latter turned her interest to others.

Where are we, then, at this point in the analysis? We have to agree with Brunswick that she has come to the end of her investigation. The full exploration of the repressed material seems to validate the initial construction. The traumatic seduction no longer seems to be a fantasy but a real event. The early sexual intrusion could be a sufficient explanation for the depth and the repression of the attachment to the first object. Moreover, all the additions in the course of the analysis itself have considerably modified, if not reversed, the initial assumptions. To take only the last example, the existence of early vaginal masturbation means something other than the masculinity indicated by clitoral masturbation: the denied vagina is not the unknown vagina but the repressed one (cf. Abraham's letter of December 26, 1924 in Freud and Abraham 1907–1926).

And the case has demonstrated that the patient's jealousy toward her husband is overdetermined. He is envied as bearer of the phallus, and the second dream reveals the wish to castrate him, for he appears as the third man in the dream: he has the same name and has a bald spot on top of his head behind which is a tuft of blond hair like that of the sister. The patient herself makes the analogy between the tuft of blond hair and her sister's brown pubic hair. Envied for the attributes she herself lacks (in the dream she robs him of them and saves them for her sister), the man is also envied as lover of the stepmother in accordance with the projection of the patient's homosexuality (it is not I who love her, but he; cf. Freud 1911). Finally, Brunswick notes that he appears in several dreams as a substitute for the sister, and so it is inevitable that he too is the object of the patient's jealousy: since she doubted the sister's fidelity, she doubts his as well.

Penis envy, as it is gradually explained in this case, is defined as a quest for the phallus more on the level of *being* than of *having* (cf. Lacan 1958a). One's own castration is nothing compared to the only castration that counts and that one denies, that of the first female object. As we see here, only the betrayal of the loved sister, her fault, could take on the meaning of castration for the patient, were she to admit it. Admitting it would mean recognizing that she had been neglected as a love object because she could not satisfy her sister's *jouissance*. The primary trauma has less to do with the early sexual intrusion, or even with the function of being the object of the Other's *jouissance*, than with the helplessness experienced in the face of the sister's vanishing desire that the patient could not retain. It has become clear in the dreams, where her history is played out instead of being remembered, that the husband has taken the sister's place. Going beyond what Brunswick says, we may infer that he was therefore called upon to reactivate this trauma and its traumatic consequence: the patient has already been unfaithful to her sister (with the older friend) in revenge for the abandonment.

The analyst emphasizes throughout that the injustice the patient felt she had committed toward her sister in agreeing to make her the instigator of the sexuality she condemns, or, worse, the one who is responsible for the patient's present distress, is the most severe resistance in the treatment. The patient had already borne the brunt of injustice when, as a child, she was accused by her playmate, and she likened this to the infidelity that continued to burden her. On the one hand, she was the guilty party, on the other, she was afraid to recognize guilt as coming from the Other. This infidelity on her part was just a shifting onto herself of what she attributed to the Other and did not want to see, even though in the dream of the orgy she took revenge, identifying with the dead woman who would pursue all the men. The unconscious infidelity, Brunswick is certain, is also the main motive for the intensity of the transference: the patient can be unfaithful to her sister through the analysis with a woman and the ensuing transference. The first betrayal comes from an Other; if, in this dream, the patient willingly followed the man who had brown hair like that of the analyst in the preceding dream, the man who led her into a house like the analyst's, she did so in order to avenge herself against the unfaithful one, either the sister or the husband.

Thus vengefulness and anger in response to this betrayal are represented on the stage of the dream but are withheld from repetition in the analysis. Isn't it the case that recognizing them would amount to admitting the abandonment—and the dephallicization—that befell her after the seduction? Here is where Brunswick locates the heart of the repressed homosexuality: there is something that the patient does not wish to see or believe. And, since Brunswick has noted the terms of the belief that the patient preferred to maintain in its stead, we can relate this to the screen memory from the opening phase of the treatment, in which, when the patient was 2, her sister forbade her to look at what she could not keep from staring at, namely the pubic hair that concealed the lack of the phallus, veiling both its absence and its presence. If the patient was so fascinated, Brunswick says, it is because she wanted to believe that a phallus was hidden there. Let us think ahead at this point. The decisive issue in the third paranoid phase, the phase that marks the completion of the analysis, will involve the same belief that is impossible to renounce. Brunswick will ask the patient whether the ultimate motive for her uncooperative attitude toward her analyst is the resurgence of this old anger against her sister, anger in which, up to now, she had always refused to *believe.*

In the first two paranoid phases of the transference (the jealousy and the negative transference), the signs of aggression were perceptible. However, before the anger ascribed to the analyst after the interview with the husband could be admitted by the patient as her own, there had to be an interval even after the interpretation was made. The patient likewise refused to acknowledge the death wish that Brunswick tried to explain to her as lying behind the concern she manifested toward the analyst. This shows how necessary it was for there to be at least two repetitions, first in symptoms and dreams, then in the transference, before symbolization and interpretation became possible. There is movement in both directions, since the dreams repeated what would then have to be replayed in the transference in order to be decoded and admitted, and certain transference phenomena preceded material that had to be repeated in dreams before the interpretation could be accepted. Thus the analyst was able to see the hate underlying the patient's unease. And we can go further on the basis of Brunswick's indications and conjecture that unconscious anger and revenge were also present in the suspicion of theft the patient ascribed to the analyst and her household. For she held to this suspicion; it was not at all certain, she stated in response to Brunswick's assurances, that she had not deprived the analyst of something. In this way she bore the burden of an original sin, along with its consequences in the form of the suspicion directed toward herself. And the criminal act that she complained of being accused of—without, however, denying responsibility for the actual damage done, whether or not it was visible—anticipated vengeance and retaliation: if she herself lacked something, then the Other, here the analyst, must lack it as well, even if the lack is not apparent.

As we have seen with the deciphering of the third dream (the masturbation of female animals) the patient's confessions did not lead to an accusation of her sister. On the contrary, they served only to revive her memory of her own deficiency. At issue is not so much jealousy, which had already been admitted, as the child's anger and hate toward the sister, who, after having seduced her and won her attachment, ended up betraying her. If this realization does not emerge, Brunswick shows, it is because the analyst has been emphasizing something else. The prominence of the delusional jealousy had led her to focus on the mechanisms of projection and on repressed homosexuality, relegating to the background the mechanisms of delusional persecution, although the analyst was aware of them. She finally comes to understand the delusion, because it happens that her overall aim was accurate, but it was the result she obtained that made her aware of what she had done, the means that had to be used, and what was involved in the patient's "refusal."

Following the revelation of the material on the sister's role (vaginal masturbation of the child in the service of her own *jouissance*), the patient persists in her blindness regarding any fault on the sister's part; she herself, she says, behaved in a perverse way. But she misses the next session with no pretext other than a sewing job to be finished for a friend of the analyst. Brunswick seizes on the flimsiness of this excuse to reproach the patient and, she says, to make the persecutory delusion come to the surface. How, she asks the patient severely, could she have offended her this way? It is she, the analyst, who ought to be angry. Or was she trying to make her jealous by paying more attention to a sewing job than to her analysis? Unless, she suggests, this was all about the old anger at the sister that she had always *refused to see* up to now . . . ?

It is at this point, where Brunswick goes beyond the process of projection, that we see how accurate she was in formulating what the patient had not been able to articulate for herself. The patient then relates the hallucination she had experienced the preceding day, at the exact time of her missed session. Sensing laughter in the street, she had thought she saw her sister mocking her as she had done back in the past when busy with the boys around her. She remembered that, at that moment, she had had a clear wish that the sister were dead.

With this clinical evidence, Brunswick recognizes that she ought to have taken into account what Freud (1911) said about Schreber: what the subject excludes or rejects returns in the real as a hallucination; what is abolished within comes back from without. Here the excluded hatred returns in the real in the form of persecution.

We then witness an astonishing comprehension of her delusional mechanisms on the part of the patient, at the same time
as the delusion itself resolves. She admits that she is, at present,
jealous of a young man who is in analysis with Brunswick and
who clearly represents her sister's male friends. And, Brunswick
says, the patient grasps the analogy between the current situation and the past one to the point where she can easily see that
she had turned to her stepmother, her father's second wife, to
take revenge on the sister who had abandoned her. It was just
at this later time that the stepmother had become a substitute
for the sister and an object of jealousy. And the patient finally
accepts the interpretation of the death wish toward the analyst
that she had formerly denied. She herself associates her symptoms (the humming in her head, her eyes popping out) with
her sister's madness, and she also understands that the feeling
she had, as a child, that she was being mocked was just her interpretation of what was in fact indifference toward her. At the
same time, and for the first time, the patient is freed from the
fits of helpless rage that she had experienced since childhood.
She is able to think calmly and without undue grief about her
dead sister.

Although, taken in itself, the account of the end of this analysis
leads us to see it as a successful treatment of a psychotic, Brunswick
is much less certain, as cautious about her therapeutic success as
about a diagnosis that she goes on discuss. In support of a cure,
however temporary, she reports that, at the time the case was
written up, there had been no relapse (in a year and three months
in the German edition, two years in the English edition prepared
later). The patient had adapted to her surroundings, having
satisfying physical relations with her husband and accepting the
behavior of her stepmother and mother-in-law, even though her
particularly unfavorable material and familial circumstances
remained unchanged. Though her husband's mother no longer
slept in the same bed as the young couple, the two women continued to share a bedroom, a kitchen, and the attention of a man
who did not conceal his preference for his mother. The husband's
undeniable neurosis had obviously had an effect on the young
woman's suspicions, Brunswick agrees; she had transferred to her

stepmother what she noticed about the neurotic link between her husband and mother-in-law. Her delusion thus had some basis in reality, since her mother-in-law constantly kept an eye on her. But Brunswick makes it clear that the fact that there were real reasons for jealousy or for the feeling of being observed did not prevent jealousy or a sense of persecution from becoming delusional.

Nevertheless, she says, the relatively short period of time without relapse does not allow us to say that the cure has been permanent, in that she does not preclude the possibility that the improvement was a final effect of the transference. We must also note the argumentative force of the last part of her paper, in which she sets forth not only the results she obtained but also the objections that might be raised, objections to which she replies. Moreover, she recognizes that she ended up in an unexpected place; thus, in retrospect, the fact that clinical evidence takes precedence over theoretical presuppositions explains the confusion we may experience in reading the text.

In assuming the risk of undertaking this treatment, Brunswick was interested in more than the mechanisms of paranoia in a woman. Given the uniqueness of this case, in which incestuous trauma played such a large role, she is not certain that repressed homosexuality is a regular feature of paranoia. She can only state, without generalizing, that even where the homosexuality in question does not have the typical form of active identification with the father but is a contingent and, above all, passive fixation on the early same-sex object, we see the development of a paranoid psychosis.

If we follow her argument, the first surprise is that the repressed homosexuality she had presupposed has nothing to do with the Oedipus. It is not a regression, an identification in place of love after the failure of the demand addressed to the father, but instead a fixation to the phallic female object and a developmental arrest. The second surprise is that Brunswick was able to resolve this psychosis by means of analysis. She herself is astonished at this result that goes beyond both her expectation and her ability to theorize what had occurred.

She is certain as to the facts. And this conviction, which she is not yet able to transform into knowledge, seems to me to account for the thoroughness with which she sets forth her analytic work. She wants to reproduce the facts in the real order or disorder in which they appeared, so as to retrace their exact sequence and their relation to each of her interventions. If she presents her results in the form of questions, we may suggest that she does so by choice and not out of ignorance or an inability to conduct the case herself. The procedure in which she sets forth the successive revelations in the treatment demonstrates the connection between her interpretations, her handling of the transference, and the resolution of a psychosis in the kind of patient for whom psychoanalysis had been thought to be ineffective. Her attempt to report the case with maximum transparency is intended to lead all her readers, not only Freud, to verify her findings on the basis of the evidence.

It is remarkable that she manages to transmit as generalizable clinical experience a case in which she might well have gotten stuck, given the discrepancy between her expectation and what she found, and that she is able to make sense of this in terms of both the need for a time of understanding and the need for technical modifications in view of the particularity of the case.

I should admit at this point that what interests me about this case is that it enables us to go beyond Freud in understanding some of the formulations that originate with him. For it seems to me that it is in this paper that the meaning of castration and the nature of the fantasy of the phallic mother have found clinical support and explanatory value for the first time, and this in a text that is not by Freud but by one of his students. Likewise, and paradoxically, it is with this case of a female patient in which the Oedipus is missing that I think we can better understand what Freud meant by the Oedipus and why he gave it a central role.

Let me explain. Although a concern to validate Freud's postulates orients Brunswick's work, what she discovers goes far beyond this aim. It is no longer a question only of illustrating certain concepts or implementing a technique, but, without her having intended this or even noticed it, of demonstrating indirectly the effectiveness of a way of thinking that Freud could not have developed except on the basis of clinical experience. But we must not forget Freud's relative discretion with regard to this case, though we may consider it to be decisive for the modification and radicalization of his positions between 1925 and 1931–1932 on the issue of femininity and the tie to the mother. In other words, we must explain the enigma of his not having stressed the implications of this paper, either for what he himself undoubtedly took from it beyond what he acknowledges, or for its clarification of basic notions that had been hard to grasp from the clinical point of view.

What does Freud say about this case? One sentence in the 1931 paper, two in the 1932–1933 lecture. He does not name Ruth Mack Brunswick in his references to the analytic literature on female sexuality at the end of the 1931 text. And although he refers to Brunswick's paper at the beginning of this article, he does so as an aside by way of illustrating his own insights. In the same paragraph he mentions the difficulty he has in getting an analytic grasp of the first tie to the mother that is so well repressed; he ascribes this difficulty to the paternal transference that he, as a man, evokes in women, who take refuge in the tie to the father. He contrasts this with the transference to a mother substitute that enables Helene Deutsch or Jeanne Lampl-de Groot to gain access to the preoedipal period when archaic repressed material relating to the mother returns in the treatment.

But he says nothing about the treatment that is most probative from this point of view, is entirely oriented to this type of homosexual transference, and is decided on the basis of such a transference. It cannot be a coincidence that the name of Ruth Mack Brunswick arises a few lines further on, but it does so in another context (the preoedipal fixation that Freud suspects is at the origin of paranoia). The entire 1931 paper makes us wonder why, where we would rightfully expect a reference to the work of this analyst, it never comes, whether Freud is talking about the intensity and duration of the first bond, the observation that some women never arrive at the Oedipus, or the obstacle to achieving the Oedipus posed by the original fixation on the maternal object.

And yet, when we read Brunswick, it is clear that it was her clinical experience more than any other that persuaded Freud to consolidate his position on the importance of this period that had been neglected up to then. We may recall that even in 1925 he was still speaking only of the prehistory of the Oedipus complex, a prehistory that he had first inferred from the persistent attachment of some women to their father, an attachment in which the wish for a child by him remains in full force. He had drawn the conclusion that the Oedipus is a secondary formation in girls, preceded by the effects of the castration complex. But, when he speaks of the tie to the father in the 1931 paper, he says that in cases where it is especially strong there was first a phase of exclusive and equally intense and lasting attachment to the mother that had been previously underestimated.

The strength of penis envy and onanism are now no longer the only elements that explain the difficulty of the passage to the father via the penis = child equation. Everything is displaced toward the point that has not been examined up to now, the primal attachment to the mother. Though there is support for this displacement in the clinical cases mentioned by Deutsch and Lampl-de Groot, it seems that the archeological metaphor used by Freud to characterize the intensity of repression and the depth of forgetting most nearly describes the effect produced by the material in the treatment Brunswick reports.

Don't Freud's silence about the formal and theoretical originality of Brunswick's observations and the brevity and incompleteness of his comments suggest why he misunderstands this case and its underlying theory of psychosis? For it is astonishing, when we read it, that it does not contain what is said to be there. What is ascribed to it—a theory of the origin of psychosis in the pathological tie to the mother—is not to be found, and this for two reasons. The first is that the source of psychosis and what causes its outbreak are very clearly distinguished. Although the origin comes from a fixation to the feminine-maternal object, the cause is more circumscribed: it involves marriage, the encounter with a man and with a sexuality that reactivate the original traumatic sequence of seduction, abandonment, and infidelity. The second reason is that the origin itself, in the pathological relation to the mother or her substitute, is specifically characterized by Brunswick. It is a fixation to a *phallic mother*. What has not occurred, therefore, is the intervention of a father or other third party as castrator of the mother (here, the sister) and bearer of the phallus. This valuable observation about the phallic mother needs to be added to Freud's statements in 1931 and 1932–1933: the oedipal situation presupposes the symbolic operation of castration.

Brunswick's demonstration, lacking in Freud, is primarily concerned with the connection between castration and the Oedipus. It proves that there can be no Oedipus, no access to what is can be desired and symbolized on the part of the father, as long as the first object remains untouched by castration but occupies the place of the phallic mother with feminine attributes (the beautiful blond hair) and masculine ones (the pubic hair concealing the phallus) at the same time. The persistence of the patient's infantile sexual theories is strictly dependent on this non-phallicization of the first love object. If she herself is castrated, this is because she was punished for masturbating. But this punishment is just her own and does not apply to all other women. Those others, who make fun of her, are obviously not afflicted by this weakness. And the first dreams show that the analyst, a fortiori, is presumed to have what the patient lacks (she is the foreigner who gives her her pants), since she occupies the place of the loved sister.

Neither an inventory nor a synthesis of the forms of the castration complex in women, Brunswick's article can be seen as a detailed clinical account of what is going on in a girl's refusal of castration. Let us recall the stages. There is a perception that at first has no effect, the screen memory in which the patient sees her little brother whose power of erection she admired. Then a castration threat coming from the sister after the patient had exhibited herself to gain her attention. The threat causes the perception of sexual difference to take effect. There follow the admission of her own castration and the hate for those who have a better lot than hers (the dead brother, the sister's male friends). But the process stops there. She refuses the generalization of this negative trait, especially when it comes to her sister.

We recall that she also refused to believe in any guilt on the sister's part. In this sense, the symbolic and imaginary registers of castration are correlated. And what Brunswick is aiming at in the treatment, with the recognition of the guilt of this incestuous Other and the hate that the patient should direct outward toward her instead of experiencing it as persecution, bears a strong resemblance to a symbolic castration of the lawless Other.

This *jouissance* of the Other threatens the subject much more than the castration that might come from a parent who has the phallus. This is exemplified in the dream of the rooster who claimed all the hens and in whom the patient recognized her husband: a figure of the unbridled *jouissance* of a primal father who possesses all women and all rights. It is not coincidental that this figure arose at the time when the analyst found that she had to reproduce the patient's delusional jealousy in the transference. The envied husband was the successor to the phallic sister who knew no limits, who, in her mental retardation and early prostitution, claimed all men for herself. The fantasy of the phallic mother and the myth of the father of the primal horde resemble each other in that they both show the lawlessness of *jouissance.*

Thus Brunswick has shown what castration is: it is what puts an end to the devouring *jouissance* of the Other, a fantasy that gives rise to anxiety that, as Melanie Klein emphasized again and again, is not the same as castration anxiety. And Brunswick has shown what the Oedipus is in relation to castration and *jouissance*: it is a recognition of the law, to which the mother herself is subject, in the mythical image of a figure coming between her omnipotent desire and the child's dependence. Paradoxically, this demonstration comes from the reverse direction, in a case where the Oedipus is missing. In sum, we arrive at an exact understanding of the Oedipus by way of its absence, that is, by way of psychosis.

Not only does this extremely detailed case render obsolete what Freud had been saying about the lack of material on the development of the girl, but it also proves that what he had been saying all along on this topic had come not, as he later claimed, so much as an inference from the boy's development as from the neurosis of women he had analyzed. What he lacked should be formulated in a different way. First, he did not have the opportunity to follow in detail the treatment of a woman that would show the extent to which the terms "phallic phase," "castration," and "Oedipus" are as relevant as for a man. Second, and above all, he did not see that the connection of these three elements is decisive for structure (that is, neurotic or psychotic), since it is the analysis of a psychosis in a woman that shows the link between the Oedipus and castration.

We can see how this contribution that goes a step further than Freud also goes beyond a mere play of concepts. Though the phenomena themselves could be conceptualized, their empirical proof goes further and "forces" theorization, showing where the ideas need to be extended or modified. It is clear, from this perspective, that it is this case—and this case alone, even without Brunswick's theorization of it—that reveals two levels of the relation of the subject to the phallus. The aspects of *being* and *having* are, to be sure, intermixed, and they sometimes alternate with one another. At the beginning, in the first phase of the treatment, the analyst tends to stress where the material relative to castration occurs on the side of *having* (imaginary possession or privation). Yet the other value of the phallus is legible in the screen memory of the sister who abandons the patient for others. Recalling her exclusion, the patient laments this abandonment more than the accompanying castration threat. The lament returns when the analyst tries to explain to the patient that the sister may well have withdrawn because, in devoting herself to prostitution, she was attempting to rid herself of the habit of masturbation that disgusted her. And the lament returns in the form of hate, displaced onto boys: the patient detests them, less for what they have than because, in taking away her sister, they threaten her with *being less.* She would no longer be, like the boys, an object adequate to the sister's desire.

The patient's comment that comes almost immediately after this interpretation, a comment about her mistreatment at the hands of her stepmother, is also understood in the register of *being* by the analyst: anything is better than being neglected. If there is masochism here, or regressive libidinization of castration (being beaten = being castrated), this is because it does not matter very much whether one has or does not have the phallus, is or is not castrated, as long as one still is something, even if that something is the stepmother's anal object, mistreated like a dog. This phallic value on the level of *being* a desirable object seems to me to be especially evident in the dream of the orgy. The identification with the phallic sister enables the patient to possess all the men, including those the sister preferred: she is not less than her.

This twofold aspect of the meaning of the phallus is not spelled out as such in Freud. There is a phase where, in her dreams, the patient passes from *being* to *having*, from the recognition of the sister's refusal of love as a sign of the patient's inadequacy (or castration) to the recognition of male privileges. This passage from *being* to *having* does not have a determinative effect, however, because the fleeting admission of a "more" in the other sex is soon doubly denied by the imaginary maintaining of the phallus in the female love object and by the patient's hate of men, not so much because of what they have as because they monopolize the attention of the sister or the loved woman. The problematics of penis envy and castration are displaced. What we clearly see here is that the problem for the girl confronted with her first (feminine) object is the same as for the boy: one has to be able to provide the *jouissance* of this Other, to have or to be what it takes to satisfy her.

In contrasting this case with the work of Jeanne Lampl-de Groot and with Freud's remarks, we may also note that phallic activity or wishes addressed to the sister are less important in this case than subjection to her *jouissance*. Brunswick explains this dependence on the Other's love and *jouissance* as an early excess of *jouissance*, an infinite nostalgia for a fusion that, from the beginning, makes the child a fulfilling or an inadequate object (cf. Lacan 1958b, p. 198).

Another example of what this empirical report contributes beyond what theory could provide has to do with maternal prohibition and with the superego that, according to Freud, is weaker in women than in men. Though Brunswick was not looking for this, we see it in the twistings and turnings of the treatment. We may recall that what Brunswick was trying to do was, above all, to verify whether the thesis of repressed homosexuality could be sustained in a case of female paranoia. Her models here were Freud's "A case of paranoia running counter to the psycho-analytic theory of the disease" (1915a) and certainly "Some neurotic mechanisms in jealousy, paranoia, and homosexuality" (1922b). We must agree with Freud's reasoning in the 1915 case: if the mother of childhood is really the original persecutor behind the figure of an older superior with the same white hair as the young woman's mother, a figure herself overlapping with that of the lover, the originary fantasy that we can discern in the chance incident (the click that disturbed their lovemaking) has to do with the guilt of oedipal identification of the lover with the patient's father, the patient herself with her mother, overheard by a third party.

Now, what is evident in the case analyzed by Brunswick is that the oedipal configuration—having coveted the place of the mother in order to be possessed and loved by the father—is not necessary for the feeling of having betrayed the first love object. If the subject imagines that she was at one time able to satisfy the mother or her substitute, then seeking this gratification with another object, whether from spite, vengeance, or nostalgia, is itself enough to bring on guilt. The inference we can draw from this clinical case gives a new dimension to the maternal prohibition of *jouissance*. Any turn to another object, male or female, would constitute a betrayal of the mother, the first object to whom one must be wholly devoted; hence the remorse and guilt connected with sexuality.

Brunswick provides clinical evidence both for the validity and coherence of Freud's postulates on female sexuality and, beyond his reconsideration of the girl's tie to her mother, for his obstinacy in maintaining concepts inappropriate to femininity.[1] But I was able to see this only through a process of analysis in the chemical sense; that is, I had to decompose and recompose the elements of the case before I could see how Brunswick obtained her results through a certain way of handling the treatment, and how this related to points I had emphasized though Brunswick was not interested in them. In this sense, my reading of the case is not aligned with the chief concerns of the analyst who experienced it directly.

The facts are mentioned by Brunswick, but often in the form of separate ideas, as yet unconnected. Thus, although she orients the treatment in the direction of a symbolic castration of the Other, she does not explicitly theorize the impossibility of hate for the first object (the phallic sister), the patient's fixation in unconditional love for her, and the refusal to see her as castrated, as lacking. The reader is left to infer the connection between the attachment and the refusal of castration and to theorize it on the basis of the effects of the treatment, which have to be reassessed. But it is necessary to do this, since, at the end of the analysis, there is a definite possibility of separation from the sister and from the analyst, which suggests that something on the order of castration has taken place. We can discern this castration in what is in effect a replication of the sister's death, once that death is symbolized in the retroactive confession of hatred (the hallucinated death wish). The recognition of hatred, which up to than had been denied, entails the recognition that the love object is at fault, dethroned from her omnipotence. We know that this is true because, when the patient agrees that her sister was guilty and hence is no longer phallic, there is an end to the persecution coming from an Other who enjoys without fear of sanction.

Thus I have examined Brunswick's case in terms of multiple cross-references between, on the one hand, the 1928 paper (which does not focus of issues of femininity) and the 1940 paper, and, on the other hand, what Freud says about the earlier text, those allusions that are so minor in comparison with what he does not say, although, as I reread him, he was heavily influenced by Brunswick in his change of position in 1931 and 1932–1933.

Freud's discretion, the meagerness of his praise, indeed, his injustice when we consider the clinical richness of the material his student presented in 1928, leads me to wonder how the case report might have caused this reaction. It is obscure on first reading, and the connections between the analyst's interpretations and their effects are often unclear. The fact that Brunswick makes certain comments only later on and, at other times, anticipates material yet to appear disturbs the linear exposition. And it was possible to see these formal defects as indicative of an implicit discussion with Freud: unlike Freud, Brunswick did not feel the need to spell out each point that she set forth, since her primary reader could be presumed to know what was at issue. Similarly, the fact that she states her uncertainty about the results of the treatment, preserving its experimental character, could be seen as a request for supervision addressed to Freud. Despite her clinical astuteness and the confirmation she got in the treatment itself about the validity of her decisions, one might reproach her for not being able to do without Freud's approval. Her thematization of the material in the first part of the case report, instead of orienting her readers and making them aware of her approach, thus has the effect of diluting and devaluating the part that is her distinctive contribution and innovation; we lose the thread of the construction that she is so intent on making (though its aims are made clear at certain points).

Moreover, although we do not attach so much weight to this possibility today, it may be that Freud had a role in the conduct of this analysis. This is suggested by the indications, in the case report, of a request for approval that Brunswick is addressing to Freud more than to others in the analytic community. From this perspective, what at first seemed to be a wrongful appropriation, on Freud's part, of the results of a treatment conducted by someone else takes on a different meaning: he supervised more than he lets on, and thus we may add to his statement, in the 1931 paper, that he has not yet seen such a case through to completion the qualification "except indirectly, through Ruth Mack Brunswick." Likewise, his reticence about the case and the diagnosis could be explained by the proximity of their work. Perhaps he had nothing further to say, or his reconsideration of his earlier hypotheses also entailed a reconsideration of hypotheses so closely connected to his own.

But this closeness between Freud and Brunswick lost its explanatory power for me when I realized the discrepancy between the implications of the 1928 paper—the very paper, and, in my opinion, the only paper, that puts an end to all the challenges to Freud's conceptualization of femininity—and Freud's restrained reaction to it. For Brunswick, as for Freud, her report was simply a confirmation of a phase of archaic dependence on the mother. Brunswick herself did not emphasize the demonstrative force of her paper any more than Freud did. It remains for us, then, to go further. The closeness that may have caused Freud's silence is not so much Freud's silence toward his student as Freud's silence toward his own statements and Brunswick's toward hers.

In this sense, my thesis that a retroactive effect is an integral part of the theorization of facts or of clinical experience is especially relevant here. A certain distance is necessary between experience and theorization. What we take from this text is not what the author foregrounds and goes far beyond Freud's reading of it. It has been hard for us to orient ourselves in Brunswick's case report, because we are too far from it, having brought later theory to bear on it, while Freud underestimated it because he was too close to it. Brunswick's 1940 paper confirms this need for a time of understanding. This paper is, in part, an effect of the 1928 article. As Brunswick says herself, it is the result of work begun in 1930 in collaboration with Freud, the point of origin being her study of a case of delusional jealousy that had unexpectedly provided a great deal of information on a hitherto unknown period, the preoedipal.

Note

1. There was a lively polemic in Freud's own time concerning some terms he used: "castration" (cf. Jones 1927); "phallic phase" (cf. Jones 1932); "primacy of the phallus" (to which some contrasted the early awareness of the vagina and thus of the innate "femininity" of the little girl in place of her native "masculinity," as claimed by Karen Horney, Melanie Klein, Josine Müller, and Ernest Jones); and primary or secondary "penis envy" (cf. Jones' [1932] distinction between the protophallic and deuterophallic phases). This polemic is customarily regarded as a dividing line between Freud and Jones (cf. Chasseguet-Smirgel 1964), but I would see the issue differently. Jones seems to me to be following Klein, or even Horney, on these matters.

22 Primitive Identification and Castration

The term "preoedipal" became necessary following Ruth Mack Brunswick's clinical observations (1928a), and, in her 1940 paper, "The pre-oedipal phase of the libido development," she claims to have been the first to use it. It is true that it does not appear as such in the German text, but it occurs twice in the English-language version. Moreover, the need to rethink the girl's relation to her mother, and especially the process and meaning of the mother's castration, had its origin in the first version and, as we see very clearly in the 1940 paper, converged with the work of Melanie Klein, shifting the issues through its puzzling finding of the fixation of the subject in a passive position. As Brunswick noted in her conclusions, what seemed to involve activity in the patient's masturbation of female animals was instead a repetition of a situation that had been experienced passively—specifically, we may add, in the patient's submission to her sister's requirements. This contrast of passivity and activity (and the alternation between one and the other) takes on an additional meaning once we no longer think of it in terms of the analogy with femininity and masculinity that bothered Freud, but in relation to the primordial activity of the mother as the reverse of the original passivity of the child. From this point of view, if we investigate what became pathological in the patient described in the 1928 case, we may be able to define what is "normativizing" in the passage to activity, what activity involves, and why it is necessary. What the 1940 paper newly affirms is essentially this: for every child, boy or girl, the necessary and normativizing activity comes about through the primitive identification with the active mother.

Once we recognize that the basis of the 1940 paper is the clinical problem that arose in the case reported in 1928, it is no longer justified epistemologically or historically to discuss the two texts independently of one another. The only reason to consider the two separately is that, in the first of them, the notion of the pre-oedipal, the prehistory of the Oedipus complex, is not the point of departure. Brunswick comes upon it, but she was not looking for it. In the second paper, however, it is precisely this concept that she is trying to situate and legitimize. Right from the outset, she is seeks to justify the creation of a new term instead of simply modifying those already available, for example, *active Oedipus complex* toward the mother, *passive Oedipus complex* toward the father.

As we have seen, the two papers are close to one another, and this is also true insofar as they both qualify Freud's statements of 1931 and 1932–1933. The echo of the shared thinking of Freud and Brunswick in the 1930s is undeniable in Freud's need to specify, in 1932–1933, that the girl's penis envy is to be located between the desire for a child from the mother and the desire for a child from the father, the latter coming afterwards and presupposing the mother's castration, in other words, the recognition of the father as bearer of the phallus. Brunswick, for her part, notes in the 1940 paper that the active wish for a penis (the wish to possess one) and the passive wish for it (to receive it from a man) come from the same source, the first relation to the mother: one wants both to have a penis for her and to get one from her. Another point that may reflect their common work is Freud's view, from 1931 on, of the girl's first identification with her mother as active, an identification with the mother's activity toward her; thus doll play is in no way a proof of early femininity in the sense of an awakening of maternal feelings, but, on the contrary, in its reversal of roles between mother and child shows that the role of the father is not at all recognized and is of no importance at this stage. The further explanations Freud offered in the 1932–1933 text regarding the girl's masculinity complex are in accordance with this view: the masculine identification can be understood either as identification with the father (a regressive identification after the failure of the Oedipus, or the transient one that every girl experiences after she becomes aware of her mother's castration and refuses it), or as an identification with the phallic mother.

It is difficult to determine the extent to which these are Brunswick's notions or Freud's own. For example, everything having to do with the sexual nature of the child's reaction to his mother's physical caretaking—the mother's role as the first seducer who is blamed for later prohibiting what she herself at first aroused—is amply developed in Brunswick's paper. Even if they did not come first, what suggests that her formulations were at least contemporaneous with those of Freud, not just a repetition or redeployment of them, is that she reports in the 1928 paper (and Freud alludes to this in 1931) that the child's rage reaction to enemas inflicted on him, enemas experienced as a rape, are the regressive anal equivalent of genital orgasm. Such a reaction, in my view, may explain the otherwise incomprehensible rage of the patient in the case report of 1928: this was a similar regression, since, as we saw, Brunswick locates the libidinization of the stepmother's mistreatment in the anal register in which orgasm can be misrecognized.

Freud's two papers on femininity were certainly influenced by the work of Ruth Mack Brunswick, and we must not give credence to the impression that she is merely repeating what Freud had written more succinctly but more firmly in 1931 and 1932–1933. Still, this might be true in the sense that, at the time Brunswick was preparing the final edition of her old notes for the 1940 piece, Freud's papers had already been published years ago, though, conversely, what Freud presents so concisely in these years is strongly influenced by their shared reflection following the publication of Brunswick's clinical case in 1928. In Brunswick's 1940 paper, part of the theorizing of the exclusive relation to the mother recalls earlier ideas put forth by Freud, and the very construction of the piece shows the effects of Freud's prior publications.

The paper has two phases. In the first, Brunswick logically and chronologically situates the preoedipal in relation to the Oedipus, the difference between them being the passage from dependence and passivity vis-à-vis the active, phallic mother to independence and activity through identification with her. In the second, she explains this preoedipal period as an exclusive relation to the mother in which there is no triangulation as yet, the father being regarded as a rival while the child is passionately attached to the mother.

But the connection between these two aspects is not presented in the form of a demonstration. It is as though the priority of Freud's publication had become a priority of ideas that Brunswick no longer has to prove or demonstrate. Thus we do not find here what is constantly present in Freud, namely the concern to persuade a reader or listener, to set forth a train of reasoning for someone. This dimension of address was perceptible in Brunswick's 1928 paper, where she asked questions, answered them, and argued her positions. There is nothing of the sort in the 1940 text. Though it does not lack rigor, we might say that it is missing a certain vitality. For, if it were really a question of reconsidering the Oedipus as the core of neurosis, as had been the case nine years earlier, these high stakes would have called for more enthusiasm. But in the absence of a progression in reasoning, we lose a sense of how much is at issue and how deeply Brunswick is engaged in it.

The rhetorical weakness of the paper is all the more regrettable because in other ways its theorization is quite precise. A simple shifting of emphasis is enough to shed new light on familiar statements, as when Brunswick points out that, while the girl must give up one sexual object for another and one genital for another, the boy also has a hard task, in that he must change not his love object or sex organ but his attitude toward his first object, his mother. Thus the originally passive boy must, if he is to be healthy, develop an active mode of relating to women. Another important point is Brunswick's drawing a connection between the active Oedipus, which concerns the mother for both sexes, and the interest in the parents' sexual relations, that is, in the role of the father, the third party who drives the child away from the exclusive relation to the mother: as soon as the boy's or girl's active Oedipus is established, parental intercourse becomes a matter of intense interest and jealousy. In addition, there is a similarity between the girl's passive Oedipus and that of the boy, in that it is always addressed to the father. And we must note the special significance attached to the girl's penis envy (the girl's realization that, without the penis, she is unable to win her mother) and to her consenting to be castrated by the father or to libidinize this castration. She accepts it because she has made the right choice: an object who is guaranteed to posses the penis and whose love makes castration worth the price.

And we must not forget that this 1940 paper is so striking in the way it clarifies some Freudian concepts that it is easy to forget its connection to the 1928 piece, even though that text is mentioned at the beginning. And, as I have noted, this is the only text that shows us what we are up against in the Kleinian concepts of archaic anxieties and aggression against a devouring and castrating mother. This effect of interpretation of one text on a series of others, thanks to one or two formulations, is no doubt coincidental and subjective. How does it manage better than any other contribution, including Freud's, to explain what is much more alien to our way of thinking than the Oedipus, namely the meaning of castration—specifically, the castration that is not attained by the primal mother with whom Melanie Klein is concerned in her child analyses?

Brunswick first states the facts about the passage from passivity to activity, and she relates them to other facts, such as the coinciding of the child's aggressivity and his gaining independence from his mother. Then she locates the facts in a reconstruction of development before she spells them out conceptually. The result of this change of libidinal position, in which the child substitutes activity for passivity (gradually doing for himself what the mother had done for him), a change that is strongly fought for, is that the mother becomes less necessary, if not superfluous, and all her injunctions and prohibitions are felt as threats to the newly acquired activity. She is threatening because of all the restrictions she places on the child and because of the omnipotence he ascribes to her: she can do everything, and she possesses everything that is desirable. This idea of maternal omnipotence, Brunswick says, lasts up to the end of the preoedipal period, at which time the child recognizes sexual difference and the mother's castration. Thus the concept of castration takes on a new intensity. It not only defines the lack of the male organ, an imaginary defect associated with the infantile notion of coitus, but it is also a symbolic limit. Yet the two registers are interdependent, since it is insofar as the mother is imaginarily deprived of all the enviable traits that had been attributed to her that she no longer has all power and all rights. Thus castration marks the end of the mother's omnipotence, the limit set to her whim, the law imposed on the unbridled, devouring *jouissance* of the first object on whom one is dependent.

It is surprising that, at this point in her definition of terms, Brunswick does not refer to the clinical experience that proved the necessity for conceptualizing castration in these two registers, imaginary and symbolic. Surprising, that is, only if we ignore the difference between, on the one hand, clinical data and the conduct of a treatment and, on the other, the theorization that can come only afterwards. Surprising only if we forget that the symbolic castration that, in my view, Brunswick tried to bring on in this treatment of paranoia in a woman was immediately apparent to us as such. But I have stressed that it took me a long time to perceive it in the fault of the sister that Brunswick was trying to get the patient to acknowledge, and even then I risked this interpretation only to the extent that Brunswick herself notes the elements that indicate the imaginary rejection of the sister who substituted for the maternal object. And I was assisted by the conceptual cross-referencing of both papers one to the other, the effect of later formulations on the clinical observation that preceded them and the clinical assurance that oriented the later theorization. Perhaps this is the answer to our question about why it is Brunswick who sheds light on the concept of castration for psychoanalysis and for the conduct of a psychoanalytic treatment: her speculations are entirely based on the clinical experience that she is so concerned to understand and transmit.

But how, beyond Freud's omission, are we to explain the lack of effect on the analytic milieu in general of these two papers of Brunswick's on femininity and the role of the mother? The 1928 paper is mentioned as a reference to Freud, a student's work that illustrates the validity of a theory already put forth by him. As for the second paper, perhaps it appeared too late for Freud's approval, or other analysts sensed a reticence on Brunswick's part in deferring publication, or the debate on femininity in the preceding decade had lost its currency.

The first paper has become canonical without being considered in its own right, and hence it has been open to misunderstanding. The other has always been neglected, despite the fact that it alone provides a rigorously Freudian account of the tie to the first (maternal) object. Why should this be so?

It seems to me that an initial reason for this lack of influence on the part of the student who worked most closely with Freud is a problem of belief, as when we too automatically place faith in the judgment of a master, even if that master is Freud. If, as it seemed, Freud "displaced" silence regarding an as yet unpublished text (the work he had undertaken together with Brunswick) onto another, the "Supplement to Freud's 'A history of an infantile neurosis'" (Brunswick 1928b) that had already appeared when he mentioned it in 1937, we can understand how this may have been interpreted as a repudiation. Similarly, if all along there has been an inadequate understanding of the full import of Freud's views on femininity in 1931 and 1932–1933, isn't this because the texts he mentioned have not received the attention they deserve? The more or less doctrinal way in which he presents these views can lead the reader to forget that the results obtained from clinical experience are the fruit of hypotheses, disagreements, and controversies to which he was attempting to being clarification. In giving him credit in advance, we were not able to grasp the issues in the debate, his reasons for privileging one point or the other. We lost the sense of his approach and the advance it represents, because we did not examine the context of his theoretical efforts.

But the very fact that he makes decisions and takes sides in accordance with his experience of the validity of this or that contribution shows the scientific nature of his method. He retains only what interests him, refutes what contradicts the results he trusts on the basis of his clinical work and his theorization of the facts, and does not bother to criticize what seems unimportant to him.

His 1931 paper on femininity, where the papers he criticizes are mentioned only at the end, cannot be interpreted solely in terms of strategy. Freud reversed the usual order of debate, in which the logical argumentation of one's position is deployed first in order to anticipate and negate any possible objections. But this strategy of avoiding polemics, if it is indeed a strategy, has another aim. What Freud is concerned to do in 1931 is to note the gains that have been made, even though they are as yet limited in scope and all has not been said. His theoretical standpoint represents a consideration and a selection of the hypotheses of others as well as his own, and it is in no way presented as the ultimate and irrefutable truth. He backs up his statements with evidence and argument, but the firmness of his tone and the choice of a subjective form of utterance (the "I" that he uses) are not inconsistent with his awareness that the contributions he mentions have, taken together, served to modify his initial proposals.

The second reason for the relative silence surrounding Brunswick's papers has less to do with belief or transference (unconditional love for the presumed knowledge of the founder) than with the way knowledge is gained and constituted in psychoanalysis. Though some contributions have been forgotten and others retained, the fact that a given disagreement or deviation is anticipated (as Freud does) or is explained after the fact (as I am trying to do) should not be seen as disparaging the approach it represents, however risky, confused, or even mistaken it may seem to be later on. That approach may turn out to be more fruitful for general reflection, and for the emendations it made possible, than other works that, at first glance, were more rigorous and more orthodox but only confirmed what was already known without offering anything new.

The papers of Ruth Mack Brunswick are exemplary in this regard, since they show the problems of fidelity both on the level of reception in the analytic community and on the level of theorization. As long as we assume that they offer only what Freud says about them, and that this is all we need to know, we will not see what is there. And if the quality of the student reflects more on the master than on his disciples, one may neglect papers that seem to reflect discredit on him.

Is some form of overt polemic or discord necessary for the exercise of thought? Why does fidelity seem so ineffective or even sterile? Clearly stated opposition arouses interest and calls more systematically for a response. Thus, paradoxically, error can be productive at first, on the epistemological level and also strategically. This productivity may be more evident, in the short run, than the finesse and subtlety of shifts that, concealed by fidelity, can be assessed only later on. This is why the prejudices and the misapprehensions or incomprehensions of one or the other colleague were more useful in stimulating Freud to refine his thought than the applied work, however intelligent, that merely extended and confirmed what he had already formulated—which is what he says about Ruth Mack Brunswick.

Afterword:
How the Meaning of
the Oedipus Changed

When it comes to the debate on female sexuality, the liberties of style and the form and simplicity of the questions asked by the analysts who were pupils or contemporaries of Freud in the years from 1915 to 1930 can seem surprising to us today. A statement by Freud, or by a colleague, was not necessarily taken as the ultimate truth that called only for exegesis but instead as a stimulus, a call for verification or contradiction. Contributors set out with their own issues, based on clinical experience, and, in a sense, were not overly concerned about the orthodoxy of their proposals. It thus became clear that, though Freud advanced what seemed to be new concepts, this was partly due to what came back to him from his pupils, inviting him to think about his initial reflections, about what might be missing or confusing, what had to be modified in view of the responses he was getting. This reflexive return was inspired by the discrepancies he noticed among his own remarks, those of his near disciples that did not seem very far from his, and the use to which these were put, sometimes very different from what he had intended.

On the other hand, we surely must see this period as one of great fecundity, when every research effort could make a contribution and take on meaning. This is true for Freud, who found a way to reassert his positions or to correct them on the basis of the misinterpretations to which they led certain colleagues, but it was also true for others, who took what seemed best to them as long as the theoretical edifice was not so much a dogma as a construction to be explored and enriched. Any sanctions, whether from the analytic community or from Freud himself, did not have the weight in those years that they may have had before or afterwards. This is so because, if Freud felt any reservations or disagreement, he was careful to justify them; what he rejects, he says, does not correspond to what he himself has encountered. The nuance may be a rhetorical one, but it made a difference: disagreement was not stigmatized as blindness. Jones's and Horney's papers after 1931 is proof of this, and we may add that they illuminate, if only by insisting on misunderstanding it, what Freud had not yet redefined in a convincing way.

Moreover, it may be that sometimes the very failure to be acknowledged by Freud lends substance to an analyst's work. Consider the broad extent of Melanie Klein's efforts, in which, though she had to pay a price, she never yielded on the issues she had staked out for herself, and compare it to the thinness of production of the equally talented Ruth Mack Brunswick after she was no longer sustained in her exclusive address to Freud. In this little drama of psychoanalysis, the transference must come to an end and one must step forth as oneself, with no guarantees. This can lead to an injustice in the short term, when we consider that it was Brunswick's two papers that enable us to sort out confusion. I have stressed how useful I found the later one, dated 1940, especially with regard to the castration of the mother as marking the end of her omnipotence, in shedding light on what I had not understood when reading Freud, and in showing that Freud and Brunswick were not deaf to the objections of Melanie Klein: he redefined the Oedipus, she focused on the primitive identification with the mother. And it was only through Brunswick's clinical report of 1928 that I could really make sense of Freud's insistence on the soundness of the notions of the phallic phase, castration, and the Oedipus in theorizing the reconstructed development of the girl and the boy alike. This detailed exposition of a case made it clear, in retrospect, how meaningful these concepts are as reference points of psychic structure and diagnosis.

Freud was the first to call attention to his mistakes, his prejudices, and his difficulties in seeing what was involved in the development of the girl. Thus it is paradoxical that he has been reproached for what, in a way, he predicted himself in trying so hard to offer the necessary modifications without retreating from the reconstruction he had in mind. This paradox can be explained by the context of the ten years between 1925 and 1935, when psychoanalytic thinking about female sexuality was following the paths that Freud had previously marked out between 1915 and 1925. But his colleagues resisted what he had gradually been suggesting. For the most part, they did not understand what Freud (1923b) called the castration of the mother and the primacy of the phallus. A fortiori, they rejected the idea of the girl's penis envy (even its "positive" side, as Karen Horney pointed out in 1926) and the period of identification with the father that Freud described as necessary for the passage from masculinity to femininity. We must note that he does not liken penis envy to a masculinity that would be harmful to the girl; for him, it is female desire par excellence.

I have tried to show how the resistance to this conceptualization of the woman's castration complex came about on the basis of the hypotheses of another analyst, Abraham, to whom I gave a central place on account of a single page taken from a text that Freud does not mention, though almost all the analysts he cites in 1931 refer to it. This silence seemed to me to represent a criticism on Freud's part, which suggested to me that the debate on femininity had to be refocused. It was not, as has always been said, played out between Freud and Jones but between Freud and Abraham. I ventured to see this criticism of Abraham by Freud as the source of a series of omissions, imprecisions, and errors in his concise summaries of other analysts' papers at the end of the 1931 paper on female sexuality. Thus I saw this paper of Freud's not as the final stage of his discoveries but rather as an attempt, albeit an indirect one, to respond to and critique the contribution of each colleague. I found here an effort to recapture what he felt had escaped him, if only because the theorizations of femininity that referred to the developmental reconstructions and "fictions" proposed by Abraham ran the risk of forgetting the only direction in which analytic thought can be applied: as deduction from effect to cause, not vice versa.

The reference to the works of others in 1931 no longer has the same meaning it did at the time when, having just emerged from his splendid isolation, Freud knew that everything was still coming from him. From now on, he can no longer refocus or readjust to his own way of thinking what has been developed in the work of others. The contributions he mentions no longer have the status of confirmations that he can integrate into his own texts. On the contrary, they indicate the diversity of perspectives and the process by which truth is recognized in psychoanalysis: as a correction of prior errors. Error can persist despite the possibility of knowledge, or beyond the localized emergence of this knowledge, because it is related to repression, one of the pillars of the edifice of psychoanalysis. And the truth can emerge only if one is prepared to reckon with the time needed for the work of the unconscious.

Thus I have tried to explain that the continued misunderstanding of Freud's views on femininity stems from the lack of the distance and time required for working through (*Durcharbeitung*). Freud's contemporaries could have avoided this kind of haste in drawing conclusions only if they had been able to grasp the epistemology that Freud himself came to discern only gradually. We too needed time, and certainly—whether we realized it or not—we also needed the effect of Lacanian theorization.

Why do women love men and not their mothers? This is what Freud was asking when he understood that the attachment that the girl, like the boy, has to undo is an attachment to the mother, and that this fact no longer allows us to conceptualize her love for the father on the model of the boy's love for the mother. The Oedipus has taken on a new meaning: for both sexes, it is now the relation of active love directed toward the mother.

References

Abraham, K. (1916). The first pregenital stage of the libido. In *Selected Papers of Karl Abraham*, trans. D. Bryan and A. Strachey, pp. 248–279. London: Hogarth, 1927.

—— (1917). Ejaculatio praecox. In *Selected Papers of Karl Abraham*, trans. D. Bryan and A. Strachey, pp. 289–298. London: Hogarth, 1927.

—— (1920). Manifestations of the female castration complex. *International Journal of Psycho-Analysis* 3:1–29, 1922.

—— (1924). A short study of the development of the libido, viewed in the light of mental disorders. In *Selected Papers of Karl Abraham*, trans. D. Bryan and A. Strachey, pp. 418–501. London: Hogarth, 1927.

Aparicio, S. (1985). Les psychoses dans la psychanalyse freudienne. Dissertation, Université de Paris.

Braunschweig, C. M. (1926). Zur Genese des weiblichen Über-Ichs. *Internationale Zeitschrift für Psycho-Analyse* 12:163–184.

Breuer, J. and Freud, S. (1893–1895). Studies on hysteria. *Standard Edition* 2.

Brunswick, R. M. (1928a). The analysis of a case of paranoia (delusions of jealousy). *Journal of Normal and Mental Diseases* 4:70–95, 1929.

—— (1928b). A supplement to Freud's "A history of an infantile neurosis." *International Journal of Psycho-Analysis* 9:439–476.

—— (1940). The pre-oedipal phase of the libido development. *Psychoanalytic Quarterly* 9:293–319.

Chasseguet-Smirgel, J., ed. (1964). *Female Sexuality*. Ann Arbor, MI: University of Michigan Press, 1970.

Cottet, S. (1982). *Freud et le désir du psychanalyste*. Paris: Navarin.

Deutsch, H. (1925). The psychology of women in relation to the functions of reproduction. *International Journal of Psycho-Analysis* 6:405–418.

—— (1930a). The significance of masochism in the mental life of women. *International Journal of Psycho-Analysis* 11:48–60.

—— (1930b). Der feminine Masochismus und seine Beziehung zur Frigidität. *Zeitschrift für Psycho-Analyse* 16:172–184.

—— (1932). On female homosexuality. *Psychoanalytic Quarterly* 1:484–510.

—— (1944–1945). *The Psychology of Women*. New York: Grune and Stratton.

—— (1973). *Confrontations with Myself*. New York: Norton.

Fenichel, O. (1930). The pregenital antecedents of the Oedipus complex. *International Journal of Psycho-Analysis* 12:141–166, 1931.

—— (1931). Über Homosexualität. *Psychoanalytische Bewegung* 3:511–536.

—— (1934). Further light upon the pre-oedipal phase in girls. In *Collected Papers of Otto Fenichel*, pp. 305–319. New York: Norton, 1953.

—— (1936). The symbolic equation: girl = phallus. *Psychoanalytic Quarterly* 18:303–324, 1949.

Ferenczi, S. (1924). *Thalassa, a Theory of Genitality*. Albany, NY: Psychoanalytic Quarterly.

Freud, A. (1926). *The Psycho-Analytic Treatment of Children*. London: Imago, 1946.

—— (1936). *The Ego and the Mechanisms of Defence*. London: Hogarth.

Freud, S. (1892). On the theory of hysterical attacks. *Standard Edition* 1:151–154.

—— (1894). The neuro-psychoses of defence. *Standard Edition* 3:41–61.

—— (1896a). Further remarks on the neuro-psychoses of defence. *Standard Edition* 3:157–185.

—— (1896b). The aetiology of hysteria. *Standard Edition* 3:187–221.

—— (1896c). Heredity and the aetiology of the neuroses. *Standard Edition* 141–156.

—— (1900). The interpretation of dreams. *Standard Edition* 4/5.

—— (1901). The psychopathology of everyday life. *Standard Edition* 6.

—— (1905a). Three essays on the theory of sexuality. *Standard Edition* 7:123–243.

—— (1905b). Fragment of an analysis of a case of hysteria. *Standard Edition* 7:1–122.

—— (1907). Obsessive actions and religious practices. *Standard Edition* 9:115–127.

—— (1908a). Some general remarks on hysterical attacks. *Standard Edition* 9:227–234.

—— (1908b). Hysterical phantasies and their relation to bisexuality. *Standard Edition* 9:155–166.

—— (1908c). On the sexual theories of children. *Standard Edition* 9:205–226.

—— (1909a). Analysis of a phobia in a five-year-old boy. *Standard Edition* 10:1–147.

—— (1909b). Notes upon a case of obsessional neurosis. *Standard Edition* 10:151–249.

—— (1910). Leonardo da Vinci and a memory of his childhood. *Standard Edition* 11:57–137.

—— (1911). Psycho-analytic notes on an autobiographical account of a case of paranoia (dementia paranoides). *Standard Edition* 12:1–79.

—— (1912). Contributions to a discussion on masturbation. *Standard Edition* 12.239–254.

—— (1912–1913). Totem and taboo. *Standard Edition* 13:1–161.

—— (1913a). The disposition to obsessional neurosis. *Standard Edition* 12:311–326.

—— (1913b). Two lies told by children. *Standard Edition* 12:303–309.

—— (1913c). An evidential dream. *Standard Edition* 12:267–277.

—— (1914a). From the history of an infantile neurosis. *Standard Edition* 17:1–122.

———— (1914b). On the history of the psycho-analytic movement. *Standard Edition* 14:1–66.

———— (1914c). On narcissism: an introduction. *Standard Edition* 14:67–102.

———— (1914d). Remembering, repeating, and working through. *Standard Edition* 12:145–156.

———— (1915a). A case of paranoia running counter to the psycho-analytic theory of the disease. *Standard Edition* 14:261–272.

———— (1915b). Instincts and their vicissitudes. *Standard Edition* 14:109–140.

———— (1916a). On the transformation of instinct as exemplified in anal erotism. *Standard Edition* 17:125–133.

———— (1916b). Some character types met with in psycho-analytic work. *Standard Edition* 14:309–336.

———— (1916–1917). Introductory lectures on psycho-analysis. *Standard Edition* 15/16.

———— (1917). Mourning and melancholia. *Standard Edition* 14:237–259.

———— (1918). The taboo of virginity. *Standard Edition* 11:191–208.

———— (1919a). A child is being beaten. *Standard Edition* 17:175–204.

———— (1919b). The "uncanny." *Standard Edition* 17:217–256.

———— (1920a). The psychogenesis of a case of homosexuality in a woman. *Standard Edition* 18:145–172.

———— (1920b). Beyond the pleasure principle. *Standard Edition* 18:1–64.

———— (1921a). Psycho-analysis and telepathy. *Standard Edition* 18:173–193.

———— (1921b). Group psychology and the analysis of the ego. *Standard Edition* 18:65–143.

———— (1922a). Dreams and telepathy. *Standard Edition* 18:195–220.

———— (1922b). Some neurotic mechanisms in jealousy, paranoia, and homosexuality. *Standard Edition* 18:221–232.

———— (1923a). The ego and the id. *Standard Edition* 19:1–59.

———— (1923b). The infantile genital organization. *Standard Edition* 19:139–145.

———— (1924a). The dissolution of the Oedipus complex. *Standard Edition* 19:171–179.

———— (1924b). An autobiographical study. *Standard Edition* 20:1–70.

———— (1924c). The economical problem of masochism. *Standard Edition* 19:155–170.

———— (1925a). Some psychical consequences of the anatomical distinctions between the sexes. *Standard Edition* 19:241–258.

———— (1925b). Negation. *Standard Edition* 19:233–239.

———— (1926a). Inhibitions, symptoms, and anxiety. *Standard Edition* 20:75–174.

———— (1926b). The question of lay analysis. *Standard Edition* 20:177–250.

———— (1929). Civilisation and its discontents. *Standard Edition* 21:57–145.

———— (1931). Female sexuality. *Standard Edition* 21:221–243.

———— (1932). New introductory lectures on psycho-analysis. *Standard Edition* 22:1–182.

———— (1932–1933). Femininity. Lecture 23 in New Introductory Lectures on Psycho-analysis. *Standard Edition* 22:112–135.

———— (1937). Analysis terminable and interminable. *Standard Edition* 23:209–253.

———— (1960). *Letters of Sigmund Freud,* ed. E. L. Freud, trans. T. and J. Stern. New York: Basic Books.

———— (1972). *Sigmund Freud and Lou Andreas-Salomé: Letters,* ed. E. Pfeiffer, trans. W. and E. Robson-Scott. New York: Harcourt Brace Jovanovich.

Freud, S. and Abraham, K. (1907–1926). *The Letters of Sigmund Freud and Karl Abraham, 1907–1926,* ed. H. C. Abraham and E. L. Freud, trans. B. Marsh and H. C. Abraham. New York: Basic Books, 1965.

Hamon, M.-C. (1986). Des pudeurs. *Quarto. Bulletin de la cause freudienne en Belgique* 25:17–23.

Horney, K. (1922). On the genesis of the castration complex in women. *International Journal of Psycho-Analysis* 5:50–65, 1924.

———— (1926). The flight from womanhood. *International Journal of Psycho-Analysis* 7:324–339.

———— (1932). The dread of women. *International Journal of Psycho-Analysis* 13:348–360.

Jones, E. (1927). The early development of female sexuality. *International Journal of Psycho-Analysis* 8:459–472.

———— (1932). The phallic phase. *International Journal of Psycho-Analysis* 14:1–33.

Klein, M. (1923). Infant analysis. *International Journal of Psycho-Analysis* 7:31–63, 1926.

———— (1925). A contribution to the psychogenesis of tics. In *Contributions to Psychoanalysis, 1921–1945*, pp. 117–139. London: Hogarth.

———— (1926). The psychological principles of early analysis. In *Love, Guilt, and Reparation and Other Works, 1921–1945*, pp. 128–138. New York: Macmillan.

———— (1927a). Criminal tendencies in normal children. *British Journal of Medical Psychology* 7:177–192.

———— (1927b). Symposium on child analysis. *International Journal of Psycho-Analysis* 8:370–377.

———— (1928). Early stages of the Oedipus complex. *International Journal of Psycho-Analysis* 9:167–180.

———— (1929). Personification in the play of children. *International Journal of Psycho-Analysis* 19:193–204.

———— (1932). *The Psycho-Analysis of Children*. London: Hogarth.

———— (1935). A contribution to the psychogenesis of manic-depressive states. *International Journal of Psycho-Analysis* 16:145–174.

———— (1940). Mourning and its relation to manic-depressive states. *International Journal of Psycho-Analysis* 21:125–153.

Lacan, J. (1955–1956). *The Seminar of Jacques Lacan. Book III. The Psychoses*, ed. J.-A. Miller, trans. R. Grigg. New York: Norton, 1993.

———— (1956–1957). *Le Séminaire. Livre IV: La relation d'objet*, ed. J.-A. Miller. Paris: Seuil.

———— (1958a). The signification of the phallus. In *Ecrits. A Selection*, trans. A. Sheridan, pp. 281–291. New York: Norton, 1977.

———— (1958b). On a question preliminary to any possible treatment of psychosis. In *Ecrits. A Selection*, trans. A. Sheridan, pp. 179–221. New York: Norton, 1977.

—— (1960). The subversion of the subject and the dialectic of desire in the Freudian unconscious. In *Ecrits. A Selection*, trans. A. Sheridan, pp. 292–325. New York: Norton, 1977.

—— (1966). *Écrits*. Paris: Seuil.

—— (1970). Radiophonie. *Scilicet* 2/3.

Lampl-de Groot, J. (1928). The evolution of the Oedipus complex in women. *International Journal of Psycho-Analysis* 9:332–345.

Mannoni, O. (1969). *Clefs pour l'imaginaire*. Paris: Seuil.

Millot, C. (1984). Le surmoi féminin. *Ornicar?* 29.

—— (1988). *Nobodaddy. L'hystérie dans le siècle*. Paris: Point Hors Ligne.

Stärcke, A. (1921). The castration complex. *International Journal of Psycho-Analysis* 2:179–201.

van Ophuijsen, H. W. (1924). Contributions to the masculinity complex in women. *International Journal of Psycho-Analysis* 5:39–49.

Wajeman, G. (1982). *Le Maître et l'Hystérique*. Paris: Navarin/Seuil.

Index

Abraham, K., 3, 5, 31, 89, 94, 151, 154, 229
  and Klein, 127–130, 141, 143–145, 173
  on object-love, 113–126
  on premature ejaculation, 66–67
Addictions, need underlying, 18–19
"Aetiology of hysteria, The" (Freud), 13, 19
Aggression, 17, 74
  repression of, 200–201
  toward parents, 140–141, 145–146
Amphimixis, 67–68
Anal eroticism, 67–68
Anal phase, 65, 73–74, 99–101, 123
Anal-sadistic phase, 17, 36, 65, 149–150
  fantasies of, 167, 172
  Freud development of theory of, 14, 20

"Analysis of a case of paranoia, The" (Brunswick), 177, 179–215, 217–219, 221–222, 228
"Analysis terminable and interminable" (Freud), 176
Andreas-Salomé, L., 10, 123
Anus, 65, 71, 123
Anxiety, 36, 85, 140, 166, 172
Anxiety hysteria, 14, 98

Beating fantasies, 15, 17, 27, 81, 104, 155, 170
Biting, 70, 116, 124
Body, represented by parts, 117–118, 132
Braunschweig, C. M., 5
Breast, 65, 121. See also Weaning
  loss of, 125, 129–130, 132, 143–145, 148, 155, 167–168
  and relation with mother, 89, 117, 138
Breast-feeding. See Nursing

Brunswick, R. M., 5, 217
  on castration as symbolic, 157–
    159
  and Freud, 31, 127, 175–178,
    218–225, 228
  report on female paranoia case,
    179–215
Buttocks, mother represented by,
  117

Cannibalistic stage. *See*
  Incorporation
Castration, 43, 116, 124
  consent to, 69, 221
  denial of, 25, 64, 69, 88, 187–
    188, 193, 197
  effects of mother's, 38–39, 153–
    154
  ending mother's omnipotence,
    135–138, 178
  in Freud's papers, 21, 27–28
  of girls, 25, 27, 66
  as imaginary and symbolic, 221–
    222
  as love, 107, 109–111, 155, 170,
    221
  masochistic desire for, 65, 74
  by mother, 99, 132–133
  of mother, 5, 41–42, 65, 80–81,
    91, 103–104, 108– 110,
    136–138, 218–219
  in Oedipus complex of girls *vs.*
    boys, 27, 55, 130–131
  in perception of sexual
    difference, 22–24
  refusal of, 124, 155–156, 162,
    208, 212–213
  relation to Oedipus complex
    and *jouissance*, 209–210
  as symbolic, 157, 159, 209

weaning as model for, 57–62,
  70, 121, 130, 166
Castration anxiety, 9, 150, 163
  causes of, 58–59, 132, 139–140
  effects of, 9–10, 95–96, 140
  girls', 43–45, 121
  and identification with phallus,
    45–46
Castration complex, 94, 125, 156,
  169
  in girls, 1–2, 40, 46, 147
  in Oedipus complex of girls *vs.*
    boys, 9–12, 46, 207
  relation to masculinity complex,
    50–51, 58
  vs. castration anxiety, 9, 209
Castration threat, 24, 170, 189, 208
Child
  anal, 101, 149–150
  desire for, 122, 218
  desire for father's, 17, 25–27,
    36–38, 37–38, 40–42, 75,
    172
  parents' love for as narcissism,
    115
Childbirth, feminine masochism
  in, 73
Children
  psychoanalysis with, 140–141,
    166
  sexuality of, 17, 22–24, 26
"Contributions to the masculinity
  complex in women" (Van
  Ophuijsen), 49–51, 49–54
Conversion symptoms, 79

Da Vinci, L., 159–162
Death wish, 15–16, 16, 201–203,
  213
Defenses, 140. *See also* Repression

Delusional jealousy, 175, 179, 190–191, 197, 209

Delusions
  in female paranoia case, 182, 186, 191, 202–204
  and girls' Oedipus complex, 19–20

Denial. *See* Castration, denial of

Depressive position, 130

Desire
  of father, 101–102
  for mother, 84, 90
  of mother, 102, 137, 160–161, 163 n.1
  of Other, 199, 210–211

Deutsch, H., 30, 101, 123, 154
  Freud's relations with, 3, 5, 31, 63, 111, 175
  on frigidity, 76–78
  on homosexuality, 83–91
  on masochism of femininity, 73–82

Developmental stages, 22, 24, 31, 36, 88, 124. *See also* specific phases
  activity *vs.* passivity in, 65–66, 158–159
  object love as goal of, 114–115
  sequences in, 125, 141
  sexuality of, 17–18, 123
  timing of Oedipus complex, 165–166, 171
  transference repeating, 82

Displacement, 60–61, 63, 75, 122–124, 133, 146

"Disposition to obsessional neurosis, The" (Freud), 45

"Dissolution of the Oedipus complex, The" (Freud), 10, 23

Dora, case study of, 16, 18, 42

Dreams, 13, 59, 60
  death wishes in, 15–16
  in female paranoia case, 182–189, 193–197, 201
  vs. memories, 18

"Dreams and hysteria" (Freud), 18

"Dreams and telepathy" (Freud), 45

"Early stages of the Oedipus complex" (Klein), 127–128, 141, 166–167

Ego, 24, 62

Ego and the Id, The (Freud), 167

Ejaculation, 64, 66–67

Envy, 16. *See also* Jealousy; Penis envy

"Evolution of the Oedipus complex in women, The" (Lampl-de Groot), 50

Fantasies, 51, 56, 96, 172
  of developmental stages, 65–66
  masochism in, 73, 76
  oedipal, 74
  of phallic mother, 61, 69–70, 134–138, 163
  of possessing penis, 94–96
  sadistic, 157, 167
  transference, 192

Father, 36, 80–81, 111, 132. *See also* Child, desire for father's
  and active form of sexual gratification, 23–24, 26
  attachment of girls to, 11, 94–97
  in boys' *vs.* girls' Oedipus complex, 26–28
  as castrating, 74, 103–104, 154

Father (*continued*)
  child turning from mother to, 107, 169
  failure in female homosexuality, 86–87, 89–91
  functions of, 156–163, 218
  girl turning from mother to, 1–2, 30, 143, 146–147, 153
  girl's identification with, 42, 44–45, 115–116
  in girl's Oedipus complex, 17, 19–20, 25, 30
  and girl's relationships with mother, 36–38, 50, 120, 208
  identification and incorporation of penis of, 101, 113, 116–117, 119, 148
  passage to, 83–84, 110
  prohibition of incest by, 136, 156, 159–163
"Female sexuality" (Freud), 12, 30
Femininity, 64, 70, 156
  development of, 37–39, 89, 118, 121–122
  Freud revising theories on, 43, 109, 206
  Freud's papers on, 2–3, 5, 29–30, 49, 223–224
  masochism of, 73–82
"Femininity" (Freud), 12, 31
Femininity phase, 145–152
Fenichel, O., 5, 88, 108
  and Freud, 31, 90
  on pregenital antecedents to Oedipus complex, 93–102, 110
Ferenczi, S., 66–68, 70, 89, 128
Fixations, 217
  on father, 30, 116–117
  in female paranoia case, 190, 193
  on mother, 87–88, 177

penis envy as, 121–122
on phallic mother, 204, 208
pregenital, 52–54
vs. regression, 93
Freud, A., 10, 140, 176
Freud, S., 17, 163 n.1, 209
  and Brunswick, 175–178, 205–207, 213–214, 218–225
  Brunswick's influence on theories on female sexuality, 212–215, 219
  on castration, 155–156, 170
  clinical material on females, 13–15, 20
  criticism of Klein's theories, 127–128, 166–168, 171–173
  and Deutsch, 63–64, 73, 90–91, 111
  development of theories by, 39–40, 123, 165, 170–171, 205, 223–225
  on female homosexuality, 84, 88
  on femininity, 2, 29, 31–32, 49, 172–173, 212, 230
  on functions of the father, 136, 158–159
  ignorance of development of girls, 7–9, 12, 43, 103, 229
  interactions with colleagues and students, 3–5, 31–33, 70, 90, 93, 104, 114, 178, 227–230
  and Klein, 139, 153, 165
  Klein's departure from, 144–145, 152
  Klein's use of ideas of, 128–129, 135
  on Leonardo da Vinci, 159–162

method of revising theories, 1–4, 29–30, 32–33, 39–40, 43, 109, 125–126, 177, 223–225
on mother, 70, 147
on paranoia and repressed homosexuality, 211–212
on primacy of phallus, 118–119, 170
responses to Abraham, 113–114, 125–126
on superego formation, 167–168
on timing of Oedipus complex, 139, 165–166
use of arising ideas and emerging truths, 20–21, 25–26
Frigidity, 30, 37, 40, 68, 78
as refusal of female role, 64–65, 76–78
"Further remarks on the neuro-psychoses of defence" (Freud), 13

Gaze, and shame, 43–44
Genital phase, 67
mixed with pregenital, 148, 166–167
sexuality of, 17–18
Genitals, 22. *See also* Phallus; Sexual difference; Vagina
and displacement, 60–61
Girls, 82, 101. *See also* Oedipus complex, boys *vs.* girls
castration complex of, 9, 59
demand for penis to mother, 54, 56, 75
identification with fathers, 42, 44–45
importance of preoedipal stage to, 35–36
Guilt, 87–88, 140, 185, 208–209, 212

Hatred, 202
ambivalence with love, 129, 131–132
in female paranoia case, 188, 190–192, 198, 201, 210
for mother, 102, 107–111, 125, 137, 144, 148, 153–154, 166
for mother in female homosexuality, 84–86, 90
Homosexuality, 82, 83–91, 200
and castration anxiety in girls, 44–45
and lack of father, 160–161
repressed in paranoia, 186, 204, 211–212
women's, 15, 41–42
Horney, K., 128, 150, 155
on castration, 104, 121
and Freud, 31, 91
on partial love, 117, 122
Hostility
preoedipal, 36–37
in transference, 185, 189–191, 194–195, 197
Hysteria, 13–14, 18, 39, 42, 94, 101
and anxiety, 9, 14
frigidity in, 78–79
as repression of masturbation, 17–19

Id, conflict with ego, 24
Identification, 24, 46, 80, 109, 144, 147, 148, 168
of boys and girls, 150–152
with castration of mother, 104
with father, 42, 44–45, 81, 97, 116–117, 120, 147, 155–156
as incorporation, 113, 132
in oedipal resolution for boys, 26, 120

Identification (*continued*)
  oral-sadistic, 132, 143, 145
  partial, 116–117, 119, 144
  phallic, 45–46, 52–53
  primary (with mother), 90, 119–
    120, 122, 128, 145, 148–
    152, 178, 218
  primitive, 147, 152, 218
  refusal of, 154–156
  of whole body with genitals, 68
Impotence, 67, 133
Incest, 104, 160
  father's prohibition of, 136, 156,
    159–163
Incorporation, 143, 150
  of father, 101, 148
  of father's penis, 116–117, 119,
    151–152, 168
"Infantile genital organization,
  The" (Freud), 21, 23
Inhibitions, Symptoms, and Anxiety
  (Freud), 14, 70
Injustice, sense of, 133, 154
  in female paranoia case, 199–200
  in girls' masculinity complex,
    51–53, 58
Intercourse, 66, 68, 80, 143
  as combining infantile phases
    and fantasies, 65–66
  feminine-passive position in, 73,
    154–155
  parental (*See* Primal scene)
Interpretation of Dreams, The
  (Freud), 13, 15, 16
Interpretations, in female
  paranoia case, 184–185, 187,
  191–193, 200–201
Introductory Lectures (Freud), 8, 45
Introjection, 46, 167
  of love objects, 143–144
  of mother, 131–132

Jealousy, 27, 60, 87. *See also*
  Delusional jealousy in female
  paranoia case, 192–193, 196–
  199, 201–204
Jones, E., 31, 84, 89, 113–114, 123–
  124, 128
Jouissance, 123, 192
  altruistic, 80
  father's and mother's, 102,
    140
  infantile, 160–163, 190
  loss of, 67–68, 133–135
  mother's, 75–76, 136–138, 163
    n.1, 168
  of the Other, 197–199, 209, 211,
    213
  phallic, 39, 188
  prohibition of, 30, 88, 97
  relation to Oedipus complex
    and castration, 209–210

Klein, M., 5, 110, 124, 140, 221,
  228
  on castration, 108, 155, 209
  on femininity phase, 145–152
  and Freud, 31, 153, 165, 168,
    171–173, 176–178
  psychoanalysis with children,
    140–141
  on role of mother, 127–138
  on superego, 46, 168
  on timing of Oedipus complex,
    139–140, 165–166

Lampl-de Groot, J., 30, 55
  and Freud, 3, 5, 31, 109–110,
    175
  van Ophuijsen giving case to,
    50, 52, 54, 56
Language, 131
Latency period, 24

Libido, 65, 89
  development of, 113–126
  shift of position of, 66, 73–75,
    146–147
Little Hans, case study of, 156
Love, 211
  ambivalence with hate, 129,
    131–132
  castration as, 107, 109, 111, 155,
    170, 221
  demand for, 99, 110
  for mother, 171, 230
  partial, 117, 119, 122, 143–144
  in transference, 189–190, 196
Love object, 55, 153
  attachment to first, 195, 198,
    212–213
  giving up mother as, 56, 155,
    212, 220

Marriage, 203–204
  female homosexuality in, 85
  hostility and penis envy in, 40,
    192
  playing out of female paranoia
    in, 181–182, 188
  preoedipal hostility returning
    in, 36–37
  replaying of oedipal conflicts in,
    45, 154
  sexual difficulties in, 181, 196
Masculine identification, 169
Masculine protest, 155–156
Masculinity, 65, 88
  and girl's identification with
    father, 42, 44–45
  women's repression of, 37, 39
Masculinity complex, 77, 79, 101,
    115, 219
  as narcissistic protest, 44–45
  origin of, 27, 121

relation to castration complex,
    50–51, 58
  women's, 25, 49–51, 91, 148
Masochism
  desire for castration, 65, 74
  of femininity, 73–74, 73–82
  transformation of hatred into,
    86, 88
  of women, 63–64
Masturbation, 27
  female, 17–19, 74
  in female paranoia case, 187–
    189, 192, 195–198, 210
  girls turning away from clitoral
    sexuality, 38–39, 55
  mother's prohibition of, 46, 88,
    91
  parental prohibition of, 23–24,
    58–59, 95, 183–184
Melancholia, 130, 143–144, 166
  compared to obsessional
    neurosis, 114–115
  and primary identification, 119,
    121
Memories
  in female paranoia case, 183,
    186
  vs. dreams, 18, 194
Me/not-me, in nursing children,
    57, 59
Mirror effects, 131–132, 138, 167
Mother, 28, 31, 36, 37, 131, 175,
    209–210. *See also* Phallic
    mother
  absence of, 129, 131
  attachment to, 169, 172, 206–
    207
  being phallic through nursing,
    66, 69–70, 80
  body represented by part, 117–
    118, 132

Mother (*continued*)
  castrated, 108, 110, 155–156,
    171
  as castrating, 95–96, 132–133,
    221
  as castrating *vs.* castrated, 101–
    102, 108–109
  castration ending omnipotence,
    135–138, 157–159, 163 n.1
  castration of, 2, 5, 22–24, 65,
    103–104, 136–138, 169–
    170, 209–210, 229
  children's fear of, 150–151
  child's reversal of roles with, 84,
    90
  desire and hate for, 98–99
  father's desire for, 41–42, 149–
    150
  in female homosexuality, 83–
    88
  girl turning from, 1–2, 27, 30,
    35–36, 38–39
  girl's demand for penis to, 49–
    51, 54, 56, 75
  hate for, 107–111, 125, 144, 148,
    150, 166
  hostility toward, 15–16, 46, 145–
    146
  identification with, 128, 145,
    148–150
  love for, 171, 230
  as love object, 11–12, 119, 155
  masochistic, 80–81
  omnipotence of, 151, 221–222
  separation from, 94–97, 158–
    159, 220
  and sexual activity *vs.* passivity,
    23–24, 26, 217–218, 220
  women's preoedipal relationship
    with, 36–38, 54–55
Mother complex, 59, 70

Motherhood, 68, 71
  femininity through, 64–65
  as sublimation, 79–81
Mouth, 71, 122–123, 147

Narcissism, 30, 77, 131
  and object love, 114–115, 117
  and penis envy, 43–44
Narcissistic wound, 134
Need, in addictions and hysteria,
    18–19
"Neuro-psychoses of defence,
    The" (Freud), 13
Neurosis, 9, 13, 30, 78, 209
  masculinity complex in women,
    148
  transference, 189
  from unresolved Oedipus
    complex, 17, 93, 109
Neurotic genital problems, 67
New Introductory Lectures (Freud),
    14, 29
Nostalgia
  for fusion with Other, 211
  for mother, 160, 162–163
Nursing
  being phallic mother through,
    66, 69–70, 80
  deprivation in, 129

Object choice, 30, 75, 110, 120, 171
  girl changing, 146–147
  and penis envy, 43–44
Object love, 113–126
Obsessional neurosis, 9, 14, 45–46,
    79, 114–115
Obsessions, 13–14, 19
"Obsessive actions and religious
    practices" (Freud), 14
Oedipal conflict, weaning as cause
    of, 166–168

Oedipal fantasy, 74
Oedipal prehistory, 11
Oedipus complex, 1, 9, 14, 24,
146, 167, 205–206
actlvity *vs.* passivity of, 220–221
boys', 35, 45
boys' exit from, 26, 110, 119–
120, 169
boys *vs.* girls, 9–11, 15–17, 24–
28, 35–36, 46, 55, 109, 130,
168–169, 220–221
and castration anxiety, 23–24
early, 128–129
entry to and exit from, 130–131,
155–156
girls', 16–17, 19–20, 30, 41–42,
146, 165, 207
girls entering, 2, 75, 108
redefinition of, 209, 230
resolution of, 26, 87
similarities of boys and girls, 8, 15
timeline of, 139–140, 171–172
as unresolved, 36, 45, 93
of women, 13, 209–210
"On female homosexuality"
(Deutsch), 63, 82
"On transformation of instinct"
(Freud), 15
Oral frustration, 147, 168
Oral penis envy, 119
Oral phase, 65, 95, 101, 119–120,
123
penis envy as fixation in, 121,
122
vagina as mouth in, 65–66
Oral symptoms, 98, 119, 124
Orality, 89, 141, 145–147
Oral-sadistic phase, 96, 115, 117,
143, 149
fantasies of, 167, 172
identification in, 132, 145

Klein's theories of, 129–130
penis envy as, 113, 124
Other, the, 45, 87
abandonment by, 189
and betrayal, 194, 200–201
castration of, 59–60
desire of, 199, 210–211
jouissance of, 197–198, 209, 213
maternal, 28, 133–135, 138

Paranoia, 136, 175, 177
female, 13–15, 46, 179–215
phases of, 189, 200
repressed homosexuality in,
186, 204, 211–212
Paranoid projections, toward
mother, 166
Parents, 16, 24, 52–53, 58–59, 115.
See also Father; Mother; Primal
scene
Penetration, 70, 116
Penis. *See* Penis envy; Phallus
Penis envy, 17, 39–40, 77–78, 172,
207, 218, 221
and desire for a child, 122, 172
in female paranoia case, 192,
199
of girls, 1–2, 11–12, 27
in masculinity complex, 51, 55
as misogynist, 145
as oral sadism, 113, 119
origin of, 116, 120–121, 124
and peculiarities of femininity,
43–44
pushing girl toward father, 37–39
Phallic mother, 9–10, 117–118,
161–163
fantasies of, 61, 69
identification with, 219
love for, 153, 208
omnipotence of, 134–138

Phallic phase, 170
  activity *vs.* passivity in, 65, 69
  of boys *vs.* girls, 36, 46
  of girls, 54–55, 110, 147
  vs. femininity phase, 145, 150
  of women, 209–210
Phallus, 9–10, 64, 121, 129. *See also*
    Penis envy
  as active *vs.* passive organ,
      65–66
  being *vs.* having, 100, 199, 210–
      211
  belief in women's, 184, 187,
      193, 195, 197, 200
  breast as, 57–58
  fantasies of possessing, 94–96
  father's, 116–117, 135, 149–150
  girl's demand to mother for,
      49–51, 54, 56, 75, 108
  hatred of husband for
      possessing, 192, 198–199
  and identification, 45–46, 109–
      110
  incorporation fantasy of, 113,
      119
  primacy of, 21, 53, 58, 67–68,
      111, 118–119, 152, 170–
      171, 229
  symbolism of, 42–43, 158
  on women, 148, 188–189
Phobias, 9, 14
Pleasure-ego, 62, 67
Postphallic stage, 74
"Pregenital antecedents to
    Oedipus complex, The"
    (Fenichel), 93
Pregenital fixation, 52–53, 54
Pregenital phase, 93–102, 148,
    166–167
Prehistory, of Oedipus complex,
    26, 177–178, 207

Preoedipal period, 30, 35–37, 217
  attachment to mother in, 1,
      109–110, 139, 175–178,
      206–207
  relations with mothers of female
      homosexuals, 84, 86
  "Pre-oedipal phase of the libido
      development, The"
      (Brunswick), 177, 217–223,
      228
Primal scene, 55, 180, 221
  castration anxiety from, 139–140
  child's interpretation of, 156,
      158, 170
  in girls' Oedipus complex, 19–
      20, 41
  seen as sadism, 80–81, 140–141
  as trauma for child, 116
Primitive ego, 62
Primitive paranoia, 136
Privation, 146
  of breast, 155, 168
Projection, in female paranoia
    case, 191–192, 201–202
Psychoanalysis, 20, 186. *See also*
    Freud, method of revising
    theories
  with children, 140–141, 166
  chronology in, 139–140, 166,
      171
  development and expansion of
      theories in, 123, 223– 225,
      227–230
  Fenichel's methodology in, 99–
      100
  Freud's own, 9
  with masochistic women, 77–78
  power and limits of, 76–78
  retroactive theorizing in, 108,
      214–215
  retrospection in, 83–84

termination of, 176, 203–204
treatment of female paranoia
case in, 179–215
use of arising ideas and
emerging truths, 20–21,
25–26
"Psycho-analysis and telepathy"
(Freud), 14, 16
Psycho-Analysis of Children, The
(Klein), 141
*Psycho-Analytic Treatment of Children,
The* (A. Freud), 140
"Psychogenesis of a case of
homosexuality in a woman,
The" (Freud), 15
"Psychology of women in relation
to the functions of reproduction, The" (Deutsch), 63–71
Psychosis, 207
female paranoia case as, 182–
183, 191
and lack of Oedipus complex,
209–210
resolved through analysis, 204–
205
Puberty, active *vs.* passive sexuality
of, 65
Punishment, 146, 156

Rage, at mother, 219
Rape
enemas as, 219
fantasies of, 73–75, 155
Reaction formation, 15–16
Receptivity, of girls' sexuality,
146–147
Reconstructions, 81, 114, 123
in interpretation of dreams, 18–
19
order of events' emergence in
analysis, 139–140, 141

in treatment of female paranoia,
180–181, 184, 186, 188
Regression, 17, 139
due to castration anxiety, 123–
124, 140
in female homosexuality, 84,
89
and fixation, 84, 93
to pregenital stages, 73–74,
119–120
Religion, symbolism of, 56
Repetition, in female paranoia
case, 190, 191
Repression, 24, 37, 51, 77, 172,
187, 207
and castration anxiety, 9–10,
189
in female paranoia case, 193–
194, 198, 200–201
of homosexuality, 186, 204,
211–212
of masturbation, 17–19, 27, 38–
39
Resistance
in female paranoia case, 185,
189, 191–193, 200–202
Freud's to understanding
development of girls,
7–9
Retroactivity, 23, 104, 108, 134,
162, 165–166, 171
Retrospection, in psychoanalysis,
83–84
Rivière, J., 31

Sadism, 61, 89, 143, 149. *See also*
Anal-sadistic phase; Oral-
sadistic phase
at/by parents, 146, 167
parental intercourse seen as,
80–81, 140–141, 156

Screen memories, 60, 86
  in female paranoia case, 184–
    186, 210
  repressed material's return
    with, 51, 53
Secrets, and masculinity complex
  in women, 51
Seduction, 18
  in female paranoia case, 183–
    184, 188, 192–193
  in girls' fantasies, 36–37
  by mother, 159, 160, 175
Sexual arousal, girl's fear of,
  19–20
Sexual difference
  breasts *vs.* genitals, 61
  child's perception of, 22–24, 39,
    74, 109, 148, 208
  child's response to, 39, 51, 130,
    132–134
  consequences of discovery of,
    25–26, 108
  denial of, 116
  girl's perception of, 121, 169–
    170
  in unconscious, 117, 156
Sexual inhibition. *See* Frigidity
Sexuality, 13, 16–17, 64. *See also*
  Oedipus complex
  activity *vs.* passivity of, 65–66,
    68–70, 80, 89, 195, 217–
    218, 220
  childhood, 22–24, 26
Shame, 30, 43–44
"Significance of masochism in the
  mental life of women, The"
  (Deutsch), 63, 71
"Some character types met with in
  psycho-analytic work"
  (Freud), 50–51

"Some psychical consequences of
  the anatomical distinction
  between the sexes" (Freud),
  10, 25–26, 35–36, 83, 90, 107
Stärcke, A., 5, 31, 57–62, 121
Sterility, as refusal of female role,
  64, 76
Studies on Hysteria (Freud), 9
Sublimation, of maternity, 79–81
Superego, 27, 45, 97, 146, 167
  castration anxiety in formation
    of, 10, 24–25
  formation of, 167–168
  of women, 43–44, 46, 211
"Supplement to Freud's 'A history
  of an infantile neurosis'"
  (Brunswick), 223
Symbolism, of repressed material,
  187
Symbolization, 19, 144, 172, 187, 197

"Taboo of virginity, The" (Freud),
  15, 37, 44
Therapists, 30
  male *vs.* female, 2, 12, 54
  and power and limits of
    transference, 76–78
  transference to female analysts,
    84–87, 91
Thinking, of unconscious, 20
Three Essays (Freud), 7, 11, 39
Toilet training, 52–53, 94–96,
  129–130, 133
Transference, 82, 200
  to female analysts, 84–87, 91
  in female paranoia case, 179–
    181
  to male *vs.* female analysts, 2, 12,
    50
  negative *vs.* positive, 194–197

paternal *vs.* maternal, 30, 206
power and limits of, 77–78
Transference dreams, 183–185,
187, 196

Unconscious, 20
fantasies as, 81, 104
sexual difference in, 117
Urethral eroticism, 52–53, 67–68

Vagina, 68
erogenization of, 64–66, 69
masturbation of, 196, 198
vs. mouth, 65–66, 122–123, 147

Van Ophuijsen, H. W., 56, 137
and Freud, 3, 5, 31
on masculinity complex, 49–54,
58

Weaning, 129, 133
as castration, 57–62, 70, 121,
130
as cause of oedipal conflict,
166–168
Wolf Man case, 11, 123–124, 156,
170, 176, 180–181
Womb, desire to return to, 69–70,
85, 90